Islamic Banking and Finance in Europe: The Case of Germany and United Kingdom

Muhammad Ashfaq

Islamic Banking and Finance in Europe: The Case of Germany and United Kingdom

A Theoretical and an Empirical Analysis

PL ACADEMIC RESEARCH

Bibliographic Information published by the Deutsche Nationalbibliothek
The Deutsche Nationalbibliothek lists this publication in the Deutsche Nationalbibliografie; detailed bibliographic data is available in the internet at http://dnb.d-nb.de.

Zugl.: Tübingen, Univ., Diss., 2017

Library of Congress Cataloging-in-Publication Data
A CIP catalog record for this book has been applied for at the Library of Congress

University of Applied Sciences Coburg was the prime supervisor and mentor of the research project.

Cover Image: Videocraft / Pixabay.com
https://pixabay.com/en/financial-district-2366081/

D 21
ISBN 978-3-631-73321-9 (Print)
E-ISBN 978-3-631-73326-4 (E-PDF)
E-ISBN 978-3-631-73327-1 (EPUB)
E-ISBN 978-3-631-73328-8 (MOBI)
DOI 10.3726/b11137

PL Academic Research is an Imprint of Peter Lang GmbH.

Peter Lang – Frankfurt am Main · Bern · Bruxelles · New York · Oxford · Warszawa · Wien

This publication has been peer reviewed.

www.peterlang.com

Executive Summary

The Islamic financial industry is an innovative branch of financial services that has evolved during the last four decades and is expanding rapidly into non-Muslim countries including Western Europe, Asia and North America. The system is regulated by a set of rules based on outlines set by the Islamic *Shari'ah.* By the end of 2014, the assets of the Islamic finance industry exceeded $2 trillion and rapid growth was witnessed, particularly after the 2008–09 financial crisis. Despite having a much larger Muslim population than the United Kingdom, Germany lags far behind in the development of Islamic banking and finance. There are several reasons for this including:

- A lack of awareness among Muslims
- A significantly small number of Islamic financial institutions
- A lack of proactive management by market regulators
- The lack of an enabling environment
- A lack of support from the government
- A low income level
- The low number of Muslim women in the labor force

The research questions posted by this study were: *What are the prospects of success for an Islamic mode of banking and finance in Germany at the retail level? What are the knowledge levels, awareness levels, and perceptions of Muslims, including Muslim umbrella organizations, toward Islamic banking and finance?* In general, there is lack of scientific research investigating the various aspects of Islamic banking and finance in Germany including research into market acceptability, consumer knowledge about the market, key Islamic banking products, regulatory challenges, the potential of retail banking, and the determinants of Islamic banking. To answer these research questions, the researcher has conducted a mixed study including quantitative and qualitative research. In the quantitative phase of this study, two surveys were performed to address retail banking consumers and Muslim umbrella organizations and to analyze the findings from a comparative perspective. As a part of qualitative study, expert interviews with 13 industry practitioners were performed, and eight Muslim organizations completed questionnaires.

A survey was used to collect data for the quantitative aspect of this mixed methods study. The responses received in 402 completed retail banking surveys revealed that a) the majority of Muslims were aware of the fact that Islamic banks avoid interest, b) an overwhelming majority declared themselves religious, c) almost two-thirds were willing to switch to Islamic banking, d) there is lack of availability of Islamic products and services, e) Giro and savings bank accounts and mortgage financing products and services were mostly desired by the respondents.

The findings of the Muslim umbrella organizations survey showed that a) Giro and savings bank accounts, and educational loans, were mostly desired by the respondents, b) there is strong demand for Islamic products, c) and the introduction of Islamic banking would bring benefits to the Muslim community. The qualitative study showed that a) the success of Islamic banking and finance in the United Kingdom is mainly due to the proactive role taken by regulators and London's role as an international financial center, b) Germany's regulatory model is different than that of the United Kingdom in that there are no market entry barriers, and the success of Islamic banking in Germany will largely depend on the operating model of Islamic financial institutions. Moreover, it is expected that growth of Islamic products and services will be slow and gradual.

Key words: *Islamic banking & finance, Shari'ah, Germany, Muslims, Interest (Riba), Retail banking*

Acknowledgement

First and foremost, I would like to thank Prof. Dr. Victor Randall from Coburg University of Applied Sciences for his great academic support and being a source of motivation. I am also grateful to Prof. Dr. Mouez Khalfaoui from University of Tübingen for his support during this study.

I would like to express my appreciation for the financial support provided by Prof. Dr. Victor Randall, and Prof. Dr. Mouez Khalfaoui, which enabled me to attend conferences and present my work and to meet the costs of data collection while conducting my research. It was very helpful to attend different research conferences. Without their help, it would not have been possible to present my results of this study at nine different international conferences.

This work would not have been possible without the support of many people in data collection especially Mehmet Can Kalkan, Sumair Ali, Chaudhary Kamran, Cihan Torun and many others. I would like to extend my thanks to Torsten Niechoj, Barbara Stoberock, Alireza Siadat, Prof. Ishaq Bhatti and Abdul Rauf for their unconditional support, as well. There are many other people who have supported this study but it is not possible to mention each name here; therefore, I would like to sincerely thank every individual who has helped me in this study even if his or her name is not included above.

I would like to especially thank all interviewees who participated in my qualitative study for their time and for their efforts in editing interview transcriptions. I would like to thank all financial institutions and organizations that provided valuable support.

Dedication

I have no words to express my gratitude to my wife Faiza Salma for taking care of the rest of the family while I was working day and night on this study. She also provided me a peace of mind, which enabled me to concentrate on this challenging task. It would have not been possible to reach this level without the sincere prayers of my parents – Muhammad Ishaq and Haleema Bibi. I would like to also thank my parents-in-law Muhammad Shafi and Zubaida Khanum for the unlimited prays for my success.

List of Abbreviations

AAOIFI	Accounting and Auditing Organization of Islamic Financial Institutions
AuM	Assets under Management
ADIB-UK	Abu Dhabi Islamic Bank UK
AWM	Deutsche Asset and Wealth Management
ATM	Automated Teller Machine
ADIB	Abu Dhabi Islamic Bank
BLME	Bank of London and The Middle East
BoE	Bank of England
BAKred	Bundesaufsichtsamt für das Kreditwesen
BAWe	Bundesaufsichtsamt für den Wertpapierhandel
BAMF	Federal Office for Migration and Refugees
ANOVA	Analysis of Variance
BaFin	Bundesaufsichtsamt für Finanzdienstleistungen /German Financial Services Authority
BIS	Bank for International Settlements
BoD	Board of Directors
BCBS	Basel Committee on Banking Supervision
BMLV	Federal Ministry of Food, Agriculture, and Consumer Protection
CSR	Corporate Social Responsibility
CICM	Commerz International Capital Management
CDOs	Collateralized Debt Obligations
CDSs	Credit Default Swaps
CIMB	Commerce International Merchant Bank
CBB	Central Bank of Bahrain
CMP	Commodity *Murabahah* Program
CPO	Crude Palm Oil
DMI	Dar al-Mal al-Islami
DIK	Deutsche Islam Konferenz

EIIB	European Islamic Investment Bank
ETFs	Exchange Traded Funds
ETPs	Exchange Traded Products
ECB	European Central Bank
EU	European Union
EEA	European Economic Area
ESCO	Esfahan Steal Company
Etisalat	Emirates Telecommunications Corporation
EY	Ernest and Young
FSA	Financial Services Authority
FSMA	Financial Services and Market Act
FDI	Foreign Direct Investment
GCC	Gulf Cooperation Council
GIFDC	Global Islamic Finance Development Center
HQLAs	High Quality Liquid Assets
HNWIs	High Net Worth Individuals
IDB	Islamic Development Bank
IBB	Islamic Bank of Britain PLC
IIT	International Innovative Technologies
IFC	Islamic Finance Council
IFEG	Islamic Finance Experts Group
IFSB	Islamic Financial Services Board
IILM	International Islamic Liquidity Management Corporation
IDMA	Islamic Derivative Master Agreement
ISDA	International Swaps and Derivative Association Inc.
IIFM	International Islamic Financial Markets
IWMR	Islamic Wealth Management Report
INCEIF	International Center for Islamic Finance
JLM	Joint Lead Manager
LSE	London Stock Exchange

KWG	Kreditwesengesetz
LBBH	Landesbank Berlin Holding AG
LMC	Liquidity Management Center
LIBOR	London Inter-Bank Offered Rate
LOLR	Lender of Last Resort
LCR	Liquidity Coverage Ratio
MGLSB	Mit-Ghamr Local Savings Bank
MENA	Middle East and North Africa
MoF	Ministry of Finance
M	Mean
MATP	Master Agreements for Treasury Placement
NCB	National Commercial Bank
NBP	National Bank of Pakistan
N/n	Sample Size
NSFR	Net Stable Funding Ratio
OIC	Organization of Islamic Countries
OPEC	Organization of Oil Producing Countries
PBUH	Peace Be Upon Him
PSP	Profit Sharing Principle
PLSP	Profit and Loss Sharing Principle
PLS	Profit and Loss Sharing
P	Pearson value commonly known as P-Value
PIA	Pakistan International Airlines
PSIAs	Profit-Sharing Investment Accounts
QIB UK	Qatar Islamic Bank UK
SRIs	Socially Responsible Investments
SDLT	Double Stamp Duty Land Tax
SSM	Single Supervisory Mechanism
SPSS	Statistical Package for Social Sciences
SMEs	Small and Medium Enterprises

SHB	Saudi Hollandi Bank
SBP	State Bank of Pakistan
THM	Tabung Haji in Malaysia
TPB	Theory of Planned Behavior
TRA	Theory of Reasoned Action
t	Value of t-test
UK	United Kingdom
UAE	United Arab Emirates
UKEF	UK Export Finance
US	United States
VAG	Versicherungsaufsichtsgesetz
VASA	Vereines arabisher Studenten und Akademiker
WIEF	World Islamic Economic Forum
ZMD	Central Council for Muslims in Germany
Zft	Zentrum für Türkeistudien

Table of Content

List of Figures

List of Tables

Chapter 1: Introduction, Background and Rationale of this Study

1.1 Introduction

The financial system includes financial intermediaries and financial markets, which play a vital role in the economic development of a given country (Majanga, 2015; Claus *et el.*, 2004; Askari, 2012). The financial system has a complex structure and consists of banks, insurance companies, stock markets, and mutual funds, and it depends on the economic stage of development of the society concerned. Efficient and effective financial systems facilitate the swift transfer of funds from savers to spenders. Savers deposit excess funds in the form of savings, while the spenders seek excess funds for spending and investment (Iqbal & Molyneux, 2005).

Islam is a complete code of life and offers solutions to a wide range of problems arising from personal, social, political, and economic situations (Mohamad *et al.*, 2014). In the view of Malkawi (2014), in Islam, there are certain rules and ethical norms that provide guiding principles for conducting business and economic activities. Islamic banking and finance is an innovative branch of financial services and one that has grown significantly during the last four decades (Alrifai, 2015). The primary motive of conventional[1] banks is profit maximization where charging interest is central to the business structure. However, Islamic bank operations are interest-free (*Riba*) and only Halal (permissible) transactions are allowed (Abu-Alkheil, 2012). The Islamic financial industry[2] is comprised of a number of components including Islamic banks, Islamic windows at conventional banks, Islamic insurance (*Takaful*), capital and money markets, and non-bank financial institutions (Askari, 2012). It should be taken into account that Islamic banks are the largest segment of the Islamic financial industry, which performs the function of financial intermediation.

Islamic banking and finance is a system regulated by a set of rules based on outlines set by the Islamic *Shari'ah*. *Shari'ah* is a set of guidelines mentioned in the *Quran*, Islam's Holy book, and is based on the concept of *Riba* (Usury) which addresses interest, uncertainty (*Gharar*), and gambling (*Maysir*), which are strictly forbidden in Islam (Nienhaus,2011a, Malkawi, 2014; Etzold & Wackerbeck, 2012; Ribera *et al.*, 2011; Etzold & Wackerbeck, 2011). Hersh (2011) stated that Islamic

1 Conventional banks include those financial institutions that are not based on Islamic economic principles. Pertinent definitions of different terminologies and concepts will be provided in chapter 2.

2 The Islamic finance industry is comprised of Islamic finance, Islamic banking, Islamic wealth management, and Islamic insurance. These sectors or segments are also part of the Islamic Economics (see further: Hunt-Ahmed, 2013).

finance has emerged as a viable alternative to conventional finance[3], and the recent financial crisis[4] has highlighted the inherent weakness in the global financial system. Ahmed (2015) highlighted the fact that the financial crisis of 2008 followed by the recession of 2009 has raised important questions about the current financial architecture and the viability of the future of the global economy.

Ethical aspects of Islamic banking appeal to a wider group of customers including ethically oriented or religious customers that are not satisfied with the conduct of Western financial institutions (Etzold & Wackerbeck, 2011). Nienhaus (2011b:1) stressed the importance of a new financial system that can ensure global financial stability by stating:

> "The world in general is in search of a better financial system that, among others, can ensure more stability, efficient allocation of resources, just distribution, responsibility of investors, risk sharing, sustainability, entrepreneurship and innovation."

Etzold and Wackerbeck (2011:18) discussed the importance of Islamic finance after the recent financial crisis as:

> "Overall, with the current banking model having come into question after the crisis and with the need to channel payments and investments from East to West in a *Shari'ah*-compliant way, the opportunities for Islamic finance in Europe are better than ever."

Alrifai (2015), stated that in the mid-1990s there were about 144 Islamic financial institutions, which were functioning mainly in Malaysia and Middle East with total assets $150 billion. Currently, this number reached over 700 institutions with total assets amounting up to $2 trillion. These institutions are working in Muslim countries and expanding rapidly into non-Muslim regions including Western Europe, Asia, and North America. According to Alshamrani (2014), the Islamic financial market is growing at a rate of 15% per annum and is currently comprised of "more than 500 Islamic financial institutions operating in over 75 countries." Thus, the Islamic finance market, which operates globally and has many institutions operating in Western countries, "is one of the fastest growing financial sectors" and was ranked as the fastest growing sectors after the recent financial crisis (Alshamrani, 2014).

---

3 Generally, conventional finance refers to a mode of finance in which there is no restriction on interest (*Riba*). A detail discussion will follow in Chapter 2.

4 The recent global financial crisis started in 2008 in the United States, and swiftly spread to other leading world economies, including Europe. The main reasons for the crisis were: too much debt in the system, uncontrolled use of financially innovative products (derivatives), greed among investors, financiers, and consumers. In the United States bailout packages of more than $700 were issued to rescue the troubled financial institutions. The European Commission proposed €200 billion European stimulus plan. The United Kingdom released a £500 billion rescue package, and the German government, issued a €112 billion bailout to Hypo Real Estate (Source: Alrifai, 2015). These are only few examples. During the same period, Islamic banks faced liquidity issues but no defaults were reported (Alam, 2013). Further details are provided in Chapter 3.

According to a recent report published by the TheCityUK (2015), the size of *Shari'ah*-compliant assets was around $2 trillion at the end of 2014. Islamic retail banks are bourgeoning through the Middle East and currently the presence of Islamic banks and asset management institutions can also be seen in non-Muslim countries such the United States (US) and the United Kingdom (UK) (Perry & Rahman, 2011). Although Islamic finance is making inroads into the industrialized West, it is not currently a threat to the conventional financial institutions as it is expected to remain a niche market. Ribera *et al.* (2011) stated that Islamic banks are gradually gaining ground in major European and American markets, especially in those countries that have large Muslim population.

According to Malkawi (2014), four factors, including influx of petrodollars, Muslim population, low penetration levels, and built-in ethical values in Islamic financial model, have contributed to the rapid growth of the Islamic financial industry. As Islamic finance prospers across Europe, many financial institutions perceive a new window of opportunity to reach additional client groups, including the growing Muslim immigrant community, in order to generate additional profits by offering ethical and *Shari'ah*-compliant banking and financial services (Wilson, 2007). Thus, financial service firms and banks do not consider the growth of the Islamic financial market around the world a threat to the traditional banking and economic system. Moreover, the financial crisis in Europe demonstrated the importance of moral values in the financial sector, which would be an argument in favor of the potentially beneficial impact the Islamic financial system has on enhancing the receptiveness to the Western, and also German financial markets (Mauro *et al.*, 2013; Guski, 2009).

The Islamic financial system prohibits charging interest (*Riba*) on loans (Askari *et al.*, 2012; Daly & Frikha, 2015). Both the borrower and the lender must share risk in any transaction. Both the provider of capital and the entrepreneur share the businesses profit and loss. Speculative behavior (*Gharar*) and gambling (*Maysir*) are not allowed in Islamic *Shari'ah* (Farooq, 2014; Azad *et al.*, 2013). Due to the involvement of speculation and uncertainty Islamic financial practices also restrict the traditional use of derivatives (financial instruments that derive their price from one or more underlying assets) (Al-Amine, 2013b). Money is seen as potential capital and thus only takes the form of actual capital when it is used in a productive capacity. Sinful products, which are banned by *Quran*, including such products as pork, alcohol, and prostitution, cannot be financed (Alrifai, 2015).

According to Azad *et al.* (2013) Islamic financial markets around the world have witnessed the rapid growth of Islamic finance in recent years and currently function parallel to the conventional financial markets. The growing acceptance of Islamic financial markets is due to the unprecedented annual growth of 12–15% and the potential for Muslims wealth. Various financial centers around the world are actively promoting Islamic banking and finance in their respective jurisdictions, and conventional players are venturing into Islamic financial activities.

It is worth remembering that the recent financial crisis was, in substance, an economic disaster caused by inherent weaknesses in the conventional financial system (Ahmed, 2009). People defaulted on consumer debts that they could not afford to pay from loans that they should not have been granted in the first place. Innovative financial instruments that enabled more participants to speculate on risks magnified the effects of the financial crisis. This made things worse by creating a bigger asset bubble (El Hussein, 2013). However, with prudent financial innovation, the magnitude of this financial crisis would have been much smaller.

Islamic finance, on the other hand, relies less on debt based financial reengineering; rather, most of its growth has been predominantly a result of the expanding economies of Muslim countries, which has resulted in more demand for *Shari'ah*-compliant products. The Islamic financial market was not adversely affected by the recent sub-prime financial crisis because it was backed by real and tangible assets (El Hussein, 2013).

1.2 Literature Review and Identification of Research Gap[5]

In continental Europe, the UK is the initiator of providing Islamic banking and financial services to fulfil the demands of the increasing minority Muslim population (Wilson, 2007). This is a result of an Arab joint venture – banks bringing Islamic finance to London during 1980's as financial institutions in the Gulf realized that re-depositing on a *Murabahah* basis could be a useful tool for managing liquidity with mark-ups generated from trade activity on London Metal Exchange (Wilson, 2007). In the United Kingdom, the Financial Services Authority (FSA) has proactively facilitated the development of the Islamic financial sector. Despite having a much larger Muslim population than the United Kingdom, Germany lags far behind in the development of Islamic finance (Bälz, 2007; Wilson, 2007; Nawas, 2013; Ernst, 2011; Etzold & Wackerbeck, 2011). There is not a single Islamic bank operating in Germany. Parker (2008) stresses that if Germany implements legislation enabling Islamic banking and finance and the government provides support Germany has a strong potential for becoming an even larger Islamic financial market than the UK. The German state Saxony-Anhalt issued a €141 million asset-backed *Sukuk* bond in 2004. The bond was listed on the Luxembourg Stock Exchange, and was the first such kind of Islamic financial transaction among European countries (Ahmad *et al.*, 2014). According to Colditz (2009) and Ernst (2011), German financial institutions have hitherto not shown strong interest in Islamic banking and finance within Germany apart from specific cases of *Sukuk* bond issuance. German banks, such as the Deutsche Bank and West LB, are offering Islamic banking products and services in the Middle East and Malaysia. However, no similar initiatives exist in Germany despite a Muslim population in excess of four million persons (Etzold & Wackerbeck, 2011).

Trakic (2012) pointed out that Germany is far behind the UK in the development and promotion of Islamic finance despite having a sizeable Muslim population.

5 Review of existing literature is conducted in detail in chapter 6 in the context of proposed empirical studies.

The main reason behind the slow development of the Islamic financial sector is the existence of '*Leitkultur phenomena*' in society and '*fatwas*'- an opinion given by some Muslim scholars, which exempted Muslim populations living in Europe from complying with *Shari'ah* guidelines in the ordinary course of life (Bälz, 2007).

To offer Islamic financial products and services within a secular environment such as Germany, several successful business models that are currently used in the United Kingdom could be adapted to the German context (Mauro *et al.*, 2013). First, already established financial institutions can offer Islamic banking and finance services based on *Shari'ah*-compliant principles. Second, a dedicated Islamic finance window might be opened by commercial banks. Third, Germany could establish a full-fledged Islamic bank, similar to the Islamic bank of Britain, to serve the needs of Muslim customers. Kuveyt Turk Participation Bank, a business unit of Turkish Kuwait Finance House, has already received a limited banking license to operate in Germany, but its application for a full banking license is still under review (Nawas, 2013). In March 2015, KT Bank AG became the first bank in Germany to obtain a full-fledge banking license to offer products and services in a *Shari'ah*-compliant manner (KT Bank AG, 2015).

Some researchers, like Schönenbach (2012), have identified various barriers regarding the development of Islamic finance in Germany. Although such barriers include low-income levels for Muslims in Germany and a low number of Muslim women in the German workforce, some German banks (such as Deutsche Bank AG and Commerzbank AG) have successfully entered into Islamic banking and financial services in various Arab countries including Saudi Arabia. However, such services are not yet offered in Germany (Parker, 2008). According to Farhoush and Schmidt (2011), Deutsche Bank AG has taken an initiative toward Islamic Banking and has established its *Bankamiz* branches, which are offering consultancy to the Turkish community and free remittances to Turkey. On the other hand, Ernst *et al.* (2013) argued that Deutsche Bank AG finds little potential for *Shari'ah*-compliant products and services in Germany. Etzold and Wackerbeck (2012) stated that several attempts have been made to establish Islamic banking in Germany but the specific nature of German banking regulations and the language barrier are primary reasons for the failure of such efforts. Generally, German officials in government offices prefer the use of German rather than English. On the other hand, Ribera *et al.* (2011) asserted that Germany is an attractive market for Islamic banks due to a Muslim population in excess of four million.

According to Ernst (2011), a lawyer in Germany, a major challenge to success is the drafting of contracts that are *Shari'ah*-compliant but that also comply with laws that are enforceable in secular courts. However, Ernst firmly believes that it is possible to draft such contracts in a manner that a judge can pass a verdict without having prior knowledge about the key *Shari'ah* principles. Similarly, Parker (2008) asserted that it is feasible to structure Islamic financial transactions in Germany.

Nawas (2013) found that 74% of German-Muslims expressed a keen interest in Islamic financial products. However, a recent survey found that 94% of German-Muslims expressed an interest only if said services are available from Islamic banks.

Despite an estimated 1.2 billion Euros in Islamic finance potential less than 5% of German-Muslims are currently using Islamic banking products (Nawas, 2013).

Guski (2009) highlighted that the German market has a reasonable potential for Islamic products but it is necessary to first create awareness in the business community and among participants in the financial industry. In this regard, an initiative from the German government will be required to setup a legal framework to take steps to promote this financial sector, as has been done in the UK and France.

One of the issues with Germany granting a license is that if any European country issues a license to an Islamic bank that license will make it possible for the bank to establish itself in any and all European countries (Khan 2014, Personal Communication, 01 February). This purpose was to mandate that the issuing country take a cautious approach that includes consulting the central banks of other countries in the European Union. This may slow down the process of introducing Islamic banking in any European country.

1.3 Problem Statement

In general, there is a scarcity of scientific research about the *Shari'ah*-compliant products of Islamic banking and finance, especially in Germany. In the post subprime financial crisis era, it is important to conduct further research assessing the knowledge, attitudes, and willingness of key stakeholders including Muslims in Germany. Furthermore, there is a lack of research regarding market entry barriers and regulatory challenges. The general perception is that a lack of willingness among regulators and political leaders to take proactive steps to address these issues, and a lack of understanding around the potential of Islamic banks in Germany, is key reasons for the underdevelopment of the Islamic financial market in Germany. Moreover, there is also lack of studies investigating the knowledge level, attitudes, and perceptions of Muslim umbrella associations related to Islamic banking and finance. The existing studies show mixed results for the potential and level of awareness of the Islamic banking and financial products and services in Germany. In addition, these studies are not current and were completed from 2003 through 2011. The topic of Islamic banking and finance has been studied from a narrow perspective.

1.4 Research Questions/Objective of the Study

The primary objective of this research study was to assess the potential of developing and offering Islamic banking products and services on a retail level in Germany. Another objective of this research was to compare the perceptions of Muslim retail consumers concerning Muslim umbrella organizations. This study also aims to identify the determinants of successful Islamic banking and finance, describe the challenges of Islamic banking in Germany, and predict the future of Islamic banking and finance in Germany and other European countries. Addressing the following research questions will be critical to reaching this objective:

Main Research Question:

What are the knowledge levels, attitudes, and practices of Muslims living in Germany toward Islamic banking products and services and what are the determinants of success of Islamic banking?

Qualitative Research Sub-Questions:

1. What are the success factors for Islamic banking and finance in non-Islamic states that have a substantial Muslim population, specifically Germany and the United Kingdom?
2. What challenges are to be expected for Islamic banking in Germany and in the European Union?
3. What will the future of Islamic banking look like in Germany and in the European Union?

Quantitative Research Sub-Questions:

1. What are the perceptions of Muslim consumers about Islamic banking and finance?
2. What are the perceptions and willingness of Muslim consumers to switch Islamic banking?
3. What are the relevant Islamic products/services of Muslim consumers?
4. What are the perceptions of Muslims in Germany concerning Muslim umbrella organizations (*Muslimische Dachverbände*) toward Islamic banking and finance in Germany?

The hypotheses addressing the quantitative and qualitative research questions are addressed in section 1.6 (below).

1.5 Significance of Research

Archick *et al.* (2011) reported that 15–20 million Muslims were living in Western and Central Europe, with 4.5 million of them living in Germany. According to a recent report of Pew Research Center (2015) Germany has the largest Muslim population in Europe (4.77 million or 5.8% of the total population). Other countries with larger populations of Muslims include France with 4.71 million (7.5%), United Kingdom with 3 million (4.8%), and Italy with 2.22 million (3.7%). Kern (2016) stated that Germany's Muslim population increased to almost six million in 2015, with 850,000 added in 2015 as they were seeking political asylum and refugee status.

According to Gassner (2003b and 2004) and Colditz (2009), Germany has more than 600,000 Muslim households, which include approximately 553,000 salaried employees who are part of the German social insurance contribution system, and around 55,000 who are self-employed. Furthermore, these households have €15 to €25 billion assets deposited with German financial institutions. The average Muslim household income is €1,769 per month, which is substantially lower than the average German household income of €2,733 (Gassner, 2003b and 2004).

According to Parker (2008), Islamic investors from Muslim countries are actively seeking investment opportunities in stable European countries such as Germany. For example, in 2007, Arab Investment Ltd. launched its investment fund, German AIL Fund 1, which had made investments worth over €400 million in real estate in cities like Berlin, Karlsruhe, and Dresden. Etzold and Wackerbeck (2012) affirmed the views of Parker (2008) and stated that the investors from Gulf Cooperation Council (GCC) had made substantial investments in Germany including:

- HDG Mansur purchased real estates in Frankfurt and Munich amounting to €190 million and Gulf Finance House invested €600 million in real estate, in 2016.
- Qatar Islamic Bank purchased real estate worth of €430 million, in 2007.
- Pramerica Real Estate bought the Munich Mall 'Das Einstein' for €160 million, in 2008.

In addition to this, Germany is among the three largest economies in the world and German trade volume with Gulf Cooperation Council (GCC) countries is much higher than the United Kingdom. Despite those facts, Islamic finance does not have a strong presence in Germany when compared to the United Kingdom (Parker, 2008).

Mauro *et al.* (2013) observed that the opportunities for further development of the Islamic financial market in Germany are encouraging. Islamic financial trade could be a viable option for Germany and would enhance its trading share with Muslim countries like Turkey. Because of the high export market share, German exporters could enhance their funding profiles by using Islamic financing solutions as alternative sources of funding. Analysis of the German Muslim population is recommended because Germany's economy plays a significant role in the economic success of the European Union and, Germany features the largest Muslim population in the European Union (Mauro *et al.*, 2013). The Islamic finance industry has experienced significant growth around the world, but a literature gap exists that leaves the context of Muslim financial participation in the European Union, specifically in Germany, inadequately explored. This research study would serve to help close that gap by contributing to the existing literature.

As mentioned earlier, despite the fact that Germany has the largest Muslim population of any country in the European Union, strong banking systems, and one of the leading global economies, it lags behind in the development of Islamic banking and finance when compared to the United Kingdom. It is important to analyze the peculiarities of the German financial market from this perspective because of Germany's strategic role in securing global and regional financial stability. It is also worthwhile to examine the success factors of Islamic banking and finance in the United Kingdom and German markets. More precisely, it is worthwhile to investigate and identify the key barriers to the development of Islamic banking and finance in Germany.

1.6 Research Hypotheses

The quantitative phase of this research study was designed to gather quantitative data pertaining to the determinants of Islamic banking in Germany and to determine the extent to which the Muslim population in Germany is aware of and actively using Islamic banking and financing in Germany. On the basis of literature review, the following hypotheses will be tested.

Hypothesis 1

H_1: Muslims living in Germany are familiar with the concept of Islamic finance.
H_0: Muslims living in Germany are not familiar with the concept of Islamic finance.

Hypothesis 2

H_2: Muslims living in Germany are familiar with the *Riba* and consider charging and paying interest is prohibited in Islam.
H_0: Muslims living in Germany are not familiar with the *Riba* and do not consider charging and paying interest is prohibited in Islam.

Hypothesis 3

H_3: Muslims living in Germany consider themselves religious.
H_0: Muslims living in Germany do not consider themselves religious.

Hypothesis 4

H_4: Muslims living in Germany will use *Shari'ah*-compliant Islamic finance products and services if provided with these.
H_0: Muslims living in Germany will not use *Shari'ah*-compliant Islamic finance products and services if provided with these.

Hypothesis 5

H_5: Muslims living in Germany report a desire for mortgage finance.
H_0: Muslims living in Germany do not report a desire for mortgage finance.

Hypothesis 6

H_6: There are market entry barriers for the *Shari'ah*-compliant products in Germany.
H_0: There are no market entry barriers for the *Shari'ah*-compliant products in Germany.

Hypothesis 7

H_7: The United Kingdom's experience with *Shari'ah*-compliant financial products provides an Islamic banking model for European countries like Germany.
H_0: The United Kingdom's experience with *Shari'ah*-compliant financial products does not provide an Islamic banking model for European countries like Germany.

1.7 Expected Results

The intended final outcomes of the research will be the identification of the determinants most important to the development of Islamic banking and finance in Germany, and the interest and willingness to use such services by the Muslim population living in Germany. This study analyses the knowledge, attitudes, and willingness of ordinary Muslims toward Islamic financial instruments and Muslim umbrella associations. The study also aims to highlight some of the important challenges which Islamic banking and finance faces in Germany and discusses the prospects of success.

1.8 Concluding Remarks

Chapter 1 is an introductory chapter in which the evolution and rationale of Islamic banking and finance was described. As is demonstrated in Chapter 1, it may be concluded that Islamic banking and finance is in the early development stage and has gained attention following the recent financial crisis. Several Islamic banks, Islamic insurance companies, and other financial institutions are currently operating in Western Europe, including the United Kingdom and Germany. From a German perspective, the hallmark of development was the establishment of KT Bank AG in July 2015. It can also be concluded that despite having the largest Muslim population in Europe, positive investment potential, strong economic relations with Muslim countries, German regulators and political leaders have not proactively explored ways to develop *Shari'ah*-compliant financial products and services, unlike the United Kingdom. Existing studies reporting the potential of Islamic banking products and services show mixed results. Therefore, this study aims to explore the knowledge, attitude and perceptions of Muslims toward *Shari'ah*-compliant financial products and services using quantitative and qualitative research tools.

Chapter 2 provides a review on the fundamentals of Islamic economics, banking, and finance. Chapter 2 also provides an overview of important Islamic contracts and instruments and draws a comparison between the Islamic and conventional financial systems.

Chapter 2: Fundamentals of Islamic Economics, Banking, and Finance: A Basic Guide

2.1 Introduction

The objective of Chapter 2 is to provide an overview of the fundamentals of Islamic economics, banking, and finance, and the underlying principles that govern Islamic financial instruments and contracts. This study is built on important theoretical concepts reviewed in this chapter. Chapter 2 will serve as a foundation for Chapter 3, which reviews contemporary challenges faced by the Islamic financial industry.

Chapter 2 is structured as follows: section 2.2 provides introductory information about Islam, *Shari'ah,* and different sources of *Shari'ah*/Islamic law. Section 2.3 discusses the origin of Islamic economics. Section 2.4 reviews Islamic banking and highlights different fundamental principles of modern Islamic banking. Section 2.5 describes characteristics and principles of Islamic banking and finance. Section 2.6 provides details about the different instruments and contracts of the Islamic financial system. Section 2.7 includes a comparative analysis between Islamic and conventional financial systems. Finally, section 2.8 presents concluding remarks.

2.2 Understanding of Islam and *Shari'ah*

The principles of Islamic economics system are based on *Shari'ah,* which is the foundation of Islam (Omar *et al.*, 2013; Abdullah & Chee, 2010). Before explaining Islamic economics and the various elements that comprise Islamic economics, including banking and finance, it is important to define and explain the concept of *Shari'ah* and Islam. In an Arabic context, the word *Islam* means *submitting will to God. Oneness of God* is the central point of Islam and states that every component and form of Muslim life, including government, laws, administration, and individual life, revolves around the central point of Oneness of God (Tarlinton, 2004).

The contemporary legal framework of Islamic banking and finance is derived from the *Shari'ah,* which describes the Islamic rules that are based on the *Quran,* the holy book of Muslims and *Sunnah,* sayings and actions of the Prophet Muhammad (Qaseem, 2016; Malkawi, 2014; Krichene, 2013). The literal meaning of the Arabic word *Shari'ah* is *path to truth or seeking guidance* (Rahman, 2005). *Shari'ah* describes divine revelations made by *Allah* through *Quran* and the teachings of the Prophet Muhammad. The word *Shari'ah* is also interchangeably used to mean *Shari'ah Islamiyah* or *Islamic law,* but in general *Shari'ah* is used in broader perspective. Malkawi (2014) makes clear that *Shari'ah* is the divine law of Islam and Islamic economics, politics, finance, and all religious and social affairs are governed by this divine law.

2.2.1 Purpose of *Shari'ah*

According to Kharoufa (2000), the aim of Islam and *Shari'ah* is the wellbeing of people, and guidance in finding the right path in this world and the hereafter. Furthermore, Kharoufa (2000) states five benefits behind the revelation of *Shari'ah,* which includes:

1) To preserve religion (Islam)
2) To preserve the soul
3) To preserve the mind
4) To preserve procreation
5) To preserve wealth

According to the teachings of Islam, everything in this universe belongs to God (Wouters, 2013). The whole philosophy of Islam circles around these areas to preserve wealth on the principles of justice and equality, and to preserve religion by following the right path (Kharoufa, 2000). The message of the *Shari'ah* is not primarily for Muslims; Islam presents itself as a universal religion that is relevant for all human beings. The above mentioned advantages of *Shari'ah* are interlinked.

2.2.2 Sources of *Shari'ah*/Islamic Law

Sources of *Shari'ah*/Islamic law can be categorized as primary and secondary (Jamaldeen, 2012). Primary sources can be further categorized as revealed and non-revealed. Revealed sources are those like the *Quran,* which was directly conveyed by *Allah* to the Prophet Muhammad. Non-revealed are the *Sunnah* and *Hadith* (Malkawi, 2014; Ahmed, 2006). The *Quran*, the word of God, and the *Sunnah* are believed to be the primary sources of *Shari'ah* (Shanmugam and Zahari, 2009). These two sources are most authentic and accepted unanimously by Muslims. The precise meaning of the word *Quran* is *recitation.* The whole foundation of Islam is based on teachings embedded in the *Quran.* The revelation to the Prophet Muhammad took about 23 years, and the *Quran* consists of 114 chapters that include 6,666 verses.

The *Sunnah* is the second integral part of *Shari'ah* (Shanmugam & Zahari, 2009). Some verses of the *Quran* are very simple to understand by ordinary persons but other verses required further information to grasp their essence. Sometimes the word *Sunnah* is interchangeably used with the term *Hadith. Sunnah* is the practical life of the Prophet Muhammad, which includes deeds, dealings, and day to day economic activities, and the *Hadith* is the collection of His words and sayings.

Secondary sources include *Ijma*, *Qiyas* and others. The word *Ijma* is originated from the Arabic word *ajma'a,* which means *to determine* and *to agree upon something* (Shanmugam & Zahari, 2009). In the view of Malkawi (2014), *Ijma* is a consensus of Islamic scholars on a point of law. Thus, it is a consensus or an agreement on a particular matter by the Muslim jurists in a given time frame, and it is referred to as the third source of *Shari'ah*. *Qiyas* means analogical reasoning and it is a systematic process of finding solutions to contemporary matters on the basis of the *Quran* and the Prophet *Sunnah*, and it is considered the fourth source of *Shari'ah* (Nomani & Rahnema, 1994). According to Malkawi (2014), *Ijtihad* is a non-revealed *Shari'ah* source of law and it means an *individual intellectual effort and wider independent reasoning*. The word *Ijtihad* is derived from the word *juh'd*, which means *to put effort to perform some activity*. *Ijtihad* can only be exercised in those situations where jurists are unable to find solutions in basic sources of *Shari'ah* (Ahmed, 2006).

2.3 Definition of Islamic Economics

According to Chapra (1996:43), Islamic economics has developed as an interdisciplinary field of study with the passage of time and through interpretation of the *Quran* by jurists, historians, commentators, and social and political reformers such as "Abu Yusuf (d. 182/798), al-Mas'udi (d.346/957), al-Mawardi (d. 450/1058), Ibn Hazm (d. 456/1064), al-Sarakhsi (d.483/1090), al-Tusi (d.485/1093), al-Ghazali (d.505/1111), Ibn Taymiyyah (d.728/1328), Ibn al-Ukhuwwah (d.729/1329), Ibn al-Qayyim (d. 751/1350), al-Shatibi (d. 790/1388), Ibn Khaldun (d.808/1406), al- Maqrizi (d.845/1442), al-Dawwani (d.906/1501), and Shah Waliyullah (d.1176/1762)."

The goal of the Islamic economic system is to balance scarce resources and unlimited human needs by efficient and effective utilization of those limited resources through high moral standards (Asutay, 2007). Many Islamic scholars have attempted to define Islamic economics and its benefits for the overall Muslim society. Choiruzzad and Nugroho (2013:958) have quoted the definitions of Islamic economics cited by Robert Hefner as:

> "Islamic Economics that asserts that Islamic traditions of law and organization provide a more just and equitable model for economic growth than do the rival systems of Western capitalism and socialism."
> "All economic activities and related efforts that are established and promoted by Islamic economy movement as part of their campaign to Islamize the economy."

Hassan (2010:222–223) cited the definition of Islamic economics given by Khurshid Ahmed, one of the prominent Islamic economists as:

> "Islamic Economics deals with the economic problems of man from a new perspective, spelling out an approach for solving the society's problems that draws upon the sources of Islamic faith, culture and tradition, while availing itself of the whole experience of humanity in the field, past and present. The uniqueness of the Islamic approach lies in the integration of moral and material, spiritual and mundane, ethical and socio-physical aspects of life. Islam stresses the development of humanity with social values, instead of only material development."

2.3.1 Origin of Islamic Banking, Finance, and Economics

Ahmad (2000) stated that the roots of modern Islamic banking and economics go back to the 1960s and 1970s in countries like Pakistan, Egypt, and Malaysia. In Egypt, two events played an important role in the advancement of Islamic banking and economics worldwide. First, the Mit-Ghamer Savings Bank (1963–67) was established on the concept of German savings banks but within the framework established in the religious injunctions of Islam. These German savings banks were formed on the concept of rural financing.

Second, the establishment of the 'Nasr Social Bank' in 1971 was an important development that aimed to uplift the standards of living for the poor. Moreover, in Malaysia, an important development took place in 1963 when 'Tabung Haji' (a financial institution with the aim to function as a *Shari'ah*-compliant financial intermediary between those who have surplus funds and those who need it) was developed. On the other hand, Alrifai (2015) argued that the origin of theories of Islamic economics and commerce dates back to the inception of Islam, and that the Islamic financial system evolved almost 40 years ago and is still considered dynamic and young. Hunt-Ahmed (2013) argued that Islamic economic theory has evolved since the 1970s but Islam as religion has existed for more than 1400 years.

According to Alim (2014), there is no doubt that the Mit-Ghamer Savings bank was the first bank in Egypt if not in the Muslim world. However, it was shut down for various political reasons in 1967. Dubai Islamic Bank, established in 1975, is widely considered the first Islamic commercial bank. The Islamic Development Bank (IDB) was also established in 1975 with the objective of stimulating cooperation among Muslim countries and implementing the financial and economic agenda of the Organization of Islamic Countries (OIC).

2.4 Islamic Banking

Ribera *et al.* (2011) stated that the contemporary form of Islamic banking evolved in recent years, although Islamic financial contracts have been in existence since the times of the Prophet Muhammad. Islamic banking is an important segment of the Islamic economic system and Islamic banks "were the first financial institutions established under *Shari'ah* principles" (Jamaldeen, 2012:56). Islamic banking shares many features and characteristics with conventional banking. However, some Islamic principles, such as the prohibition of *Riba*, quite distinctly distinguish Islamic banking practices from those of conventional banks (Alrifai, 2015).

The definition of Islamic banking is important to this discussion. Hunt-Ahmed (2013:1) defines Islamic banking as:

> "An Islamic Financial Institution (IFI) refers to any financial institution that performs Islamic transactions derived from either Islamic law or Islamic economic theory. An Islamic Bank is an institution that performs conventional banking services (or their Islamic equivalent) such as checking accounts, savings accounts, loans, and so forth."

Olaoye (2013:24) cite the definition of Islamic banking presented by prominent Islamic scholar Siddiqi as:

> "Islamic banking as the business of financial intermediation, mobilizing savings from the public on the basis of partnership and profit and advancing capital to entrepreneurs on the same basis. Islamic banking therefore, is a system of banking that complies with the principles of *Shari'ah* (Islamic law) and its practical application through the development of Islamic economics."

El-Hawary *et al.* (2004:5) considered below mentions four principles as the foundation of modern Islamic banking:

(1) "Risk-sharing: the terms of financial transactions need to reflect a symmetrical risk/return distribution among each participant to the transaction."
(2) Materiality: all financial transactions must have material finality i.e., be linked to underlying assets. It means that financial assets such as options and derivatives without backing of real assets are not acceptable.
(3) No exploitation: the transaction should be fair and transparent and no party should have undue influence and advantage.
(4) No financing of sinful activities: financing to only permissible activities in the light of the *Quran* and *Sunnah* is allowed. Therefore, financing to industries and activities such as alcohol, pork, and gambling is strictly prohibited.

Islamic banking is not solely the avoidance of *Riba;* ethical considerations also play an important role (Alrifai, 2015). Karim (2001) while discussing the characteristics of Islamic banks stated that Islamic banking was a type of universal banking with special characteristics. For instances, Islamic banks offer a hybrid of services including both investment and commercial banking, which are unique in structure and objectives when compared to conventional banks.

2.4.1 Importance of Islamic Banking for Muslims

It is important to explain that why Islamic banking, or more precisely *Shari'ah*-compliant products and services, are important for Muslims. The rationale of the development of Islamic financial institution is that Muslims want to engage in international trade and business so they might become part of the global economic system. However, the financial system is dominated by capitalistic business practices that contradict Islamic values, such as the moral prohibition of interest (Hunt-Ahmed, 2013). Therefore, it is necessary for Muslims to develop a system through which to conduct business and trade while adhering to Islamic values. Asutay (2013) pointed out that in the mid-nineteenth century Muslims tried to establish *authentic Islamic institutions.* Primarily, the purpose of establishing such institutions is to enable Muslims to adhere with the teachings of Islam while engaging in financial and economic activities.

According to Hunt-Ahmed (2013:2), "integration of religious practices into daily life by governing business under Islamic" law is important for Muslims. As previously stated in this chapter, *Allah* bestowed *Shari'ah* and Muslims are advised to follow the rules of *Shari'ah* to find the right path (Kharoufa, 2000). These rules are obligations for all Muslims and Muslims are supposed to spend their lives within the limits defined in *Shari'ah*. This also includes compliance within the context of trade and business and obedience of the rule that states that *Riba* is strictly prohibited in Islam despite the fact that *Allah* has encouraged Muslims to engage in trade (El-Gamal, 2000).

2.5 Characteristics and Features of Islamic Economic System

As mentioned earlier in this chapter, the Islamic economic system is based on a set of values defined in *Shari'ah*. Below are some of the unique features and characteristics of the Islamic economic system, which differentiate it from other prevailing economics systems including capitalism, communism, and socialism.

2.5.1 The Prohibition of *Riba* (Interest or Usury)

According to Alrifai (2015), the Islamic economic system encourages trade and commerce and emphasizes fairness and social justice. The prohibition of *Riba* (interest or Usury) is considered one of the most important elements of the Islamic economic system (Krim, 2001). As such, a significant part of the Islamic economic paradigm is based on the prohibition of *Riba*. The word *Riba* means *an increase, an unearned premium, and an excess amount that a consumer pays on a borrowed amount*.

It is widely believed among Muslim scholars that the prohibition of *Riba* draws a clear distinction between the Islamic economic system and Western financial systems as it establishes a higher threshold for ethical business conduct. Islamic financial institutions are morally, ethically, and religiously obligated to eliminate interest from their institutions (Lewis, 2009). Alrifai (2015) explained that the literal meaning of *Riba* is *effortless gain* or *the profit that is received without giving anything in exchange*. Alrifai further demonstrated that in the Western financial system, interest is an excess payment made by a customer in excess of principal amount borrowed. In Islamic finance, this excess payment, known as *Riba*, is prohibited as the exploitation of the people by financial institutions.

Likewise, the *raison d'etre* for Islamic financial institutes is to avoid *Riba*. This subject has been extensively and clearly stated in the primary sources; *Quran*, *Sunnah* and *Hadith*. Below are some of the verses from *Quran* that emphasize the prohibition of *Riba* for Muslims:

- "That which you give as interest to increase the peoples' wealth increases not with God; but that which you give in charity, seeking the goodwill of God, multiplies manifold" (Surah Rome, Verse 39).

- "And for their taking interest even though it was forbidden for them, and their wrongful appropriation of other people's money, and we have prepared for those among them who reject faith a grievous punishment " (Surah al-Nisa', verse 161). "Believers! Do not swallow *Riba*, doubled and redoubled, and be mindful of Allah so that you may attain true success" (Al Imran, Ayat 130).

In the light of the above-mentioned verses of the *Quran* the message is quite clear about the avoidance of *Riba*. References regarding the prohibition of *Riba* can also be found in the various *Hadiths* of Prophet Muhammad:

- Hazrat Jabir Ibn-e-Abdullah (RA): The Prophet, (SAWS) cursed the receiver and the payer of interest, the one who records it and the witnesses to the transaction and said: "They are all alike [in guilt]." (Muslim, Tirmidhi and Musnad Ahmad) (BankIslami, 2006:14).
- Hazrat Amr bin Al Aas (RA): "When interest based dealing becomes common among people, they will start facing draught and shortage of food. And when bribery becomes norm among people they will live under constant fear of their enemy" (BankIslami, 2006:14).

2.5.2 The Prohibition of *Gharar*

Generally, *Gharar* means *uncertainty and excessive risk*. El-Gamal (2006:58) states the definition of *Gharar* as "the sale of probable items whose existence or characteristics are not certain, the risky nature of which makes the transaction akin to gambling." *Gharar* is prohibited in Islamic financial transactions because of the lack of proper information about the subject matter, which causes uncertainty and risks. Therefore, business activities that involve concealing facts about the transactions made fall under the *Gharar* prohibition.

Furthermore, Muslim jurists have drawn a distinction between major *Gharar*, excessive *Gharar*, and minor *Gharar* (El-Gamal, 2006). In the case of excessive *Gharar*, a transaction or contract is entirely invalid according to Islamic law. However, it is not possible to completely limit the impact of minor *Gharar* (risk) in financial contracts and transactions and, therefore, minor *Gharar* is accepted.

According to Al-Saati (2003), Muslim jurists have been unable to precisely define *Gharar*. Therefore, it is difficult to comprehend it while keeping in mind all the nuances. Al-Saati quoted three aspects of the definition of *Gharar* presented by Al-Darir in jurisprudential context:

First, *Gharar* means *uncertainty* and *doubtfulness*. This term mainly arises due to lack of information about the probability of some future enforceable event. Al-Staati quoted the definition of *Gharar* as "uncertainty over the existence of the subject matter of sale." The Likewise, the *Hanafi* and *Shafi* schools of jurisprudence viewed the *Gharar* in the context of sale. Second, the *Gharar* also describes ignorance of subject matter pertaining to a sale and this aspect of *Gharar* is common among the followers of the *Zahiri* school of thought. In the words of *Ibn Hazm*, "*Gharar* in sale occurs when the purchaser does not know what he has bought and the seller does not know what he has sold." Finally, the definition of *Gharar* combines the previously mentioned two aspects of doubtfulness and uncertainty. Many Muslim jurists believe that *Gharar* takes place when one or both parties hide necessary information about the sale (Al-Saati, 2003). El-Gamal (2006:58–59) stated three important conditions concerning *Gharar,* which invalidate a financial transaction or a contract. First, major *Gharar* must be present to affect the invalidation of a contract. This means that uncertainty or an intentionally concealing of facts would have a substantial impact on the contractual agreement. Second, the potential effects of *Gharar* must constitute a financial transaction such as a sale. Finally, *Gharar* must affect the principle provisions of a contract such as price or object for sale.

There are two kinds of *Gharar, Jahalah* and *Qimar,* which are also known as gambling (BankIslami, 2006). The *Jahalah Gharar* means that the subject matter is not explicitly specified. For example, the sale of something that is concealed in such a way that the buyer cannot be fully aware of it. *Qimar Gharar* is prohibited because it contains a significant element of uncertainty. This form of *Gharar* is common practice in current times such as when dealing with prize bonds, lotteries, and speculations. In summary, *Gharar* is prohibited because it brings uncertainty and undue risk, which may destabilize Islamic financial system.

2.5.3 The Prohibition of *Maysir*

As this chapter has thus far described, in Islamic finance, *Riba, Gharar* and *Maysir* are prohibited (Nienhaus, 2011a; Chowdhury, 2015). Chowdhury (2015) argued that *Maysir* is also known as gambling or *Qimar* and is an activity that involves betting on an event where, upon conclusion of the event, one party emerges as the winner and the other as the loser. *Maysir,* or *Al-Maysir,* is unearned income and is strictly forbidden by the *Quran* and the traditions of Prophet Muhammad, as it constitutes earnings made through the games of chance (Obaidullah, 2005). In the case of *Maysir,* people tend to deliberately take risks in the hopes of reaping higher returns. In the views of Al-Saati (2003:7), "The *Quran* explicitly forbids gambling (*Maysir*) and usury." Furthermore, gambling has two dimensions. One dimension is that which constitutes the use of skills and knowledge to bet on outcomes of games such as football and horse racing. The second dimension occurs when someone gambles in casinos and bars in hopes of winning a quick gain on the money used to place the bet.

Ibn Taymiyah and Ibn Al-Qayyim were the first Muslim jurists to observe the similarity between excess *Gharar* and gambling (Al-Saati, 2003). Both believed that excess *Gharar* was a form of *Maysir* and any sale that has an element of *Gharar* will be void and considered an injustice from the perspective of Islamic law.

According to Gait (2009) the rationale behind the prohibition of *Maysir* is the high risk inherited in the activities associated with gambling and placing wagers for unearned gain. These activities are also not viewed by society as moral because individuals will earn substantial sums of money while, as a result, others will face financial loss. Therefore, gambling is an unnecessary activity because it cannot add value and contribute to national development.

2.5.4 Profit and Loss Sharing

Another important feature of Islamic finance is profit and loss sharing (PLS). Islam encourages individuals to take part in trade and other economic activities, which will help facilitate the spread of Islam to different parts of the world through the actions of Muslim traders (Hoque *et al.*, 2013). Trade and economic activities conducted by Muslim traders should be based on fair principles including PLS (Lewis, 2009). Moreover, sharing of profit is in accordance with the teachings of Islam, and this very principle has paved the way for the establishment of Islamic banking.

Kahf and Khan (1992) elaborated on the principle of profit and loss sharing by dividing it into two parts: the profit sharing principle (PSP) and the profit and loss sharing principle (PLSP). The profit sharing principle is equivalent of *Mudarabah* mode of financing where one party provides the necessary funds and other party provides the required skills to conduct business. In this case, profit sharing takes place between both parties on the basis of a contractual agreement. However, the equity provider bears all the risk in the case of a loss. In the case of profit and loss sharing the partnership is constructed in such a way that the equity provider and the non-equity provider have the right to take profits based on an agreed upon ratio. Both also have the obligation to share the risks and any subsequent losses on the basis of capital contributed. Section 2.6, which discusses Islamic financial instruments, contracts, and tools, will further expand on the concept profit and loss.

2.5.5 Asset Backed Financing

Asset backed financing is another feature of Islamic banking and finance (Kammer *et al.*, 2015). Islamic economic principles discourage financing obtained through the acquisition of debt and encourage equity and asset backed financing. According to Ahmed (2010), one of the main reasons the Islamic finance industry experienced a lower level of discourse during the recent global financial crisis was that financing made by Islamic banks was backed by real assets rather than conceptualized assets based in speculation. Islamic law prohibits dealing with *toxic products* like credit default swaps and derivatives. *Sukuk* bonds, which are backed by real assets, are one of the key instruments used for financing by Islamic banks, insurance companies, corporations, governments, and other entities.

Alrifai (2015) argued that the foundation of the global economy is based on debt and that debt is seen as a vital ingredient for endless economic growth. Alrifai also pointed out that the use of excessive debt in our financial system was one of the main causes of the recent global financial crisis. On the other hand, financing in the Islamic financial system is tied to physical assets (Alrifai, 2015). However, Alrifai acknowledged that it is not possible to change a debt-based financial system into an asset-based financial system in a short time, and stressed that the amount of debt in the system is much higher than the actual total value of the assets backing that debt.

2.5.6 Prohibition of Investment in Haram Products and Industries

The Islamic economic system is not merely a set of rules concerning the activities of conducting business but also provides an ethical framework for doing business (Ahmad, 2000). This framework presents the concepts of *halal* and *haram* in all activities related to conducting business, social, and public affairs. Furthermore, the limitations of *halal* and *haram* function as a moral filter in the conscience and subconscious of individuals working at different levels within the system. On the contrary, the moral filter in Western and capitalist societies has vanished in such cases where there is no distinction between raising money on ethical and moral grounds and raising money through, and spending money on, unethical products such as alcohol, drugs, pork, gambling, prostitution, and pornography. Because the Islamic ethical framework strictly prohibits dealing in said unethical lines of business because they are neither beneficial to the individual or society as a whole. This framework showcases the ethical and social dimensions that are the basic maxims of an Islamic economic system.

According to Wilson (2002), Islamic banks offer unique products and services that are aligned with *Shari'ah* guidelines. Moreover, Islamic banks invest the money of their customers in permissible products, thus enhancing the confidence of customers in Islamic banking. This differs from the confidence held for conventional banks that aim to build close relationships with clients, offer higher quality services, and leverage their clients' high net worth. Instead of looking for the net worth of clients, Islamic banks offer their products and services based on common faith and ethical business relationships that exist between the clients and banks.

2.5.7 Ethical Values and Rules

In the view of Alrifai (2015), in Islamic finance certain ethical values and rules are also followed by the participants of a financial transaction. The objective of imposing such ethical values and rules is to provide fairness. As such, they are equally applicable to consumers and financial institutions. Nienhaus (2011a) stated that Islamic finance is frequently portrayed as ethical finance. Moreover, it is assumed that Islamic financial activities are linked with the real economy and the parties of financial transactions share business risks. Following are the important ethical rules as adapted from Alrifai (2015):

- One cannot earn a return or profit unless one is willing to assume some level of risk.
- There is no such thing as a guaranteed return.

- One cannot lose more than one invests.
- All investors must be treated equally.
- One cannot sell what one does not own.
- In order for one's money to earn a profit, said money must be invested in something productive.
- There must be transparency in any financial dealings.
- All forms of gambling must be removed from any and all transactions; and
- Money is not a commodity.

2.6 Islamic Financial Instruments, Contracts, and Tools

The Islamic financial system operates as a financial intermediary between those who have excess resources (primarily households) and those who require them for investment purpose (primarily businesses). This important role of financial intermediation is based on the use of a number of financial instruments, contracts, and tools that have been developed over time. Islam places a great deal of emphasis on trade and encourages all participants to write down their business dealings in the form of contracts. According to Greuning and Iqbal (2008:17), the Islamic financial system uses a set of financial instruments, contracts, and tools for "real economic activities, financing, intermediation and social welfare." In early Islamic history *Sarrafs,* moneychangers, performed the role of financial intermediaries and their basic business functions were akin to a conventional bank.

As we can see in Figure 1, Islamic financial instruments, contracts, and tools can be broadly categorized into two groups. Although there is no classification of such instruments in Islamic jurisprudence, on the basis of function and common features these contracts and instruments may be grouped in a particular category. The first set of instruments is based on the principle of profit and loss sharing (investing) and consists of *Musharakah* (commonly known as equity partnership or participation) and *Mudarabah* (principal or agent partnership). This group is also known as participatory modes of Islamic financing.

Nagaoka (2010:67) quoted Qureshi who was one of the early advocators of the participatory form of business as follows: "Islam prohibits interest but allows profits and partnership. If the banks, instead of allowing loans to the industry, become its partners, share the loss and profit with it, there is no objection against such banks in the Islamic system."

Nienhaus (2015:161) states that in practice the use of a participatory mode of financing on the basis of profit and loss sharing is not very common and further mentions that "PLS financing hardly ever takes place in Islamic banks. Bad experience of pioneering banks and theoretical explanations of adverse selection and moral hazard issues in PLS financing (where the ratio of profit sharing is fixed in advance and not changed afterwards) can explain the abstinence from participatory modes of financing."

The second group of instruments (see Figure 1), contracts in which the bank has no partnership with the client, are based on non-profit and loss sharing principles that are most frequently used for financing activities. These are also called non-participatory modes of financing. For the purpose of trade financing, *Murabahah* (cost-plus sale), *Bay' Salam* (forward sale) and *Tawarruq* (cash financing) are in practice. In addition to these instruments, *Ijarah* (leasing) and *Istisnah* (construction financing) are also known as financing instruments.

In addition to these basic sets of contracts and instruments, Islamic financial institutions also use other tools and products such as *Sukuk* (asset-backed bond), *Takaful* (insurance), *Qard Hasan* (benevolent loan) and *Waqf* (endowment). *Sukuk* is one of the most important and widely used capital market products.

An independent *Shari'ah* board must authorize all Islamic financial instruments, contracts, and products. An independent *Shari'ah* board consists of a group of scholars who have expertise in Islamic law and contemporary economics, who are incorporated in an institution, and who possess the authority to check the authenticity and compliance of the instruments, contracts, and products with Islamic economic principles (Alrifai, 2015). The *Shari'ah* board thoroughly examines the structures of proposed products and issue a *fatwa* only when compliance with Islamic law is confirmed. The *fatwa* is a written approval and an established religious procedure acknowledging validity and acceptance.

In the following sections each instrument and contract of profit and loss sharing and the non-participatory mode of financing will be elaborated in detail. Critical evaluations will be provided along with practical examples, features, and frequency of use.

Figure 1: Islamic Financial Instruments, Contracts, and Tools

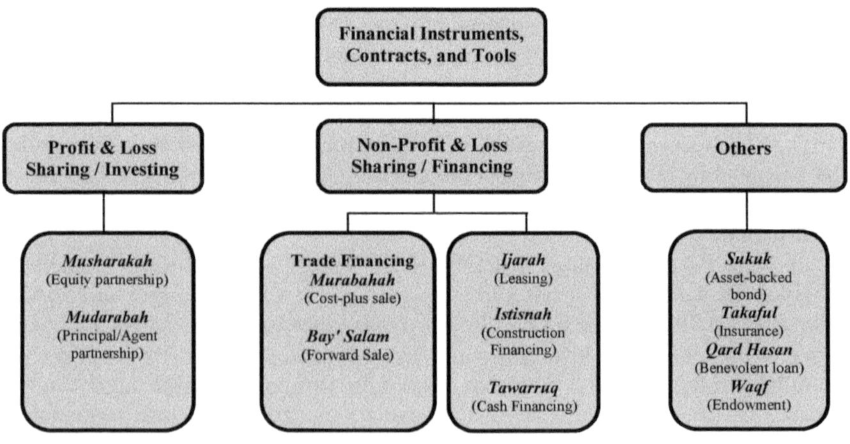

Source: Adapted from Greuning and Iqbal (2008)

2.6.1 *Musharakah* (Equity Partnership, Joint Venture)

Meaning and Definitions

The literal meaning of the word *Musharakah* is *sharing*, and it is derived from the Arabic word *shirkah*, which means *partnership*. Therefore, *Musharakah* is a kind of partnership where two or more people contribute labor and financial resources on the basis of profit and loss sharing (PSL). Iqbal and Molyneux (2005:20) defined *Musharakah* as "an arrangement where two or more parties establish a joint commercial enterprise and all contribute capital as well as labor and management as a general rule."

Historical Perspective

According to Iqbal and Mirakhor (2011), *Musharakah* is a hybrid instrument that is based on *shirkah* (partnership) and *Mudarabah* (principal or agent partnership). It should be noted that partnerships existed even before the emergence of Islam as a religion. Prophet Muhammad not only accepted it as a business contract but also extensively used it for trading purposes.

Use and Application

According to Ernst *et al.* (2013), Diminishing *Musharakah* is mainly used to finance real estate construction projects and for financing to small and medium enterprises (SMEs). Islamic banks use the *Musharakah* instrument in a number of ways and a *consecutive partnership* is one way in which it can be used (Iqbal & Mirakhor, 2011). In a consecutive partnership, deposit holders of a bank who keep their deposits for a full financial year become partners in the bank's earnings for that period, irrespective of the employment of their funds during that year. To accomplish this, an adjustment was necessary to overcome accounting challenges related to recognizing profits or losses for each depositor account.

According to Visser (2009), under a *Musharakah* contract a joint venture is created as an independent legal entity and *Musharakah* financing is deemed appropriate for long duration of projects. The financial risk is involved on the part of the entrepreneur and capital contributions may vary from project to project. For instance, the Saudi Hollandi Bank (SHB), based in Saudi Arabia, contributes capital up to 90% in a project and may require representation on the board of a financed joint-venture entity.

Musharakah has a wide range of applications in domestic trade, commerce, and agriculture (Kettell, 2011). To enable clients to trade in the local market, The Al Baraka Islamic Bank of Sudan finances on the basis of *Musharakah*. The bank and its clients form a partnership, and full cost of purchased goods is shared. A special *Musharakah* account is opened at the bank. Regarding profit distribution, the bank shares net profit with the client, and surplus profits are divided among the partners of the *Musharakah* account. But any loss is also shared among the partners in accordance to the capital contributions of each. In addition, the Al Baraka Islamic Bank of Sudan also finances the import of goods under a similar business model as that discussed above. Some other examples of diverse application of financing under *Musharakah* basis are opening a letter of credit by the Bank Islam Malaysia for its clients to import goods and by the Sudanese Islamic Bank to provide financing for agriculture.

According to Iqbal and Mirakhor (2011) *Musharakah Mutanaqisah,* commonly known as diminishing partnership, is a sub category of the *Musharakah* instrument. It is a kind of equity partnership contract that is also widely used for real estate financing. Under this contract, a capital provider, such as a bank, and a customer jointly own the property. However, the ownership held by the bank diminishes with the passage of time as the customer contributes payments.

Kettell (2011) cites several applications of diminishing *Musharakah* contracts such as: the purchase of houses, service sector purchases, small business purchases, and commercial and real estate purchases. For example, the Jordan Islamic Bank, based in Jordan, primarily uses diminishing *Musharakah* to finance the construction of commercial buildings and housing projects like the Irbid commercial market, the municipal college in Jerash, and the hospital in Zerqa.

Alrifai (2015) pointed out that since *Musharakah* financing involves high risks and early Islamic banks were not able to manage complex nature of business structures. As a result early banks took a cautious approach toward using *Musharakah.* But this instrument has gained acceptance in contemporary Islamic banking with the availability of well-educated human capital and increasing interest from Islamic bankers in the area of asset securitization.

Why less used?

Musharakah is believed to be *the purest of finance* and a particular focus has been placed on it during the early development of Islamic banking operations. However, its use in modern Islamic banking is not very common due to operational difficulties and moral hazards (Kettell, 2011). Concern from the perspective of the financial institutions stems from operational matters such as duration of a contract, ownership of assets, management of two streams of contributions, and determination of profitability. Banks avoid financing under *Musharakah* because fraudulent calculations on the part of partners may undermine the entire business venture and the reputation of the bank.

Agency problems are another cause of less usage of *Musharakah* contracts in practical life because *Musharakah* use involves profit and loss sharing, which may lead to disagreements among partners (Visser, 2009). Furthermore, in the absence of securities and collaterals banks hesitate to take undue risks in the presence of other less risky instruments such as *Murabahah* (cost-plus sale).

Andrews (2010) stated that unfeasible commercial viability of financing under the *Musharakah* principle is an important reason for its low use in the contemporary Islamic banking. Use of the *Musharakah* principle involves rigorous effort to supervise extensive business ventures and come with notably high levels of risk. Therefore, banks are not sufficiently compensated for costs incurred and risks taken.

Importance of Instrument

Due to operational difficulties and less use in modern day Islamic banking, *Musharakah* is considered an out-dated instrument despite the fact that *Musharakah* is "the most authentic form of Islamic financing" instrument (Kettell, 2011). After the recent global financial crisis, the West has become attracted toward the Islamic financial system because it was proven more resilient in comparison to the debt-based conventional financial system. Therefore, a number of scholars have called on financial institutions to base their operations on pure *Shari'ah*-based modes of financing rather than on *Shari'ah*-compliant modes.

By incorporating *Musharakah* as a core financing instrument Islamic financial institutions may also dispel the general myth that these institutions merely engage with debt-based products "under the guise of profit and mark-up" (Kettell, 2011:88). It is eminent that financial institutions will overcome problems arising from the use of *Musharakah* and begin using it on a regular basis. *Musharakah* is also inevitably important for the development of the Islamic finance industry and projection of its image as a real profit and loss sharing (PLS) economic model.

2.6.2 *Mudarabah* (Investment Partnership)

Meaning and Definition

Mudarabah is a type of equity based partnership contract that is also known as *trust financing*, and is one of the core profit and loss sharing contracts in Islamic finance. *Mudarabah* is described as a *passive partnership* because one person contributes only capital and takes no part in the management of the business. It is quite similar to the conventional limited partnership contract in which one partner contributes capital and the other contributes management skills, while profits are shared based on an agreed upon ratio (Kettell, 2011; Iqbal & Mirakhor, 2011).

Nienhaus (2015) argues that the *Mudarabah* contract is a rare Islamic financial contract where Islamic banks practice profit and loss sharing through deposit investment accounts of customers. However, in reality, use for this purpose also deviates from the genuine model of *Mudarabah* financing in that there is a building up of reserves from profits to protect against potential risks rather than depositing a share of the profits with the investment account holders.

Historical perspective

The word *Mudarabah* is originated from the Arabic word *darb fi al-ard*, which means those people "who journey through the earth seeking the bounty of *Allah*" (Kettell, 2011:67). In Islamic jurisprudence, scholars believe that *Mudarabah* instrument is based on a partnership contract which Prophet Muhammad concluded with Khadija, a businesswomen who later on married with Prophet. He travelled to Syria as an agent for her and the business. Therefore, *Mudarabah* instrument is validated through the *Sunnah* of Prophet Muhammad.

Use and Application

Kettell (2011:72) argues that *Mudarabah* is a highly recommended Islamic finance profit and loss sharing (PLS) instrument and Islamic banks use it as a mode of financing to "dentists, physicians, engineers, traders or [whomever]". Nevertheless, *Mudarabah* entails high-level risk on the part of a bank because an agent can only be made accountable in the case of negligence. Generally, banks exercise due diligence to mitigate any potential risk before entering into such arrangements. The *Mudarabah* contract is treated as a short-term partnership in Iran, and banks are advised to engage proactively in cooperative *Mudarabah* funding. However, commercial institutions are not permitted to extend *Mudarabah* funding to the private sector for the purpose of imports.

Visser (2009) found that *Mudarabah* is primarily used to fund short duration projects and trade. Therefore, it is mainly used by customers to deposits funds in banks for the purpose of earning profits. Said (2008) also stated that *Mudarabah* contracts have been used mainly for the financing of commerce. It is possible to use such contracts in other areas of the economy such as agriculture, trade, and industry.

Alrifai (2015) asserts that a *Mudarabah* contract is used in Islamic finance to fund real estate projects, angel investments, and endowments. On the other hand, Ernst, *et al.* (2013) states that *Mudarabah* is used to finance the investment projects of companies.

Why less used?

Lack of a legal framework for *Mudarabah* in commercial law in non-Muslim countries, in particular, and in Muslim countries, in general, is a considerable disadvantage in the case of disputes (Kettell, 2011). Therefore, it is recommended that Islamic banks consider all potential risks, both legal and operational. Additionally, the duration of a *Mudarabah* contract is another operational inconvenience for Islamic banks as it disrupts cash flow planning and profit accrual. Any interference on the part of banks to amend an existing contract for something as simple as a condensed timeframe to completion of the project might void the contract in its entirety.

It is more suitable to use *Mudarabah* contracts for medium and long-term financing. Visser (2009) states that it is difficult to accurately determine the amount of profits or to prove deliberate negligence on the part of an agent. In the case of serious disputes, the bank must leverage cumbersome legal procedures, which makes the use of this instrument less widespread in financial industry.

On the contrary, Alrifai (2015:126) argued that the *Mudarabah* form of financing is common and uses the words "very popular" presenting the case of mutual funds and 401 (K) plans. 401 (K) plans are retirement saving schemes for selected employees and mostly used in the United States. Furthermore, hedge funds are also an extended form of the *Mudarabah* contract where fund managers charge a certain fee along with a share in profit generated from investments.

2.6.3 *Murabahah* (Cost-plus Sale/Mark-up Financing)

Meaning and Definition

Murabahah is one of the most widely used Islamic finance instrument (Ernst *et al.*, 2013; Alrifai, 2015). The instrument is used for trade financing as was demonstrated in Figure 1 (shown earlier in this chapter). *Murabahah* is also known as cost-plus sale and mark-up financing.

Use and Application

According to Ernst *et al.* (2013), *Murabahah* is used for purchasing automobiles, electronics, land, buildings, and machines. Alrifai (2015) discussed the fact that since the inception of modern Islamic banking in the 1970s *Murabahah* has become the most used Islamic financial instrument, mainly due to its simple structure and ease of use. Shanmugam and Zahari (2009) stated that *Murabahah* financing is mainly used to finance raw materials, manufacturing equipment, and consumer goods. Said (2008) mentioned that *Murabahah* is generally used for short-term financing and is a convenient mode of financing for the agriculture industry, consumer and microfinance sectors.

Visser (2009) stated that *Murabahah* is, by nature, a trade-financing instrument, but it has an extended use in areas of business such as transportation. For instance, Pakistan International Airlines (PIA) received financing from different banks in 2002 under the arrangement of *Murabahah* contracts to buy aircrafts. Kettell (2011) explained that *Murabahah* contracts have been used for financing of mortgages, automobiles, working capital, and syndicated credits. For example, in 2005 the ABC Islamic Bank and Emirates Islamic Bank jointly financed $70 million under a *Murabahah* contract for the construction of Esfahan Steal Company (ESCO) in Iran. Similarly, several banks in Pakistan used a *Murabahah* contract as a short-term financing tool to fund $110 million to the Hub River Power Company. In 2007, Emirates Telecommunications Corporation (Etisalat) successfully won an auction of a telecom license in Saudi Arabia worth $3.256 billion under a *Murabahah* arrangement. Additionally, the Dubai Islamic Bank financed letters of credit by using *Murabahah* contracts. These examples show diverse and universal application of *Murabahah* across different industries and countries.

However, Abdul-Rahman (2010) raises two important concerns in a *Murabahah-based* transaction. As a *Murabahah* agreement entails two different transactions, a tax treatment for these transactions is quite costly, particularly in the Western world. Thus, *Murabahah* becomes an expensive financing tool compared to conventional tools. For instance, under taxation laws in the United States a higher profit charged by a bank may be considered a capital gain, which may then be taxed as such. To circumvent this issue Islamic banks include a clause in *Murabahah* contracts stating that any such tax will be passed on to the customer. Therefore, this situation may have some serious issues for *Shari'ah* sensitive customers.

Another important concern is the establishment of a special purpose vehicle (SPV) by a financial institution to comply with Western banking laws (Abdul-Rahman, 2010). Financial institutions use special purpose vehicles to buy real estate, which is then sold to a customer. Even though this strategy is workable it adds additional costs that make *Murabahah* transactions expensive. It is not possible to create asset-backed securities for secondary-market trading. However, Alrifai (2015) finds that some liberal scholars in Malaysia have permitted the resale of *Murabahah* receivables. The argument in favour of such approval is that both purchase and sale transactions are in accordance with *Shari'ah* rules and support productive businesses. However, it should be noted that Malaysian scholars have been known to apply liberal interpretation to Islamic financial principles.

Criticism and Limitations

Kettell (2011) stated that in contemporary Islamic banking, *Murabahah* financing is above 75%. However, profit and loss based financing such as *Musharakah* and *Mudarabah* comprises almost 10% of the total assets of Islamic banks. As *Murabahah* is a *Shari'ah*-compliant instrument and rules of Islamic law are not fully applied in letter and spirit, it creates "a legal embarrassment for purists in the Islamic finance industry" (Kettell, 2011:60).

According to Shanmugam and Zahari (2009) a *Murabahah* contract is not a pure Islamic financing instrument because it has a close resemblance to conventional loans. The main argument is that a *Murabahah* transaction involves only credit risk and no ownership risk on the part of Islamic bank. With *Murabahah*, the bank buys the requested product after receiving an enforceable confirmation from a customer, and a sales transaction is quickly concluded by the bank in order to avoid storage costs and mitigate other risks, including natural calamities. Furthermore, the mark-up charged by the bank is also linked to current interest-rate benchmarks such as those established by the London Inter-Bank Offered Rate (LIBOR), which is not in accordance with Islamic teachings.

Khan and Bhatti (2008) maintains a similar opinions (Shanmugam & Zahari,2009) to other scholars who consider *Murabahah* a debt based financing contract that cannot meet the legality recognized by the primary sources of Islamic law: the *Quran* and *Sunnah*. Muslim scholars like *Imam Malik* and *Imam Shafi* recognized *Murabahah* as a sale, but they did not give any ruling in the case of an increase in price for a deferred payment on a sale. Nevertheless, many Muslim scholars have contradictory views about the authenticity of *Murabahah* instrument. Some scholars deem the as non-Islamic financial instruments due to the close resemblance to conventional banking instruments.

Iqbal and Mirakhor (2011) claimed that there is a widespread misunderstanding that *Murabahah* is a non-Islamic instrument. Basically there are two causes for this confusion. First, confusion arises from the lack of differentiation between a mark-up, interest, and conventional loans. In conventional financial system, when a bank offers a loan to a customer, only the bank bears a credit risk, but with *Murabahah* transactions, the Islamic bank purchases an asset and shares the risk of price fluctuations with the customer. Therefore, an Islamic bank faces both credit and price risk because a customer may ultimately refuse to buy the requested product from the bank. Iqbal and Mirakhor (2011:85) further rectify this misunderstanding in these strong words:

> "The confusion in equating *Murabahah* with a loan is not a new one. As mentioned earlier, Arab traders posed the same question during the time of the Prophet (PBUH). The legal difference between a *Murabahah* contract and an interest- based loan is clear: the former is a sales contract in which the price is increased for deferment of payment; the latter is an increase in the amount of a debt for deferment. The first is permitted, but the second is not."

Andrews (2010) believed that *Murabahah* and *Ijara* (leasing) were among the six old modes of business and trade and that their origin dates back to a time before the inception of Islam. These instruments have played a pivotal role in trade for thousands of centuries in the Middle and Far East. Andrews further assumes that Prophet Muhammad also exercised these contracts during his life.

However, Andrews (2010) points out two differences of opinions among international scholars concerning *Murabahah*. The first concern stems from the delivery of an item purchased by a bank for a customer. For example, sometimes a customer declines to take delivery of an item purchased by a bank for reasons such as a lower available price of that item in the open market. Hence, this situation is critical for a bank and because of it some banks demand *non-refundable deposits* as a safeguarding tool. As a result, some scholars raise objection about the precautious measures taken by banks (Andrews, 2010).

Another objection that religious scholars raise is concerning whether a bank should take possession of purchased item from a third person in the first place, store it in its own warehouse, and then sell it to a customer (Andrews, 2010). But, some scholars consider the stipulation of ownership in documents of an item purchase by a bank as sufficient condition for the legality of *Murabahah* transaction.

2.6.4 *Bay' Salam* (Forward Sale)

Meaning and Definition

Bay' Salam is an advanced-sale type of contract, commonly known as a forward sale contract, is one of the most exceptional instruments in Islamic finance. Under this type of contract a seller can sell a commodity against advance payment without transferring possession and ownership of that commodity to the buyer (Omar *et al.*, 2013). Prophet Muhammad allowed this contract to enable farmers to receive money to use to purchase necessary inputs of production for farming (Iqbal & Mirakhor, 2011). *Bay' Salam* was also used to finance import and export conducted by the merchants of Arabia who were allowed to sell their commodities in advance to obtain finances for their businesses. A *Bay' Salam* contract looks similar to a conventional forward-sale contract. However, it differs in terms of payment method because in a *Bay' Salam* contract a buyer pays full price at the time of entering into an agreement and in advance of receiving the goods, and this is the main difference between *Bay' Salam* and the conventional forward-sale contract.

In the view of Kettell (2011), Prophet Muhammad allowed the use of *Bay' Salam* contracts for farmers because at that point in time *usurious loans*, which are loans that are considered exploitative because they are tied to high rates of interest, were declared *Riba* and were prohibited by Islam. Similarly, traders who could not take loans on religious grounds were allowed to use *Bay' Salam* contracts.

Historical Perspective

Islam has an old history of the application of *Bay' Salam* contracts. Visser (2009) believed that the *Maliki* school of thought allowed *Bay' Salam* contracts to trade in secondary markets in Medina. However, these contracts were exclusively limited to food items such as wheat, dates, salt, and barley. But other Islamic schools hold the view that any resale without an actual delivery or a transfer of ownership is not permitted in a *Bay' Salam* contract. Moreover, a buyer cannot lay down a penalty on the seller in the event of a late delivery. However, demand of security from a seller is permitted.

Use and Application

In contemporary economic systems *Bay' Salam* is used in a number of sectors but most importantly in agriculture (Iqbal & Mirakhor). Another important use that has gained momentum in recent years is for providing financing to entrepreneurs in small and medium enterprises (SMEs) to enable the purchase of necessary inputs of production. Therefore, Islamic financial institutions are playing an important role in economic development in various countries.

Visser (2009:61) states that *Bay' Salam* is mostly used to finance "fungible manufactured goods and for providing working capital to small traders." On the other hand, Kettell (2011) argues that a *Bay' Salam* contract poses a credit risk to a financier that is difficult to mitigate. One possible situation is that a financier may enter into another *Bay' Salam* contract with a third party to sell commodities under the same terms and condition as are agreed upon by a seller. Thus, a second contract is made. This is known as a parallel *Bay' Salam*. It should be differentiated that the financier is not actually selling the commodity and the only purpose in a parallel *Bay' Salam* is risk management. The ADCB and Dubai Islamic banks are using parallel *Bay' Salam* contracts (Jamaldeen, 2012).

2.6.5 *Ijarah* (Leasing)

Meaning and Definition

The literal meaning of the word *Ijarah* is *to give something on rent,* and leasing in conventional finance is similar to the Islamic concept of *Ijarah* (Ernst *et al.*, 2013; Lewis, 2009). *Ijarah* is the transfer of rights of use (usufruct) imbedded in a specific property or item to another person in exchange for rent payments made for a specific amount of time. *Ijarah* is not a financing instrument but rather a transfer of usufruct for an asset. Gradually, Islamic banks started using it as one of the core instruments.

In the view of Kettell (2011) and Iqbal and Mirakhor (2011), *Ijarah* has two broad meanings and uses. The usufruct of an asset is one of the important uses of *Ijarah*. Hiring professional services is the second context where *Ijarah* is used. In Arabic terminology, the employer is known as *mustagir* and the employee is called *ajir*. Generally, an *Ijarah* contract has three elements: lessor (*mujir*), lessee (*mustajir*) and payable rentals to lessor (*ujrah*).

Types of Ijarah

According to Abdul-Rahman (2010), two types of *Ijarah* contracts are used in Islamic financial circles. The first type of contract is commonly known as the rental lease or *Ijarah* where a lessor leases an asset to a lessee on the basis of rent payments for a specific period. After the agreed time, the lessee returns the asset to the lessor. The lessor calculates rent payments based on a *future projected value* of the asset, keeping in mind the timeframe and duration of the lease agreement. This practice is not fully in accordance with Judeo-Christian-Islamic law because this law is based in a theological conviction that no one can know the future except for God (Abdul-Rahman, 2010). Therefore, instead of calculating price of an asset at the end of lease contract the value should be equated with the current market price. The second type of *Ijarah* is called *lease-to-own* or *hire-to-purchase* (*ijarah-wa-imtilak* or *ijarah-wa-iqtinaa*). Under a hire-to-purchase *Ijarah* agreement, a lessee pays period rental amounts to a lessor and certain money is paid as compensation for the ownership of the asset at the end of an agreement.

Use and Application

Ijarah is the second most used Islamic financial instrument after *Murabahah*. (Alrifai, 2015). According to Iqbal and Mirakhor (2011), *Ijarah* contracts have a promising future for the Islamic financial industry with the potential to fulfil the needs of entrepreneurs and investors. *Ijarah* is also suitable for Islamic financial institutions because rental cash flows could either be fixed or variable. However, currently Islamic banks are not using the considerable market potential of *Ijarah* because it entails active engagement in the management of assets and mitigation of risks. On the other hand, *Ijarah* contracts are frequently used to finance home mortgages.

Kettell (2011) stated that *Ijarah* contracts have gained popularity during the early 1990s. Emirates Airline, a Dubai-based international carrier, received $60 million in financing to buy an A310-300 aircraft from the Al Rajhi Banking and Investment Corporation, one of the largest Islamic banks based in Saudi Arabia. The use of *Ijarah* is not concentrated to certain countries or a specific group of banks but it is widespread. The Al Baraka Investment Company uses hire-to-purchase *Ijarah* to finance industrial equipment and real estate. Islamic banks in Iran extensively use hire-to-purchase contracts for home financing and a number of products for household and industrial use.

Visser (2009) argued that *Ijarah* is not only favourite financing tool of Islamic banks and that Islamic windows of conventional banks also use it for transport sector and industry. *Ijarah* is also used for home financing but the time period of the contracts is usually longer in this case. Alrifai (2015) went on to say that *Ijarah* is the main financial tool used by Islamic banks for the securitization of leased assets, as this is permissible in Islam. Alrifai supported his claim by arguing that Islamic leasing is not a lending but rather the usufruct of an asset for specific period of time. However, conventional banks prefer to engage in lending due to a number of factors including the fact that purchasing an asset is a challenging task and ownership of an asset involves tax issues, which conventional banks try to avoid.

Some scholars believe that it is not an appropriate and approved act on the part of Islamic banks to pass on insurance costs to the lessee as part of *Ijarah* agreement (Shanmugam & Zahari, 2009). However, it is acceptable for ownership risks to be shared by the Islamic bank and lessee.

2.6.6 *Istisnah* (Construction Financing)

Meaning and Definition

Istisnah means the manufacturing of a certain commodity or asset, and is originated from the Arabic word *Sina'a,* which means *to manufacture a specific commodity* (Kettell, 2011). In an *Istisnah* contract, three terms are frequently used: *Al-mustasni* (the buyer or entrepreneur), *Al-musania'a* (the seller or manufacturer), *Al-masnoo* (the commodity or asset which is being sold or manufactured)

Difference with Bay' Salam

Bay' Salam and *Istisnah* are two exceptions among Islamic financial contracts and instruments where an asset is traded without being owned or constructed (Iqbal & Mirakhor, 2011). *Istisnah* has four distinctive differences from a *Bay' Salam* contract. First, an *Istisnah* contract involves construction or manufacturing of an asset. Second, there is no stipulation to pay full price upfront. Third, there is a possibility to revoke the contract before the commencement of manufacturing or construction begins, and finally, *Istisnah* offers flexibility regarding delivery of assets and mode of payment.

Visser (2009) stated that the *Hanafi* School of Islamic jurisprudence realized that the financing of capital-intensive products and assets such as buildings, houses, and ships is not possible without the assurance of a pending purchase by another party upon completion. Moreover, the *Hanafi* School of Islamic jurisprudence also ruled that it is lawful to make deferred payments to the financier. However, some Islamic scholars disagree with this stance and assert that, like with the *Bay' Salam* contract, the customer should pay all costs and fees in advance. However, in 1991, a group of leading Muslim scholars known as Islamic *Fiqh* Academy, legitimatized payments in the form of instalments or on a deferred date.

Use and Application

Financing based on an *Istisnah* contract is believed to be the most adaptable form of financing because it offers flexibility in terms of payment method and delivery of goods (Ernst, *et al.*, 2013). *Istisnah* contracts are useful in a number of industries such as food processing, transportation (aircraft and locomotive), and construction (Said, 2008). Islamic banks also provide financing under *Istisnah* contracts to support public infrastructure projects including the construction of roads, bridges, industrial complexes, and real estate. In the UK, the ABC International Bank, a subsidiary company of the Arab Banking Corporation Group based in Bahrain, uses *Istisnah* for construction financing in different cities including Leeds (Kettell, 2011). ABC International Bank uses the parallel *Istisnah* strategy for financing.

2.6.7 *Tawarruq* (Cash Financing/Monetization)

Meaning and Definition

The word *Tawarruq* is derived from the Arabic word *warruq,* which means *silver* (Almanaseer, *et al.*, 2014). It can be used to describe a situation in which a financier buys a specific commodity from a supplier on behalf of a customer and then sells it to the customer at a lower price. This provides an incentive for the customer to sell the commodity immediately to a third party, receiving immediate payment (on the spot) for a price equal to or slightly lower than the price paid by the financier. The customer pays the agreed upon amount to the financier in deferred instalments. Some scholars believe that in the case of *Tawarruq* the customer may sell to the same supplier. The *Hanbali* School of Islamic Jurisprudence has advocated for the use of *Tawarruq,* whereas others schools have associated it with *Bay' al-inah* contracts, which are not permitted by the majority of scholars. A *Bay' al-inah* contract is slightly different in structure from *Tawarruq*. However, the purpose of both contracts is for cash financing. In a *Bay' al-inah* contract the customer sells the purchased commodity to the same supplier. In recent years, *Tawarruq* has gained popularity due to expansion in Islamic banking and Islamic investment activities, but other Islamic banks and investment companies have scaled back on the use of *Tawarruq* because there is disagreement among Islamic scholars as to whether the tool is *Shari'ah*-compliant (Almanaseer *et al.*, 2014).

Criticism and Limitations

According to Shanmugam and Zahari (2009), in a *Tawarruq* transaction only those commodities are used that can easily be bought, sold or traded on the market, such as platinum or copper. However, under Islamic law, gold and silver cannot be traded as commodities due to their role as a medium of exchange. Some Islamic scholars view the recent use of *Tawarruq* as an undermining force for the rationale of Islamic financial instruments and contracts because of the debt underlying the transaction. Moreover, the Islamic *Fiqh* Academy has not permitted the use of *Tawarruq*. Alternatively, Ahmed *et al.* (2012), stated that the use of *Tawarruq* has been allowed by Islamic scholars but is, however, subject to certain rules because the seller is using *Tawarruq* as a tool to generate cash instead of engaging in real trade.

Siddiqi (2007:4–5), a renowned Islamic economist, stated his position about *Tawarruq* as "The introduction of *Tawarruq* into the body of Islamic economy is sure to act like a virus destroying its immune system, which could protect it from increasing indebtedness leading to speculation, monetary fluctuations, instability and inequity." This view exposes the fact that *Tawarruq* transactions result in debt and the proportions of the debt are high in relation to the value of the cash financing made available by the financier to the customer. *Tawarruq* is commonly used in the Malaysian financial market, and Islamic scholars in Malaysia have permitted the sale of debt. However, religious scholars in Gulf countries do not allowed *Tawarruq* based transactions (Siddiqi, 2007).

Andrews (2010:10) argued that the criticism on *Tawarruq* is subsiding as the Islamic banks have recognized the economic and trading benefits of it and "this form of funding has become a vital component of short term investment operations by Islamic banking using permitted commodities." However, there should be two different parties in the *Tawarruq* transaction between the times when the bank pays for the commodity and when the customer sells the commodity.

According to Alrifai (2015), the use of *Tawarruq* is against the spirit of Islamic finance because the intention of the customer is to only access cash financing instead of dealing with asset-based economic activities. This kind of instrument can be used to earn *Riba* and not all Islamic scholars approve of its use. Further, Ernst *et al.* (2013) reiterated Alrifai's (2015) arguments about the use of *Tawarruq* because Islamic banks use it as a cover to advance loans and this practice is against the socio-economic objectives of Islam.

Table 1 provides a summary of the cross-country usage of Islamic financial instruments and contracts used in different Muslim countries.

Table 1: Cross-Country Usage of Islamic Financial Instruments in Selected Muslim Countries (in %)

Country	Year	*Murabahah*	*Ijarah*	*Musharakah*	*Mudarabah*	*Bay' Salam*	*Istisnah*	*Qard Hasan*	Others	Total
Pakistan	2014	31	8	44	0	4	7	0	5	100
	2015	25	7	46	0	5	9	0	7	100
Sudan	2014	52	0	9	5	4	0	1	28	100
	2015	50	0	7	7	3	0	0	33	100
Malaysia	2014	49	24	6	0	–	0	–	21	100
	2015	50	21	7	0	–	0	–	21	100
Iran	2014	34	1	37	3	0	–	5	21	100
	2015	34	0	39	2	1	0	5	19	100
Indonesia	2014	59	6	25	7	0	0	4	0	100
	2015	58	6	26	7	0	0	3	0	100
Bahrain	2014	82	9	0	0	1	0	0	8	100
	2015	80	10	0	0	1	0	0	9	100
Bangladesh	2014	44	7	1	1	0	0	2	45	100
	2015	44	7	2	0	1	0	2	45	100
Jordan	2014	73	24	1	0	0	0	0	2	100
	2015	72	25	1	0	0	0	0	2	100
Kuwait	2014	78	17	0	2	0	0	0	2	100
	2015	80	16	0	1	0	0	0	2	100
Saudi Arabia	2014	32	15	1	0	0	0	0	52	100
	2015	33	15	1	0	0	0	0	51	100
Nigeria	2014	54	38	3	–	–	4	1	0	100
	2015	51	42	3	–	–	4	1	0	100
Oman	2014	21	41	33	0	0	0	0	4	100
	2015	18	44	32	0	0	0	0	6	100
UAE	2014	62	–	–	–	38	–	–	–	100
	2015	62	–	–	–	38	–	–	–	100

Source: Calculations[6] are based on financial reports of Central Banks and IFSB (2015). Due to rounding, sum of percentages may not be equal to 100.

6 Data is only available up to first two quarters of 2015 for countries like Jordan, Kuwait, Saudi Arabia, Nigeria, Oman and UAE.

Pakistan

It should be noted that the modes of financing in Pakistan have gradually evolved over time. For example, by the end of 2014 *Murabahah* financing was 31%, but by the end of 2015 it had fallen to 25%, as can be seen in Table 1. Despite the decline in *Murabahah* financing, it still represented a significant proportion of total financing in Pakistan. Islamic banks use *Murabahah* because the banks transfer the ownership risk to the ultimate customer and receive periodic cash flows from the customer. More importantly, banks are not obligated to share their profits with the customers under *Murabahah.*

The share of *Musharakah* represented more than one-third of Diminishing *Musharakah* in 2014 and 2015 and represented 44% of financing by the end of 2014, but this figure increased to 46% by the end of 2015. There are two main reasons for the substantial use of Diminishing *Musharakah* in Pakistan. First, as discussed in Section 2.6.1, Diminishing *Musharakah* is a popular instrument for financing real estate and SMEs. Second, Diminishing *Musharakah* is considered a less risky and more suitable instrument for Islamic banks, from a risk management perspective.

Mr. Mudassar Saleem, Assistant Director Islamic Banking Department at the central bank, State Bank of Pakistan (SBP), described the general tendencies of usage for Islamic financial instruments in Islamic banking sector in Pakistan as:

> "As far as participatory modes (i.e. *Musharakah* and *Mudarabah*) are concerned you may know that corporate clients are, in general, not willing to share their profits with banks. That's why they are very interested in availing debt-based financing from banks. As Islamic banks cannot extend cash financing to their customers they use Trade-Based financing such as Murabahah, Salam, Istisna, etc. Moreover, participatory modes involve the risk of loss for banks, but banks don't usually take exposures in these modes due to excessive risk." (Saleem 2016, Personal Communication, 30 May)

The State Bank of Pakistan (2008:159) acknowledged the issue of agency problem in the promotion of participatory modes of financing as "in fact the agency problem is one of the major factors for the reluctance on the part of banks to undertake equity based modes of financing, as it gives entrepreneurs the incentive to under-state profits."

According to Farooq and Ahmed (2013) there are a number of reasons for the lower usage of *Musharakah* financing in Pakistan: a) lack of guidelines from the State Bank of Pakistan, b) lack of interest from bank management, c) lack of experience of bank staff to handle *Musharakah* transactions, d) risk of loss due to failure of partnership, e) lack of committed, honest, and skilled entrepreneurs, f) accounting and taxation issues, and g) unwillingness of the customers to share partnership profits with the banks.

In view of the above mentioned criticisms, the State Bank of Pakistan (2013:29) urged Islamic financial institutions to increase the share of participatory modes of financing by stating:

"To encourage the participatory mode of financing, [Islamic Financial Institutions] IBI needs to refocus on asset led strategic policy by exploring the sharing based financing avenues. To this end, regulators are continuously making efforts for bringing about improvements in the *Shariah* compliance framework and harmonization of industry practices."

In light of the previously mentioned instructions of the State Bank of Pakistan to Islamic financial institutions, it is clear that regulators are keen on increasing shares of participatory financing and banks are encouraging their customers to use partnership based contracts, as the findings in Table 1 show.

Mr. Muhammad Abubakar, Customer Relationship Manager at BankIslami Pakistan Ltd. (a full-fledged Islamic bank) discussed the overall scenario surrounding the current usage of Islamic financial instruments in Pakistan, and argued that there was a lack of financing under *Musharakah* and *Mudarabah* because these instruments are participatory in nature, which requires business partnerships. Under present financial settings, Islamic banks are not fully prepared to execute partnership contracts (Abubakar 2016, Personal Communication, 11 July).

Mr. Muhammad Abubakar further asserted that most of the customers of Islamic banks in Pakistan belonged to the production and trading sectors and, therefore, *Murabahah* was a suitable instrument for their business needs. He outlined the following reasons for the use of *Murabahah*:

- *Murabahah* prices, once fixed, are final and cannot be changed in case of any early and delayed payment. Therefore, banks can project their income on the fixed income pattern
- Banks can manage liquidity related matters more efficiently due to fixed payment by clients on certain dates
- *Murabahah* is short-term in nature and offered mostly for half a year term. Any fluctuations in pricing can be taken into account in any subsequent transactions that are executed after settlement of the existing transactions
- With *Murabahah*, the client acts as an agent and procures the materials being financed by the bank, which reduces the imposition placed on the bank as the bank has no need to get directly involved in the procurement process
- *Murabahah* documentation is easily transferred to the client at the time of disbursement

Based on the above mentioned facts, it can be concluded that the operational ease of the *Murabahah* mode of financing makes it popular for Islamic banks. However, Mr. Muhammad Abubakar stated that Islamic banks are reducing the use of *Murabahah* in response to the instructions given by the central bank (State Bank of Pakistan), which were issued because Islamic scholars criticized the Islamic banks for not fully complying with Islamic law. As discussed in Section 2.6.3, according to the view of Islamic scholars, a bank should buy the commodity from the supplier and take physical possession before selling it to the customer. However, with *Muraba-*

hah, Islamic banks avoid taking possession as was highlighted by Mr. Muhammad Abubakar (above).

However, as is noted in Table 1 (above), *Mudarabah* and *Qard Hasan* remained non-existent in the Pakistan finance market. Mr. Mudassar Saleem, Assistant Director Islamic Banking Department at the State Bank of Pakistan (SBP), discussed the lack of financing under *Qard Hasan* in Pakistan as:

> "Regarding *Qard Hasan*, they are not feasible for Islamic banks as it is their mandate to earn profit for their shareholders and depositors, while the same cannot be achieved through *Qard Hasan*. It should be noted that Islamic banks are extending finances as per their risk appetite and as per prevailing regulatory framework" (Saleem 2016, Personal Communication, 30 May).

Mr. Muhammad Abubakar, Customer Relationship Manager at BankIslami Pakistan Ltd., shared the financing experience of BankIslami Pakistan Ltd. and stated that the bank offers financing for longer terms of (1–5 years) under two modes: Diminishing *Musharakah* and *Ijarah*. For short-term financing up to 180 days, *Istisnah*, *Bay' Salam* and *Murabahah* instruments are used. He further stated that Islamic banking currently had about 12% market share and that Islamic banking is a new phenomenon that is not well known by most people. The State Bank of Pakistan has taken various measures, including mass media campaigns, to educate people about Islamic banking and efforts are being made to increase the Islamic banking share to 20% by the end of 2018.

Sudan

As it can be seen in Table 1 Murabahah, mode of financing is one of the most widely used financing instruments in Sudan at 52% and 50% respectively in 2015 and 2014. Financial institutions intend to use Murabahah because such financing is easy to execute. Participatory modes of financing such as Musharakah and Mudarabah are less prevalently used for financing. For example, Musharakah financing provided 9% and 7% respectively in 2015 and 2014, whereas Mudarabah accounted for only 5% and 7% in the same period. As discussed earlier in this chapter, agency problems discourage financial institutions from engaging in participatory financing, which is also the case in Sudan.

Malaysia

Abdul-Rahman and Nor (2016) conducted a qualitative study to investigate the challenges of profit and loss sharing (PLS) in Malaysian Islamic banking. The researchers interviewed *Shari'ah* adviser and Assistant General Manager cum *Shari'ah*, head of the department at two Islamic banks. Their study highlighted several reasons for the low levels of use for participatory modes of Islamic financing, including high risk (operating and monitoring costs) associated with *Musharakah* and *Mudarabah* investments, lack of reliable business partners (agency problems), and the inadequate track records of businesses.

From the above mentioned findings, it can be concluded that Islamic banks are only willing to finance safe and less complex investments. However, *Musharakah* and *Mudarabah* financing involves issues of asymmetric information and moral hazard (Abdul-Rahman & Nor), and financing under partnership contracts burdens Islamic banks by requiring that they carry out extensive due diligence and project evaluations.

Jalil *et al.* (2013) performed a qualitative study of eight Islamic financial institutions in Malaysia to find out the challenges in the application of participatory modes of financing. The study found several reasons for the lack of participatory financing: a) a high level of risk involved in valuation of projects and companies and ownership issues in properties, b) a lack of expertise on behalf of Islamic financial institutions to oversee *Mudarabah* and *Musharakah* projects, c) a complicated documentation process, and d) an inadequate demand for participatory modes of financing from customers who are not willing to share profits with the banks.

It is worth mentioning that Malaysia is well-known for its innovation in Islamic financial products and services, but financing under *Musharakah* and *Mudarabah* is almost non-existent (Jalil *et al.*, 2013). From a legal perspective, Islamic financial institutions' ability to engage with *Musharakah* and *Mudarabah* are hindered by inadequate legal provisions in the Partnership Act of 1972 and the Islamic Financial Services Act 2013 in Malaysia.

As can be seen in Table 1, *Murabahah* financing represented almost 50% of all financing by the end of 2014 and 2015. The second most frequently used instrument, *Ijarah, represented* 21% of financing in 2015. Participatory instruments of financing, such as *Musharakah, had* only a 7% share of the market in 2015. However, instruments like *Mudarabah*, Ba*y' Salam, Istisnah* and *Qard Hasan* contributed little to no financing in the Malaysian finance market.

Mr. Rahizam Ibrahim from the central bank of Malaysia (Bank Negara Malaysia) responded to a query made by the researcher of this study about the lack of participatory modes of financing in Malaysia by stating:

> "In Malaysia, the Islamic Financial Institution (IFI) has always been encouraged to be innovative in developing its financing products based on any acceptable *Shariah* contracts. This is to ensure that the Islamic Finance Industry has a complete and wider range of products to be offered to customers in line with the aspiration to make Malaysia a one-stop center for Islamic Finance products. In this regard, the IFI is given the flexibility to adopt any *Shariah* contracts that are suitable to the institution's customer financing needs in line with institutional business and risk strategy. The IFI is required to observe the policy requirements on *Shariah* contracts issued by the Central Bank in the event that the contracts are adopted by the IFI. The overall usage of Islamic financial instruments, as per the statistics, was reflective of business and strategic decisions made by the industry players." (Ibrahim 2016, Personal Communication, 03 June)

Based on the above discussion, two conclusions related to the usage of Islamic financial instruments in Malaysia can be inferred. First, Islamic banks are interested in financing less risky projects and companies. Second, the central bank of Malaysia has not formulated guidelines to encourage Islamic banks to use participatory modes of financing. Thus, Islamic banks and financial institutions can freely decide which financing instruments to employ, as long as these are *Shari'ah*-compliant.

Iran

As can be seen in Table 1, *Murabahah* and *Musharakah* are two dominant modes of financing in Iran. *Murabahah* financing remained constant at 34% in 2014 and 2015. However, *Musharakah* financing marginally increased from 37% in 2014 to 39% by the end of 2015. It should be noted that after Pakistan, Iran ranks second in volume of financing issued using the *Musharakah* instrument. Islamic banks have also extended financing under *Qard Hasan*, but the proportion of *Ijarah*, *Mudarabah*, *Bay' Salam* and *Istisnah* is negligible.

Mr. Alireza Siadat, Iranian, origin lawyer and an Islamic finance expert at Price-WaterhouseCoopers Legal AG (a consulting firm based in Frankfurt am Main) postulated that *Musharakah* was considered a less risky instrument when compared to other forms of debt financing in the Iranian Islamic banking industry, because a bank and client become project partners and share the risk after due diligence is performed (Siadat 2016, Personal Communication, 25 May). He further supported his claim that *Musharakah* is less risky by stating that once a bank and client find a good working relationship and overcome complex management issues *Musharakah* financing becomes less risky, hence chances of default or failure are low. On the other hand, debt financing is discouraged in Iran due to an increase in the number of defaulted loans in the aftermath of the credit crunch that followed the financial crisis that began in the United States. Mr. Siadat shed further light on the use of *Musharakah* and *Murabahah* financing in Iran with the following assertion:

> "Islamic banking in Iran is highly regulated by Iranian law and the Iranian regulator (Bank Markazi). The list of services is given by these two, as well as directions on how often a bank is allowed to offer respective services. Whereas conservative and low risk services (e.g. *Musharakah* and *Murabahah*) are allowed in higher quantities."
> (Siadat 2016, Personal Communication, 25 May)

According to Iqbal and Molyneux (2005), Islamic banks in Iran are obliged to extend a specified percentage of financing using *Qard Hasan* instruments to support for community building projects. This is a provision established under the guidelines of the Iranian constitution. However, in the view of Mr. Siadat, there are no such obligations for Islamic banks in Iran (Siadat 2016, Personal Communication, 25 May). It should be noted that Islamic banks in Iran offer the highest percentage of financing for *Qard Hasan* when compared to the sample of 13 Muslim countries presented in Table 1.

Iqbal and Molyneux also stated that *Mudarabah* is one of the dominant modes of financing in Iran. However, the findings presented in Table 1 contradict this claim as there was only 3% and 2% financing under *Mudarabah* in 2014 and 2015, respectively. From the above discussion it could be concluded that Islamic banks in Iran are willing to make partnerships with clients using *Musharakah* instruments by mitigating agency problems and extending more than one third of financing with the *Murabahah* mode. These two modes are convenient and better meet the requirements of Islamic banks.

Indonesia

Ernawati (2016) stated that until recently the contribution of Islamic banking was as high as 5% in the broader banking sector of Indonesia. Moreover, the secondary data published between 2009 and 2014, by the Indonesian Financial Services Authority, indicated that the dominant Islamic mode of financing was *Murabahah,* and participatory modes such as *Mudarabah* and *Musharakah* were less often leveraged as modes of financing. The fundamental reason to extend financing under *Murabahah* is that it is a comparatively safe mode of financing. On the other hand, *Mudarabah* is risky due to asymmetric information and moral hazards (Ernawati, 2016). This study concluded that Islamic banks are, in general, risk averse financial institutions.

As can be seen in Table 1, the *Murabahah* instrument comprised almost 60% of Indonesian financing in 2014 and 2015. *Musharakah* was the second dominant mode of finance, with 26% financing in 2015. *Ijarah* and *Mudarabah* provided less than 7% financing in 2014 and 2015. But *Bay' Salam* and *Istisnah* were not represented in the market. *Qard Hasan* was used only marginally in 2014 and 2015. However, Sadr (2014) stated that several Islamic banks in Muslim countries have increased financing under *Qard Hasan,* especially in Bangladesh, Iran, and Indonesia. Based on the statistics presented in Table 1, Sadr's argument appears to be valid. However, the market share for *Qard Hasan* financing in Indonesia is very low.

Bangladesh

As can be seen in Table 1, the *Murabahah* mode of financing contributed almost half total financing in Bangladesh (44%) in 2014 and 2015, respectively. *Ijarah* accounted for 7% of total financing in the same periods. Participatory modes of financing, *Bay' Salam, Istisnah,* and *Qard Hasan* represented a relatively low percentage of total financing in Bangladesh in 2014 and 2015. It should be noted that 'other' instruments comprise nearly half (45%) of all financing in Bangladesh from 2014 through 2015. Under the 'others' instrument category, two instruments, *Bai Muajjal* (credit sale) and HPSM (Hire Purchase under *Shirkatul Melk*), represented 25% and 16% share of financing (respectively) in 2015. Also important is the practice of Islamic banks in Bangladesh to leverage additional instruments, including *Bai Muajjal* and HPSM, to satisfy local market demands and requirements.

Bahrain, Jordan, Kuwait, Saudi Arabia and Oman

In countries like Jordan, Kuwait, and Saudi Arabia, *Murabahah* and *Ijarah* are two major financing instruments, as can be seen in Table 1 (above). For example, *Murabahah* accounted for 73% and 72% of Jordan's total financing in 2014 and 2015, respectively. In Kuwait, *Murabahah* financing was comparatively higher at 78% and 80% in 2014 and 2015, respectively. Meanwhile, *Ijarah* represented 17% and 16% of Kuwait's total financing in 2014 and 2015, respectively. However, the volume of *Ijarah* financing in Kuwait's financial market is relatively low when compared to that of Jordan, but is relatively higher than that of Saudi Arabia. This is indicative of the high proportion of *Murabahah* financing in Joran.

It should be noted that Islamic banks in Jordan, Kuwait, and Saudi Arabia have extended only a marginal volume of financing using *Qard Hasan.* Moreover, participatory modes of finance, *Bay' Salam, Istisnah,* and *Qard Hasan,* are rarely used in these countries. In the case of Oman, data presented in Table 1 indicates that *Ijarah* represented highest proportionate share of market financing (41% and 44% in 2014 and 2015, respectively), followed by *Musharakah* with 33% and 32%. Moreover, Islamic banks in Oman also used *Qard Hasan* instrument. As can be seen in Table 1, *Murabahah* is the dominant mode of financing in Bahrain at 82% and 80% in 2014 and 2015, respectively). Ijarah represented 9% and 10% of total financing in 2014 and 2015, respectively. The volume of participatory modes of financing, *Bay' Salam, Istisnah* and *Qard Hasan* were negligible.

Most Muslim countries in the Middle East, with the exception of Oman, do not use participatory modes of financing as their main focus is on *Murabahah* and *Ijarah,* which can be seen in Table 1. The fundamental reason to extensively use non-participatory modes of finance is to avoid the risks inherent to *Musharakah* and *Mudarabah* transactions, which were discussed earlier in this chapter.

Nigeria

As can be seen in Table 1, in Nigeria *Murabahah* and *Ijarah* are the primary modes of financing. *Murabahah* accounted for 54% and 51% of Nigeria's total financing in 2014 and 2015, respectively. Likewise, *Ijarah* represented 38% and 42% in 2014 and 2015. It should be noted that participatory modes of financing, *Bay' Salam,* and *Qard Hasan* made marginal contributions to total financing during the same time.

Dr. Aliyu Dahiru Muhammad, Deputy Director Training and Linkages at the International Institute of Islamic Banking and Finance at Bayero University Kano in Nigeria, responded to the query made by the researcher of this study concerning the lack of participatory modes of financing with the following observation:

> "Banks and other financial institutions, Islamic or otherwise, are business oriented entities. So in terms of risk exposure they also want to minimize it or manage it. Partnership based products rely on trust between the agent and capital owner or institution as financing the agent. Unfortunately, issue of trust or lack of it is very obvious in our society nowadays. For Nigeria to increase partnership based products there is need

to overcome the legal and regulatory challenges. For instance, the capital adequacy ratio requirement, which is very high, may not allow huge investment in partnership products." (Dr. Muhammad 2016, Personal Communication, 02 June)

In Nigeria, another reason for lower usage of participatory modes of financing is the lack of experience Islamic financial institutions have in dealing with risky financial products. It should be noted that there are currently only one full-fledged Islamic bank (Ja`iz Bank Nigeria PLC) and two Islamic banking windows of conventional banks (Dr. Muhammad 2016, Personal Communication, 02 June). From this discussion it could be concluded that Islamic banking in Nigeria has only recently been established and there are currently only a few institutions offering *Shari'ah*-compliant products and services. Therefore, the main focus of these institutions is to offer risk-free financing. The central bank should encourage Islamic financial institutions to engage with participatory modes of financing, just as the central bank of Pakistan has directed the Pakistani Islamic banks to do.

United Arab Emirates

As depicted in Table 1, *Murabahah* is the dominant mode of financing in the United Arab Emirates (UAE), representing 62% of all financing issued in the UAE in 2014 and 2015. *Bay' Salam* is the second most popular Islamic financial instrument, representing 38% in the same period. It should be noted that data was not available for other modes of financing. Although the data available for the issuance of *Murabahah* and *Bay' Salam* appear to make it clear that these are the most prevalent forms of financing in the UAE. Mr. Jassim Mahadik, Officer Sharia Structuring and Coordination at Al Hilal Bank (an Islamic Bank based in Abu Dhabi), asserted that the use of *Ijarah* by Islamic banks in the UAE is a common practice because the majority of real estate financing in the UAE is based on *Ijarah* (Mahadik 2016, Personal Communication, 09 June). Mahadik further argued that in the UAE participatory modes of financing are less prevalent because of the inherent risk of *Musharakah* and *Mudarabah* instruments. However, Islamic banks in the UAE have started using Diminishing *Musharakah,* which is a hybrid product that is infrequently used because the *Ijarah* instrument more appropriately addresses client needs. For example, banks prefer to use *Ijarah* instead of *Istisnah.*

Mr. Jassim Mahadik stated that the rationale for the frequent use of *Murabahah* and *Bay' Salam* instruments by Islamic banks in the UAE is based on the ability of these instruments to better fulfil customer needs. For example, *commodity Murabahah,* and *Bay' Salam* instruments are suitable financing tools for customers needing cash. Similarly, *Murabahah* is a suitable instrument for financing the purchase of an automobile. It should be noted that *Qard Hasan* is a benevolent loan, thus it is not an attractive option for Islamic banks seeking to make a profit. For that reason, many banks in the UAE provide student loans by issuing *Qard Hasan* contracts (Mahadik 2016, Personal Communication, 09 June).

Overall Analysis

Dr. Yahia Abdul Rahman, Founder of Lariba-American Finance House and author of several books on Islamic banking and finance, cited in a personal communication dated June 6, 2016 the following four reasons for a lack of participatory modes of financing in Islamic banking:

a) Most banks want to minimize the risk and compete with the market (setting huge conventional banking industry).
b) Most bank executives and senior bankers in Islamic *Riba* Free – RF – banks have conventional banking backgrounds and training. They feel comfortable with what they have been used to while working in conventional banks.
c) Bank regulators in the countries that use *Murabahah* financing, and *Shari'ah* scholars, do not insist on a target mix between *Murabahah, Ijarah,* and *Musharakah.*
d) Lack of a clear financing model that would comply with *Shari'ah* and at the same time comply with the laws of many of these lands, which were colonies of European countries and have local laws derived from European legal systems.

Mr. Tariq Al-Rifai, former Head of Research and Investor Relations at Kuwait Finance House (one of the largest Islamic banking group based in Kuwait) and CEO at Quorum Centre for Strategic Studies (an Islamic banking and finance think tank based in London, United Kingdom), argued that Islamic banks prefer *Murabahah* because "once the contract is executed, what is left is a debt.... and banks love having debt on their books and not an asset" (Al-Rifai 2016, Personal Communication, 06 June). Al-Rifai further argued that the conventional banking model is not appropriate for Islamic finance because regulators push Islamic banks to function like conventional banks. Al-Rifai's assertions can be interpreted to imply that the main reason why Islamic banking is lacking participatory modes of financing is because the current structure of Islamic banks is not in alignment with the requirements of Islamic finance. For example, a lack of expertise for handling complex nature of partnership and joint venture contracts at the bank branch level might play a role.

Mohammed Amin, Islamic Finance Consultant and Former Partner at PricewaterhouseCoopers LLP UK, argued in a personal communication dated 07 June, 2016 that there are two main reasons why Islamic banks more readily embrace the use of non-participatory modes of financing. First, participatory modes of finance are much riskier than debt financing instruments and Islamic banks try to avoid risk and, therefore, potential losses. After all, Islamic banks are business entities just like conventional banks, and the main objective of a business is to generate profit for shareholders. If Islamic banks provide genuine equity financing they would be exposed to additional risk and would increase the capital allowed against such financings. Second, customers avoid genuine equity participation financing and prefer debt financing because equity participation involves taking on more risk, which requires higher degree of compensation to the bank and increases the cost of capital for the customer. In short, debt-based instruments are the instrument of choice in Islamic banking. From Table 1 it can be surmised that most countries prefer debt-based financing instruments and that the use of participatory modes has been less common. This is true, at least in part, due to the reasons listed above.

Jalil *et al.* (2013) outlined several suggestions to enhance participatory financing:

a) Amendments in existing legal and regulatory frameworks to encourage Islamic financial institutions
b) Government sponsored tax incentives for Islamic financial institutions, making all earnings from *Mudarabah* and *Musharakah* tax exempted because of the risky nature inherent in such transactions
c) Governments should hold Islamic financial instructions and government related entities accountable for offering specific percentages of participatory financing
d) Islamic financial institutions and relevant financial authorities should educate customers about the benefits of participatory modes of financing and the positive implications for economic development and soundness of Islamic financial system

According to Ernawati (2016), Islamic financial institutions can promote the use of participatory modes of financing by enhancing managerial skills, effectively collaborating with business partners, and overcoming administrative challenges. Moreover, regulatory frameworks that can serve as checks and balance to protect the interests of parties involved in participatory financing should be introduced.

2.7 Difference between Islamic Banking System and Conventional Banking System

In order to understand the fundamentals of Islamic banking and finance, it is important to draw a clear difference between Islamic and conventional banking systems. Among many notable differences, the element of *Riba* is the most important distinguishing factor between the financial system based on Islamic economic principles and those based in Western economic principles. Table 2 depicts the comparison of Islamic and conventional banking systems on the basis of banking practices, equity financing with capital risk, prohibition of *Gharar* and profit and loss sharing.

The Islamic banking system is based on Islamic law, whereas the conventional banking system is governed by secular banking laws (as can be seen in Table 2). Another important difference (in theory) is that banks in the Islamic banking system are encouraged to fund projects under PLS arrangements, whereas banks in the conventional banking system avoid financing on the basis of PLS. Moral values and ethics are extremely important in Islamic banking and require the financing physical assets and a prohibition of short selling. Also, in the conventional banking system credit and debt financing are common practices. One of the reasons for the recent sub-prime crisis was excessive use of debt financing. As table 2 shows, another important difference between Islamic and conventional banking systems is the application of a penalty for late payments. Islamic banks avoid imposing penalties, but conventional banks impose additional charges for late payments. Islamic banks are not allowed to get involved in *Gharar*, gambling, and financing of specific businesses such as those in the alcohol industry. However, in the conventional banking system, banks are free to finance any industry or business with few exceptions that are explicitly identified by regulations as illegal.

Table 2: Comparison of Islamic Banking System and Conventional Banking System

Business Framework	**Islamic Banking System**	**Conventional banking System**
Banking Practice	Based on *Shari'ah* laws, *Shari'ah* scholars ensure adherence to Islamic laws and provide guidance.	Based on secular banking laws and financial practices of respective countries.
Equity Financing with Capital Risk	Islamic banks provide equity capital to a project or venture. Losses are shared on equity participation while profits are shared on a pre-agreed ratio. Management of the enterprise depends upon the type of financing provided. Examples are *Mudarabah* and *Musharakah* etc.	Although Venture Capital companies and investment banks take equity stakes and management control of an enterprise for providing start-up finance, commercial banks that are the primary lenders do not have this facility.
Prohibition of *Gharar*	Transactions deemed *Gharar* are prohibited; it denotes varying degree of deception on the price and quality of goods. E.g., derivatives, which are prohibited in Islamic finance.	Trading of all financial instruments including derivatives are allowed in conventional banking.
Profit and Loss Sharing	All transactions are based on this principle, returns are variable depending on bank performance, and consumers can participate in the profit upside in a more equitable way than receiving a predetermined return.	Returns to customers are irrespective of bank performance and profitability. Customer is treated only as a depositor and does not get any other compensation other than interest.
Balance Between Moral and Material Requirement	The requirement to finance physical assets, which banks usually take ownership of before resale, reduces over extension of credit.	Excessive use of credit and debt financing can lead to financial problems.

Business Framework	Islamic Banking System	Conventional banking System
Penalty/Late Payment	Penalties on late payments are prohibited. If penalties are levied they must be rechannelled to charities.	Fees are typically charged for late payments.
Ethical Transaction	Transactions and activities that involve engagement with unlawful business sectors such as gambling and brewery are not allowed.	Besides money laundering and the financing of criminal activities, how customers utilized borrowed funds is typically unrestricted.

Source: Adapted from Djennas *et al.* (2015) and International Finance Magazine (2015)

2.8 Concluding Remarks

The legal framework of Islamic banking and finance is based on *Shari'ah*. *Quran* and *Sunnah* are considered primary sources of *Shari'ah* and *Ijma*, *Qiyas and Ijtihad* are considered secondary sources. The Islamic banking and finance is a financial system that prohibits the use of *Riba* (interest), speculation, and excessive uncertainty in business transactions. *Riba* means effortless gain or profit, and *Shari'ah* prohibits excess payment other than the principal loan at a predetermined rate.

As far as the origin of Islamic banking is concerned, the Mit-Ghamer Savings Bank was the first to put Islamic economic principles into practice in 1963 in Egypt. Important characteristics and principles of Islamic banking and finance are the prohibition of *Riba* (interest), *Gharar*, *Maysir* and the use of profit and loss sharing (PLS). *Musharaka*, *Mudarabah*, *Ijarah* and *Murabahah* are the key instruments of Islamic finance. In practice, *Murabahah* is the most widely used instrument in the Islamic financial industry and are under scrutiny due to criticism by several *Shari'ah* scholars because of the close resemblances to conventional cost-plus sale contracts.

The fundamental difference between the Islamic and the conventional banking system is the governance structure. The Islamic banking system is based on *Shari'ah* laws and religious scholars ensure that Islamic banks adhere to these laws in letter and spirit. On the other hand, the conventional banking system is based on secular and national laws of the respective countries.

The following chapter provides a review of the important topic of risk management in Islamic financial institutions, wealth creation, and wealth management in the context of Islamic banking and finance.

Appendix Chapter 2

Figure 2: Timeline of Evolution of the Islamic Banking and Finance

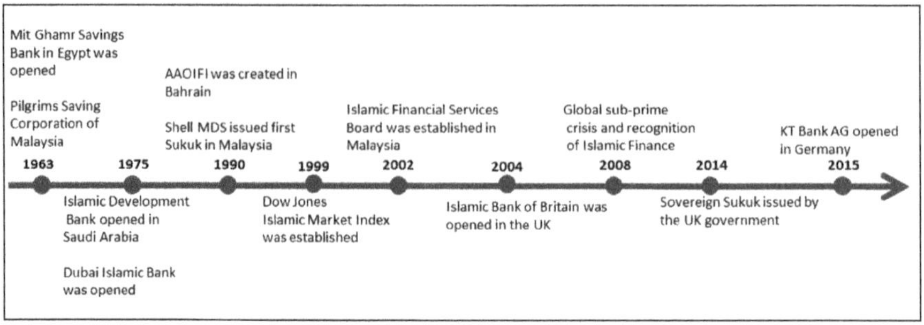

Source: Adapted from Jamaldeen (2015)

Figure 2 shows the timeline of the evolution of Islamic banking and finance. In 1963, two Islamic banking and finance experiments were made in Egypt and Malaysia. Mit Ghamr Savings Bank, which was opened in Egypt, was considered the first Islamic financial institution. However, Islamic banking and finance activities were formally started with the establishment of Islamic Development Bank, commonly known as IDB, in 1975. The Islamic Development Bank strives to foster the economic and social development of its member Muslim countries. It is worth mentioning that, also in 1975, the Dubai Islamic Bank was opened. The Dubai Islamic Bank is considered to be the first commercial Islamic bank.

In 1990, the Accounting and Auditing Organization of Islamic Financial Institutions (AAOIFI) was established to meet industry demands and formulate accounting and auditing standards. In the same year, the first *Shari'ah*-compliant *Sukuk* was issued in Malaysia by Shell MDS. In 1999, the Dow Jones Islamic Market Index was launched to provide services to those investors that were willing to invest according to Islamic principles. In 2002, the establishment of Islamic Financial Services Board (IFSB) in Malaysia was an historic development. (The IFSB is an international standard-setting body for the Islamic financial industry that oversees the regulatory and supervisory matters of Islamic financial institutions.) As can be seen in Figure 2, the Islamic Bank of Britain PLC, the first full-fledged retail bank in Europe, was opened in the United Kingdom in 2004.

During the sub-prime global crisis, many scholars and financial institution executives viewed Islamic banking and finance as a viable financial system. In 2014, the United Kingdom became the first Western country to issue a sovereign *Sukuk*. As Figure 2 shows, Islamic banking and finance continued making inroads into Europe, and KT Bank AG became the first European bank to establish a full-fledged *Shari'ah*-compliant bank when it opened in Germany in 2015.

Chapter 3: Risk Management and Islamic Wealth Creation and Wealth Management

3.1 Introduction

The Islamic banking and finance industry is young but its rapidly growing footprint has gained the attention of financial leaders in all major regions of the global banking environment. The Islamic banking and finance industry has developed rapidly over the past two decades (Bacha, 2014), especially in the Middle East and South East Asia. Unprecedented growth and expansion of Islamic financial activities along with cross-border business transactions has brought to light several challenges facing the Islamic financial industry. The aim of Chapter 3 is to investigate the nature of such challenges and to discuss how industry participants have responded and what initiatives have been undertaken to overcome the challenges.

Chapter 3 begins with a brief introduction of the risk management practices leveraged by Islamic financial institutions. This chapter also provides a discussion of derivatives from an Islamic finance perspective, describes the application of derivatives as tools for risk management, reviews the issues arising from the use of derivatives in Islamic banking, and explains the features of *Shari'ah*-compliant derivatives. Chapter 3 provides also a brief overview of the different Islamic derivatives currently in existence including the *Bay' Salam* (forward contract), *Bay' Uran* (down payment), *Khiyarat* (option by stipulation), and *Mubadalatul Arbaah* (Islamic profit rate swap).

Section 3.6 of Chapter 3 addresses the issue of liquidity risk management for Islamic financial institutions, and emphasizes the importance of effective liquidity risk management, causes of liquidity risk, and current industry practices. The discussion of risk management is followed by an overview of the institutions supporting liquidity risk management with *Shari'ah*-compliant liquidity management tools.

A detailed overview of the implications of the Basel III framework for Islamic banks is provided, followed by a discussion of the importance of wealth creation and wealth management from an Islamic perspective. Finally, Chapter 3 contains an overview of the unique features of wealth creation and distribution in the Islamic economy and concludes with a chapter summary.

3.2 Risk Management in Islamic Finance

Risk management practices are becoming increasingly important for financial intermediaries and Islamic financial institutions amid volatility in global financial markets (Al-Amine, 2013b). Risk is indicative of uncertainty in the degree to which one might suffer loss resulting from an action or decision made without consideration for risk mitigation. Hedging is one way in which risk can be mitigated. Hedging can be defined as "an act of protecting an asset or investment from the uncertain market" (Razif *et al.*, 2012:155). Risk management is a process that involves identification and quantification of potential risks that results in the act of selecting the tools appropriate to managing the potential risks. In the view of Hassan and Kayed (2009), the risk management process involves hedging and speculation. Speculation (*Gharar*) is forbidden in Islam (Ahmad *et al.*, 2014). Nordin *et al.* (2014) stated that risk management is in with the objectives and teachings of Islam, which encourage the protection of wealth. Ahmad *et al.* (2014) argued that the concept of risk is well recognized in Islam and that Islamic teachings urge calculated risk taking in business activities.

Abdullah (2007) explained that risk management plays an important role for Islamic banking institutions by minimizing adverse consequences, providing a system of checks and balances, and addressing the unique characteristics or risk. Thus, risk management is essential for the identification, measurement, monitoring, and mitigation of risk. The Islamic Financial Services Board (IFSB) released a standardized declaration on risk management that recognized the paramount importance of risk management in Islamic financial institutions. Nordin *et al.* (2014) argued that more than 300 Islamic financial institutions are working in more than 75 countries, which creates the need for effective risk management processes that might require hedging. Hedging becomes especially pertinent for business and financial transactions involving foreign exchange when such transactions introduce circumstances in which fluctuating currency values and volatile prices are a prominent feature of the financial system (Nordin *et al.*, 2014).

3.3 Importance of Derivatives in Islamic Finance

Because the risks faced by conventional and Islamic financial institutions are similar, Islamic financial institutions have adopted many of the risk management tools used by conventional financial institutions (Al-Amine, 2013b). However, Islamic financial institutions should be very cautious in the adoption and application of such instruments as derivatives because the vast majority of Islamic scholars explicitly denounce the use of derivatives. One reason why derivatives were denounced was because of the negative role they played in the recent financial crisis and because derivatives are structured in such a way that they violate core principles of Islamic law that prohibit hedging.

Alshamrani (2014) argued that more than 500 Islamic financial institutions currently operate in more than 75 countries and pointed out that Islamic finance is the fastest growing sector of the financial industry, growing at a rate of 15% per year. Therefore, the industry at large is not in a position to ignore the use of Islamic financial derivatives. Likewise, Islamic financial institutions cannot afford to ignore the pivotal role that derivatives play in conventional financial systems (Al-Amine, 2013b). Damak and Volland (2008:29) highlighted this issue by stating:

"The management of market risks is made more difficult for Islamic banks due to the limited number of risk management tools/instruments available to them. For example, it is difficult for an IFI to use hedging instruments such as derivatives as they are generally forbidden."

Hassoune (2010) highlighted the importance of derivative instruments for Islamic financial institutions:

"If employed with care, derivatives can enhance efficiency in IFIs through risk mitigation, thereby making them more competitive as well as appealing to customers. However, their application in Islamic finance is highly controversial for reasons of speculation and uncertainty, two practices forbidden under *Shari'ah*."

Innovation in the Islamic financial industry is needed to address the challenges Islamic banks are facing as they work toward applying risk management practices in accordance with *Shari'ah* principles (Hassoune, 2010). The Islamic financial industry must strive to create innovative products rather than mimicking non-compliant instruments such as conventional derivatives. Malkawi (2014) stated that the principles of Islamic law discourage blind and uncontrolled use of financial derivatives in Islamic finance.

In the following section, the application of derivatives in Muslim countries is examined.

3.3.1 Slow Growth of Derivatives in Muslim Countries

(Al-Amine, 2013b) argued that the economies of most Muslim countries are dependent on commodities such as oil, but surprisingly these Muslim countries have not realized the importance of developing a *Shari'ah*-compliant derivative market to hedge financial risks associated with trading in commodities. Although an overwhelming majority of the Organization of Oil Producing Countries (OPEC) are Muslim (Venezuela in the exception), only a few have taken steps to develop derivative markets. Two examples of Muslim countries that have taken steps to establish derivative markets are Saudi Arabia and Malaysia (Al-Amine, 2013b). A Saudi company, Aramco Trading, uses futures (a type of derivative), and Malaysia has established a derivative market for the palm oil industry.

In 2008 in a talk at the Harvard School of Law, Dr. Shamshad Akhtar, Governor of the State Bank of Pakistan (SBP), emphasized the authenticity and innovation in Islamic finance from a regulatory perspective. Shamshad highlighted the fact that, despite on-going debate concerning derivatives in Islamic finance, some Islamic financial institutions have used derivatives in a *Shari'ah*-compliant manner. For example, Standard Chartered and Bank Muamlat Malaysia structured an Islamic cross currency swap worth $10 million, and Citigroup floated a 5-year $230 million currency profit rate swap (Akhtar, 2008). Moreover, Citigroup is working to issue a profit-rate swap. Meanwhile, Malaysia is the only Muslim country that is using credit derivatives (Ahmed & Khan, 2007; Al-Taani, 2013). Annuar (2015) stated that in 2007 The Central Bank of Malaysia, Bank Negara Malaysia, took the initiative to issue the first Islamic Derivative Master Agreement (IDMA). The purpose of IDMA was to foster the application of derivatives and facilitate the development of hedging in the Islamic financial market. Uberoi and Evans (2008) discussed the acceptance of Islamic derivatives in the Malaysian market and postulated that this acceptance was mainly due to permissions given by the *Shafi* school of Jurisprudence. Motani (2013) pointed out that, with the passage of time, some Islamic scholars have come to understand the significance of hedging instruments for risk management in Islamic financial institutions. Moreover, there is a widespread understanding among stakeholders of the Islamic financial system and Islamic scholars that current market volatility necessitates the use of hedging instruments for risk mitigation.

Reasons underlying the underdeveloped derivative market are discussed in the following section.

3.3.2 Reasons for the Underdeveloped Derivative Market in Islamic Finance

Unsolved issues surrounding the use of *Shari'ah*-compliant derivatives exist in Malaysia and Saudi Arabia. Recently, various *Shari'ah* authorities and Islamic institutions have geared efforts toward reaching a consensus about whether the emerging derivatives markets are *Sharia'ah*-compliant (Al-Amine, 2013b). Authorities and institutions taking an interest include the *Fiqh* Academy based in Makkah, the Islamic *Fiqh* Academy based in Jeddah, the Permanent Research Committee of the Board of Great Scholars in Saudi Arabia, and the Accounting and Auditing Organization of Islamic Financial Institutions (AAOIFI). These deliberations and discussions have resulted in the prohibition of derivatives (Al-Amine, 2013b). However, as Jobst and Sole (2012) pointed out, there are other financial instruments available that may serve the same purpose as derivatives while meeting the standards of *Shari'ah*.

A closer investigation revealed the following reasons for the prohibition of derivatives in Islamic finance:

- Derivative instruments are based on speculation and uncertainty and both are expressly prohibited by Islamic law (Al-Amine, 2013b)
- Lack of consensus among Islamic scholars about the use of derivatives (Al-Taani,2013; Al-Amine, 2013b; Malkawi,2014; Iqbal *et al.*, 2012)
- Element of interest is the cornerstone of conventional derivatives, although they are widely prohibited under Islamic law (Al-Amine, 2013b)
- Misuse of derivatives, as was witnessed in the recent global financial crisis
- Derivatives are prone to speculation (Kamaruzdin, 2014), which is prohibited by Islamic law

Derivatives were labelled as "weapons of mass destruction" by billionaire investor Warren Buffett in 2013 after their role in the 2008–09 global financial crises (Alrifai, 2015). Since the crisis, the derivative market has shown 20% growth annually with a current global volume worth around $700 trillion. The negative consequences of derivatives are evidenced through the example of JP Morgan, the world's leading investment bank, and a London-based affiliate known as the London Whale when the two speculated with assets valued at $67 million and lost $6.2 billion. Derivatives normally result in zero-sum payoffs because at the time of contract the collateral underlying the transaction does not physically exist. This leads to excessive uncertainty and gambling by the parties of the contract (Jobst & Sole, 2009). In the non-existence or non-possession of assets, derivatives give rise of counterparty risks (Jobst & Sole, 2009).

Although there arc compelling reasons behind the underdevelopment of derivative markets in Islamic finance, the perceived need for such financial instruments may give rise to the development of *Shari'ah*-compliant derivatives for future use. The following section discusses the proposed features of potential Shari-ah-compliant derivatives markets.

3.3.3 Proposed Features of *Shari'ah*-Compliant Derivatives Markets

Al-Amine (2013b) argued that there are four clear restrictions that make it unlikely that a *Shari'ah*-compliant derivative market can be developed. First, Collateralized Debt Obligations (CDOs), a complex credit risk derivative product and Credit Default Swaps (CDSs), are not allowed in Islamic law due to the prohibition on interest and the sale of debt (Veremyev *et al.*, 2012). A Collateralized Debt Obligation (CDO) is a complex credit risk derivative product, while a Credit Default Swap (CDS) is a credit risk derivative leveraging a bond as the underlying asset. The Credit Default Swap is described as "an insurance against possible losses due to credit default events." The extensive use of Collateralized Debt Obligations and Credit Default Swaps in recent years paved the way for the global financial crisis of 2008 through 2009. Second, no speculative activities should be allowed in the foreign exchange market because Islam stresses the role of money as a medium of exchange. Third, there is no space for *Gharar* or *Maysir* activities. Fourth, unlike in conventional financial systems, a *Shari'ah*-compliant derivative market should be built on equity-based instruments.

Al-Taani (2013) stated that creating a *Shari'ah*-compliant derivative market for the Islamic financial industry would require three steps. The first step would require structuring standardized contracts by eliminating *Gharar* and counterparty default risk. For this purpose, it would be essential that such derivatives be tradable on exchanges just as any other standard contract. The second step would be to ensure that market participants avoid gambling and short selling, and that they enter into the market with the objective of hedging risks instead of participating in speculation for the purpose of profit making. Finally, the third step requires the inclusion of a physical settlement mechanism for the determination of contract completion (Al-Taani, 2013).

The following sections provide examples of *Shari-ah*-compliant derivatives.

3.4 Examples of *Shari'ah*-Compliant Derivatives in Islamic Finance

Forwards, futures, options, and swaps are the four main types of derivative instruments (Iqbal *et al.*, 2012; Al-Amine, 2013b). One of the important benefits of derivative instruments is that they are excellent tools for hedging risk (Kamaruzdin, 2014). Bennett and Jain (2015) pointed out that derivatives adhering to Islamic financial principles such as avoiding speculation and leveraging real-world collateral backing have been developed over the last ten years. Alshamrani (2014) stated that hedging instruments such as *Bay' Salam, Bay' Urban, Khiyarat* and *Mubadalatul Arbaah* may constitute the alternatives of conventional derivatives in Islam. Al-Taani (2013) similarly argued that despite an on-going debate about the permissibility of derivatives in Islam, profit rate swaps, profit rate options, cross currency swaps, and FX swaps are being used as *Shari'ah*-compliant derivatives in Islamic finance. On the other hand, Malkawi (2014) discussed the idea that *Bay' Salam, Bay' Istisnah, Bay' Urban, Khiyarat,* and third-party guarantees are some of the derivatives which are partially acceptable in Islamic finance. Iqbal *et al.* (2012) explained that Islamic and conventional financial institutions face similar kinds of risks and reasoned that some of the conventional financial tools and instruments can be used in Islamic finance. Moreover, there are certain options contracts to hedge against risks that may be used in Islamic finance. In the following section, some of the *Shari'ah*-compliant derivative instruments are discussed.

3.4.1 *Bay' Salam* as an Alternative to Conventional Forward Contract

A forward contract is an agreement between two parties whereby one party sells an asset to another party at an agreed upon price to be paid at a future date (Djenic *et al.*, 2012; Al-Taani, 2013; Rizvi & Lahsasna, 2012). The use of forward contracts as hedging tools against uncertain fluctuations in asset and commodity prices is widespread in the financial markets. Mohamad and Tabatabaei (2008) held a similar opinion and explained that forward contracts were developed to support trading activities and provide a safeguard against the movement of prices.

Contrary to the above discussion concerning the use of forward contracts, Rizvi and Lahsasna (2012) highlighted the fact that Islamic contract law accentuates the possession of an asset at the time the contract is initiated. This principle prohibits the use of conventional forward contracts in Islamic finance when and if the seller does not present the asset at the time of sale. Al-Amine (2013b) found that there was a lack of consensus among Islamic scholars about the potential benefits of forward contracts in Islamic finance. Some scholars argue that Islamic contracts such as *Bay' Salam* and *Istisnah* are similar to conventional forward contracts. According Malkawi (2014), a *Bay' Salam* contract is the most similar to the conventional forward contract.

Commodity trading is an ancient business activity that dates back to some 2400 years to the ancient Greeks (Malkawi, 2014). A *Bay' Salam* contract is structured using a *Murabahah* commodity and, in certain situations, may be used as an Islamic derivative (Global Islamic Finance Report, 2011). The use of commodity *Murabahah* in Islamic finance is heavily scrutinized, but most Islamic scholars argue that in the absence of other equivalent instruments commodity *Murabahah* is allowed.

Obaidullah (2005) argued that *Bay' Salam* is a convenient Islamic forward contract for hedging. Similarly, Bacha (1999) stated that *Bay' Salam* is almost identical to the conventional forward contract except for the fact that with *Bay' Salam* the buyer of the product pays full price upfront at the time the agreement is made and with the conventional forward contract there is flexibility regarding the payment and full or partial payment may be made at the time the contract is initiated. As discussed in Chapter 2, the *Bay' Salam* is the exception in Islamic finance whereby the sale of a product or commodity is allowed without the actual existence or physical possession of the product. Moreover, the initial purpose of *Bay' Salam* was to facilitate trade among and by farmers.

El-Gamal (2006) discussed that a *Bay' Salam* contract can be used in Islamic finance provided it meets certain conditions, specifically the exclusion of *Gharar* and *Riba*. Dali and Ahmad (2005) found that forward contracts are permitted in Islamic finance if the conditions of *Bay' Salam* contracts are fulfilled, which includes the receipt of full advance payment at the time of the transaction. But, futures and options contracts do not fit these requirements and are not in accordance with Islamic law.

Ehsan (2012) stated that the use of forward contracts for the purposes of speculation is prohibited but recognized that futures contracts can be used in Islamic finance if due diligence is followed to guarantee payment of a reasonable amount of money in advance of receiving a good. In the view of Al-Amine (2013b), a conventional forward contract "is a valid contract by the way of analogy to" *Bay' Salam*. Thus, in complying with certain Islamic law provisions a *Bay' Salam* contract could be used in place of derivatives for the purpose of risk management in Islamic finance.

3.4.2 Use of Options as Derivative Instruments in Islamic Finance

Another form of derivative used in trade is the *option*. An option is a contract in which the buyer has the right, but not the obligation, to buy (call option) or sell (put option) an asset at a specific price (strike price) on a future date (Banks, 2011). Options are one such financial derivative in today's financial market (Elahi & Aziz, 2011). Nordin *et al.* (2014) stated that options contracts are used to hedge market risk, but a number of scholars are against the use of options in Islamic finance.

Options are widely used in conventional financial markets, but a lack of understanding around the intricacies of options hinders the application of options contracts in Islamic finance. Iqbal *et al.* (2012) stated that options are frequently used to satisfy four main objectives. First, options provide a risk management tool that leverages a minimum purchasing cost and gives the buyer protection against price fluctuations. Second, options are more flexible than futures contracts because unlike the futures contract the options contract does not obligate the holder to buy the product at a future date. Third, options are used to reduce the cost of hedging. Fourth, options can be used according to the individual risk profiles of a customer.

In the view of Iqbal *et al.* (2012), in Islamic finance three main arguments are raised against the use of options: gambling, excessive speculation, and prohibition of the payment of premium for the right to buy or sell an option asset. Chapter 2 provided a review of the basic maxims of Islamic finance that prohibit gambling and speculative activities in financial dealings. In the following section, an analysis will be made about the permissibility of *Bay' Urban* and *Khiyarat;* two types of contracts in Islamic finance that are considered equivalent to conventional options.

3.4.3 *Bay' Urban* (Down-Payment, Deposit, or Earnest Money)

The meaning of the Arabic word *Urban* is *down payment or deposit for the future transaction* (Al-Taani, 2013). Malkawi (2014) argued that a buyer pays in advance some money (a deposit or down payment) to the seller, which is intended to secure the purchase of a commodity at a specific time in the future. If the buyer finds a more economically favorable deal in the meantime the buyer has a right to cancel the previous contract and purchase the product from the alternative source for the lower price. However, in doing so the seller is not required to return the down payment. In this way a *Bay' Urban* contract is similar to a conventional options contract with which a buyer secures the purchase of a commodity on a future date and for a specific price by providing a premium to the buyer as a guarantee (Malkawi, 2014). Based on this similarly, a *Bay' Urban* contract may be used in Islamic finance as a substitute for conventional options.

Al-Taani (2013) argued that the *Bay' Urban* is analogous to call options because the buyer loses the down payment if the option is not exercised by the date established in the contract. Contrary to this, Malkawi (2014) maintained that a *Bay' Urban* contract differs from a conventional call option because the down payment for a call option is a payment in addition to the amount the buyer pays for the commodity whereas the down payment for a *Bay' Urban* contract is deducted from the purchase price of the good and is not money received in excess of the sale price of the commodity. Iqbal *et al.* (2012) held a similar opinion to that of Al-Taani (2013) and argued that a call option is similar to a *Bay' Urban* contract if certain conditions are fulfilled. For example, the option cannot be detached from the underlying asset, which avoids the creation of a derivative. Furthermore, The Accounting and Auditing Organization of Islamic Financial Institutions (AAOIFI) (a body that formulate accounting and auditing standard) has, as stated in its Standard 1: Trading Currencies, allowed the use of *Bay' Urban* contracts in Islamic finance

There is a considerable lack of consensus among Islamic scholars about the acceptance of *Bay' Urban* contracts as *Shari'ah*-compliant derivative instruments (Al-Taani, 2013). Iqbal *et al.* (2012) pointed out that the legality of *Bay' Urban* contracts are arguable. For instance, *Hanabli* scholars consider it a valid contract but all other Islamic schools of jurisprudence consider it an invalid contract. Kamaruzdin (2014) stated that although there are mixed views about options, many scholars believe that *Bay' Urban* contracts are an acceptable derivative instrument for Islamic financial transactions.

3.4.4 *Khiyarat* (Option by Stipulation)

Iqbal *et al.* (2012) stated that the word *Khiyar* means *choice or option. Khiyarat* is a contract in which one party has an absolute right to confirm or reject the contract within the agreed upon time frame. This type of contract provides equal advantage to both parties through protection against price fluctuations or viability of the underlying asset (Malkawi, 2014). The *Khiyarat* contract can be used as an alternative to the conventional options contract because the ethical features inherent in it differentiate it as an ethical choice. For example, under a *Khiyarat* contract one or both parties have the right to review the agreement whereas rights and obligations of financial significance are ignored when entering into a contract for the conventional option (Malkawi, 2014).

In summary, there is lack of consensus among scholars about the ethical and legal application of down payments in financial transactions, and concerns about the use of gambling and speculation are still unsettled. Ahmed and Khan (2007) stated that although options contracts serve as an important tool for risk management the Islamic *Fiqh* Academy has prohibited their use in Islamic finance.

3.4.5 *Mubadalatul Arbaah* (Islamic Profit Rate Swap)

A *swap* is an agreement in which two parties commit themselves to exchange sets of cash flows on scheduled future dates for a specific period of time (Chisholm, 2004). Swaps contracts are useful for the Islamic financial industry as long as they comply with Islamic law. Both parties in a swap agreement receive net financial gain because a steady stream of cash flows is created in both party's assets and liabilities structures (Ahmed & Khan, 2007).

Islamic profit rate swaps (PRS) are derivative instruments and were recently structured to support financial institutions so that they could exchange cash flows in order to hedge against risks (Annuar, 2015). Jobst and Sole (2009) mentioned that in 2005 Islamic profit rate swaps were developed by the Commerce International Merchant Bank (CIMB), based in Malaysia. Profit rate swaps facilitate the ability of financial institutions to manage exposure to fixed and floating rates of return. The International Swaps and Derivative Association Inc. (ISDA) and the International Islamic Financial Markets (IIFM) jointly worked to develop the first ISDA/IIFM *Mubadalatul Arbaah* (profit rate swaps) in 2012 (Bennett & Jain, 2015).

(Henceforth the acronym ISDA/IIFM is used in reference to the partnership between the International Swaps and Derivative Association Inc. (ISDA) and the International Islamic Financial Markets (IIFM))

Uberoi and Evans (2008) argued that Islamic profit rate swaps could be structured in a *Shari'ah*-compliant manner by using reciprocal *Murabahah* transactions founded on *Wa'ad* (unilateral promises). (As discussed in Chapter 2, Islamic scholars have allowed the use of *Murabahah*-based transactions in Islamic finance). In *Wa'ad* transactions, parties to the transaction promise to swap fixed and floating cash flows on specific future dates. Al-Taani (2013) highlighted the fact that the reference of *Wa'ad* can also be found in the *Quran*, and it literally means *to promise, to pledge, or to firmly intend.* As such, the use of *Wa'ad* is in accordance with Islamic law. Mohamad *et al.* (2014) stated that *Wa'ad* is a useful contract used in Islamic markets today and obligates contracted parties to complete the arranged transaction.

In summary, Islamic financial institutions are seeking ways to manage financial risks through securitizations, loan structures, and project financing (Uberoi & Evans, 2008). Moreover, Islamic financial institutions have developed a number of swap derivatives including Islamic profit rate swaps, Islamic currency swaps, and Islamic total return swaps. All are Islamic commercial instruments employing contemporary financial techniques. However, Jobst and Sole (2009) stated that there are still some controversial views among Islamic scholars about Islamic total return swaps and other swaps that are structured on the basis of *Wa'ad.*

3.4.6 Way Forward for Islamic Derivatives

In the contemporary globalized world of finance, unprecedented advancement in technology and cross-border trading activities have made exhaustive risk management systems mandatory for financial institutions. Some Islamic instruments have derivative features therefore; it is possible to apply Islamic principles in the development of derivative contracts for the Islamic financial industry (Rizvi & Lahsasna, 2012). *Bay' Salam* and *Bay' Urban* are two examples in this regard.

The preceding sections discussed the absence of uniform principles and consensus among Islamic scholars for the validity of various derivative instruments and pointed out the legal challenges surrounding the development of this important component to the success of the Islamic financial industry. Regulatory and standards setting organizations have recently started to pursue options for standardizing practices across regions in hopes of promoting the use of Islamic derivative instruments. It should be noted that the Islamic financial model differs from the conventional model in the areas of ethical dimension and risk sharing. However, the limited availability of universal risk management products may slow or halt growth for Islamic finance (Bacha, 2014).

In the following section liquidity risk management, which is one of the most critical challenges for Islamic financial institutions, will be discussed in detail.

3.5 Managing Liquidity Risk in Islamic Financial Institutions

Islamic financial institutions face credit, market, operational, strategic, reputational, and regulatory risks (Parashar, 2014). Liquidity risk, which arises from a mismatch of maturities on assets and liabilities, is an inherent risk faced by all banks. Liquidity refers to readily available cash or assets that can be easily sold to obtain cash. In the context of financial institutions, liquidity is the ability to immediately meet "cash and collateral obligations at a reasonable cost" (Khalid, 2015:34).

The Bank for International Settlements (BIS) Committee on Banking Supervision (2008:1) defined liquidity as follows: "Liquidity is the ability of a bank to fund increases in assets and meet obligations as they come due without incurring unacceptable losses." Parashar (2014:140) cited a similar definition of liquidity from a bank's point of view, "liquidity is the on-going ability to accommodate liability maturities, to fund asset growth and to meet other contractual obligations in a timely and cost effective fashion." These definitions demonstrate that the implications of liquidity are significant because customers place full trust and confidence in the ability of financial institutions to provide expedient repayment of money deposited.

3.5.1 Importance of Effective Liquidity Management for Islamic Banks

Ali (2013) argued that excess liquidity is a major hurdle to competitiveness, whereas dearth of liquidity is the most frequent cause of bank failure. Ali further stated that recent history provides examples of several conventional bank failures, and at the present time several Islamic banks are experiencing financial distress. For example, a 2001 liquidity crisis among conventional banks in Turkey forced the closure of *Ihlas Finans*. Historically, conventional banks have more frequently faced liquidity problems than have Islamic financial institutions, and during the global financial crisis that began in 2007 a number of conventional banks experienced financial distress or insolvency, and some went bankrupt (Ali, 2013). Some Islamic banks involved in the wholesale investment business also experienced difficulties.

The Bank for International Settlements (2008:1) emphasized the importance of effective liquidity management:

> "Effective liquidity risk management helps ensure a bank's ability to meet cash flow obligations, which are uncertain as they are affected by external events and other agents' behavior. Liquidity risk management is of paramount importance because a liquidity shortfall at a single institution can have system-wide repercussions. Financial market developments in the past decade have increased the complexity of liquidity risk and its management."

Conventional banks and Islamic banks face liquidity risk as a result of an imbalance between maturities of assets and liabilities (Sobol, 2013). Islamic banks experienced liquidity risk when they fail to honor financial commitments and therefore incur additional costs and losses (Global Islamic Finance Report, 2014). *Mudarabah* and *Musharakah* experienced credit defaults and fluctuations in rates of return that caused liquidity issues at Islamic financial institutions. Ali (2013) argued that Islamic banks might face additional liquidity risk stemming from *Shari'ah*-compliant contracts and instruments if such contracts and instruments are exercised using conventional banking policies and practices. Islamic financial institutions are comparatively less profitable compared to conventional financial institutions because of the underdevelopment or non-existence of interbank exchanges and money markets and a lack of government backed securities (Parashar, 2014). In the following section an attempt is made to understand the causes of liquidity risk for Islamic banks.

3.5.2 Causes of Liquidity Risk

Archer and Karim (2014) argued that liquidity risk poses existential threats to financial institutions. Islamic banks are facing liquidity risk for a number of reasons such as:

1) Islamic banks have limited options to use *Shari'ah*-compliant money market and inter-bank instruments because "*Murabahah, Wakalah* and *Salam Sukuk* are not tradable in most Islamic financial centers" and money market instruments are not in line with Islamic law due to the Islamic prohibition of *Riba* (Al-Amine, 2013a:123; Sulaiman *et al.*, 2013:254). Moreover, these instruments have debt obligations and the sale of debt is not permitted under Islamic law.
2) Another source of liquidity risk for Islamic banks is the shallow secondary market caused by the buy-and-hold culture (Al-Amine, 2013a). For example, the *Sukuk* instrument is tradable in the secondary market, but short supply forces investors to buy-and-hold *Sukuk* instead of actively trading the instrument. Recent rapid growth and development of *Sukuk* might help Islamic banks minimize liquidity risks.
3) The limited number of market participants also poses liquidity risk for Islamic banks (Sulaiman *et al.*, 2013).
4) Because Islamic banks must currently function in the conventional banking environment, Islamic banks face the issue of buying and selling short-term instruments to meet reserves established by the central banks and the absence of a lender of last resort (LOLR) facilities (Al-Amine, 2013a). According to a survey of 24 Islamic financial regulators and supervisors, conducted by Chattha and Halim (2014), only six countries or jurisdictions have developed dedicated *Shari'ah*-compliant Lender-of-Last Resort (LOLR) facilities for local Islamic financial institutions. However, such facilities are vital for overall soundness and stability of a financial system (IFSB, 2015).
5) The current accounts held at Islamic banks are demand deposits and can be withdrawn by customers without prior notice, which creates a level of uncertainty for Islamic banks (Mohammad, 2013).
6) Islamic banks also face liquidity risk arising from certain instruments and contracts (Sulaiman *et al.*, 2013). For example, the customer may refuse to take the

delivery of a commodity in a *Murabahah* contract, as was discussed in Chapter 2. Furthermore, many contracts including *Bay' Salam* can only be traded at par value.

7) Islamic banks have excessive liquidity compared to conventional counterparts due to the use of profit and loss sharing (PLS) instruments (Al-Amine, 2013a). Excess liquidity reduces the profitability of Islamic banks. In 2007 Standard & Poor's calculated the average liquid-to-total asset ratio of Islamic banks from Gulf Cooperation Council at 30% compared with 18.1% for conventional banks in the same region. The 2015 International Financial Stability Report issued by the Islamic Financial Services Board showed that Islamic wholesale banks had maintained liquidity ratios above 20% since 2012.

3.5.3 Liquidity Management in Practice for Islamic Financial Institutions

Liquidity management for Islamic financial institutions has been an important concern in Islamic financial circles, and the lack of tradability for *Shari'ah*-compliant short-term instruments further raises questions about the soundness of Islamic financial institutions. According to a recent report released by the Islamic Financial Services Board (2015), the Islamic finance industry requires a minimum of $400 billion in short-term liquid securities for proper capital management. Currently, most of the Islamic banks rely on two methods of liquidity management: bilateral investment-based (*Mudarabah*) deposits and commodity *Murabahah*.

3.6 Role of Supporting Institutions in Overcoming Liquidity Management Challenges

According to Al-Amine (2013a), global regulations and infrastructure provide a solid starting point to effectively manage liquidity. Islamic financial institutions and religious scholars should work together to create a consensus about the viability of proposed *Shari'ah*-compliant instruments. Overcoming the challenges of liquidity management requires action by Islamic financial institutions and market stakeholders. The following section discusses several different institutions that could play a role in meeting this challenge, and highlights several institutions that have been established to help address the challenges of liquidity management in Islamic finance.

3.6.1 The International Islamic Liquidity Management Corporation

In 2010, the Islamic financial industry witnessed an historical development with the establishment of the International Islamic Liquidity Management Corporation (IILM). Based in Kuala Lumpur, the primary objective of the International Islamic Liquidity Management Corporation is to foster cross-border liquidity management for Islamic financial institutions through the issuance of short-term *Shari'ah*-compliant financial instruments (Bank Negara Malaysia, 2010; Archer & Karim, 2014). This significant move was the result of the recommendation of the High Level Task Force on Liquidity Management, initiated by the Islamic Financial Services Board Council in March 2009. The membership of the International Islamic Liquidity Management Corporation is open to banking and financial market regulators including those of the central banks, monetary authorities, financial regulatory authorities, and government ministries.

Currently, the membership of the International Islamic Liquidity Management Corporation is comprised of 12 central banks, two multilateral development institutions, and the applicable regulatory authorities. Included in the membership are the central banks of Indonesia, Kuwait, Luxembourg, Malaysia, Mauritius, Nigeria, Qatar, Turkey, and the United Arab Emirates, along with the Islamic Development Bank Group (Bank Negara Malaysia, 2010; Önal, 2013).

In April 2013, to provide short-term liquidity solutions to Islamic financial institutions, the International Islamic Liquidity Management Corporation launched the *Sukuk* program. This program facilitated the issuance of the first *Sukuk*, which was rated A-1 by Standard & Poor's (Archer & Karim, 2014). This development is considered the most important step toward overcoming the liquidity management challenge for three reasons: it was the first *Shari'ah*-compliant short-term *Sukuk* that was denominated in US Dollars, it was linked with tangible sovereign assets, and a liquid secondary market was established by the multi-jurisdictional primary-dealer network (Bank Negara Malaysia, 2013a).

Archer and Karim (2014) cited a number of additional milestones achieved by the International Islamic Liquidity Management Corporation including the issuance of a three-month US Dollar-denominated $490 million *Sukuk* in August 2013, and the issuance of a six-month *Sukuk* worth $400 million in August 2014. By the end of August 2014, a total of $5.33 billion *Sukuk* had been issued by the International Islamic Liquidity Management Corporation, which demonstrates the success of the *Sukuk* Program. However, the International Islamic Liquidity Management Corporation *Sukuk* Program also brought to light the following important challenges.

One of the most pressing challenges is the identification and accessibility of underlying sovereign assets for the *Sukuk* issuance, because no government finds it convenient to sell and buy back the same assets. Conditions imposed by Islamic law that require that the resale of assets must be at fair price rather than market price also presents a hurdle. Archer and Karim (2014) cited several related challenges including:

- Enhanced complexity of compliance with Islamic law, and fulfilling rules and regulations of different states with diverse regulatory and tax laws
- Lack of well-trained staff to structure different *Sukuk* programs while employing technology
- Limited availability of highly rated instruments such as A-1 by Standard & Poor's
- Lack of awareness among stakeholders about short-term liquidity management instruments, and inadequate use of financial technology in liquidity management

Varying interpretations of *Shari'ah*, in relation to liquidity management instruments, presents a major challenge for the International Islamic Liquidity Management Corporation (Bank Negara Malaysia, 2013a). The International Islamic Liquidity Management Corporation faces various challenges including inadequate cross-border liquidity infrastructure, a lack of availability of tradable short-term assets, a lack of transparency, and the need for sophisticated technology. According to Basu *et al.* (2015), there is also a lack of information about whether the *Sukuk* issued by the International Islamic Liquidity Management Corporation is backed by its member countries and can be liquidated through repo transactions. Moreover, it appears that such *Sukuk* are corporate rather than sovereign.

3.6.2 The Islamic Financial Services Board

The Islamic Financial Services Board is an international standard-setting organization that was established in 2002 in Kuala Lumpur and began operations in March 2003 (IFSB, 2016). One of the key responsibilities of the Islamic Financial Services Board is to facilitate the formulation of international supervisory and regulatory standards in accordance with Islamic law and to ensure that such bodies are designed to ensure soundness and stability of the Islamic financial system. By the end of April 2013 the Islamic Financial Services Board had 187 members spread over 43 jurisdictions, which included 57 regulatory and supervisory authorities, 8 international inter-government organizations, and 122 professional financial firms and industry organizations (Haron, 2012). Adebayo and Hassan (2013) argued that the Islamic Financial Services Board played an instrumental role in enhancing prudence and transparency among Islamic financial institutions and issued 12 standards, guiding principles, and technical notes covering areas such as risk management, capital adequacy, and Islamic money markets.

Following are the major objectives of the Islamic Financial Services Board, which are adapted from Haron (2011:3):

- "Develop standards and recommend implementation
- Provide guidance for effective supervision and regulation and develop risk management and disclosure criteria
- Establish standard international financial oversight bodies in corporations and member countries
- Enhance and coordinate initiatives to develop instruments and procedures for efficient operation and risk management
- Facilitate capacity building and development of human capital
- Undertake research and establish a database"

Al-Amine (2013a) expressed a belief that the Islamic Financial Services Board was keen on addressing liquidity management issues in the Islamic industry through the establishment of risk and liquidity management standards. Haron (2012) discussed the fact that the Islamic Financial Services Board was aware of the importance of sound liquidity management and asserted that the International Islamic Liquidity Management Corporation was established in 2010 for the purpose of issuing highly rated inter-government *Sukuk*, which would help bring Islamic capital and money markets into the mainstream of global finance. IFSB-12: Guiding Principles of Liquidity Management, a standard that was established in March 2012 to educate Islamic financial institutions about the vigorous management of liquidity, guides regulatory and supervisory authorities to effectively monitor such institutions. Aziz (2016) argued that the achievement of the Islamic Financial Services Board has provided the necessary foundation for the Islamic financial industry to experience continuous growth across various jurisdictions. However, the Islamic Financial Services Board has yet to play an important role in the convergence of the varying practices used to manage investment accounts (known as profit sharing investment accounts) among member countries.

3.6.3 Liquidity Management Center in Bahrain

As mentioned earlier, liquidity management is a key challenge for Islamic financial institutions. To tackle this issue the Liquidity Management Center (LMC), an active secondary trading platform, was established by the Bahraini government to provide support to financial institutions for liquidity management (Bacha & Mirakhor, 2013). The Liquidity Management Center was founded in 2002 and is managed by The Central Bank of Bahrain (CBB). The aim of the Liquidity Management Center is to provide financing and investment platforms that foster the robust growth and development of Islamic capital markets (Liquidity Management Center, 2016).

According to Parashar (2014), the Liquidity Management Center developed the inaugural structure of its short-term *Sukuk* Program (STSP) with to offer investors a tradable low-risk liquidity management product. The introduction of the short-term *Sukuk* program represents the first such experiment. The Liquidity Management Center in conjunction with other agencies has developed a portfolio of asset-backed corporate and sovereign *Sukuk* instruments to support the short-term *Sukuk* program (Parashar, 2014). By the end of 2009, the total value of short-term instruments in the *Sukuk* program was $250 million.

Al-Amine (2013a) argues that the Liquidity Management Center slowed its activities in the three years following the recent financial crisis and has decided to establish itself as a fully-fledged investment bank dealing mainly with *Sukuk*. The agency faces a viability challenge because its own equity paid up capital and asset size is quite small (Parashar, 2014). Furthermore, primary Islamic capital markets are relatively small, which could pose a challenge to the expansion plans of the Liquidity Management Center.

3.6.4 International Islamic Financial Markets

The International Islamic Financial Markets (IIFM), founded in 2002 through the joint efforts of the Islamic Development Bank (IDB), Autoriti Monetari Brunei Darussalam, Bank Indonesia, The Central Bank of Bahrain, and The Central Bank of Sudan and Bank Negara Malaysia is another institution supporting the Islamic finance industry, particularly in the development of Islamic capital and money markets (IIFM, 2016). The main function of the International Islamic Financial Markets, in the context of liquidity management, is to ensure harmonization of standards pertinent to Islamic financial instruments (Al-Amine, 2013a). The International Islamic Financial Markets issued standards on *Murabahah*, *Tahawut* (netting), profit rate swaps, and liquidity management. Vizcaino (2015) stated that the International Islamic Financial Markets also issued standards on Islamic cross currency swaps in order to meet the growing demand of cross-currency transactions at Islamic financial institutions. This standard can be used for multiple purposes including interbank treasury placements, *Sukuk*, trade, and corporate finance transactions. It should be taken into account that since 2002 the International Islamic Financial Markets has issued seven standards.

In 2014, because the International Islamic Financial Markets (IIFM) was gaining a reputation for being a standard-setting body, the Board of Directors (BoD) of the International Islamic Financial Markets made a strategic decision to include corporate finance and trade finance in its mandate (Alvi, 2015). This move was intended to provide standards and unified documentation for the development of the Islamic financial industry as a robust, transparent, and vibrant industry.

According to Adebayo and Hassan (2013), to achieve unification of Islamic capital and money market products, documents, and standards the International Islamic Financial Markets (IIFM) issued the IIFM Master Agreements for Treasury Placement (MATP). The Master Agreements for Treasury Placement helps to minimize legal and operational costs, provides an efficient standardized documentation process (as compared to costly bilateral approach), and ensures strenuous negotiation and constant *Shari'ah* involvement for the Commodity *Murabahah* (Alvi, 2009).

Following are the major benefits of the International Islamic Financial Markets, which are adapted from Adebayo and Hassan (2013:85):

- "Acting as a standard setting body with regulatory heritage
- Addressing the standardization needs of the industry
- Providing a universal platform to market participants through global working groups for the development of the Islamic capital and money market
- Facilitating *Shari'ah* harmonization in documentation, products, and processes
- Establishing a *Shari'ah* advisory panel consisting of renowned scholars, hence ensuring wider *Shari'ah* acceptance"

In the following section, several liquidity management tools and instruments that are being used in the Islamic finance industry are discussed.

3.7 Liquidity Management Tools and Instruments

According to Khalid (2015), the following are important tools and instruments at the disposal of Islamic banks for liquidity management:

- *Sukuk*
- Inter-bank *Musharakah/Mudarabah-based* pools

- Commodity *Murabahah* transactions
- Trading and hedging currencies
- *Shari'ah*-compliant equities and mutual funds

Table 3 provides information about some of the existing financial instruments available to Islamic banks for the purposes of liquidity management. The Commodity *Murabahah* instrument is a short-term liquidity management tool with a maturity that varies from one week to six months and is widely used by Islamic banks (Önal, 2013). Interbank *Mudarabah*, Interbank *Wakalah*, and Islamic repo have short-term maturities of less than three months. However, it should be noted that Islamic banks use Islamic repo only domestically and these instruments are unrated. *Sukuk* is used both for short-term and long-term liquidity management. The following section will elaborate on details provided in Table 3, below.

Table 3: Existing Financial Instruments Available to Islamic Banks for Liquidity Management

Central Bank and other Islamic Financial Institutions	Duration	Local/ International	Rating
Idle Cash	Unlimited	Either	
Commodity *Murabahah*	1 week-6 months	Either	Counterparty Rating
Interbank *Mudarabah*	Overnight-1 month	Either	Counterparty Rating
Interbank *Wakalah*	1–3 months	Either	Counterparty Rating
Islamic repo	Overnight-1 Month	Local	Unrated
Long-term *Sukuk*	More than 1 Year	Either	Rated
Short-term *Sukuk*	Various Maturities less than 1 Year	Local in few countries (e.g., Bahrain)	Rated

Source: Adapted from Archer and Karim (2014)

3.7.1 Commodity *Murabahah*

The Commodity *Murabahah* is the most widely used interbank tool available to facilitate the transfer of funds from institutions experiencing a surplus in liquidity to those that require additional resources (Önal, 2013). Using the infrastructure provided by the London Metal Exchange, the Bursa Malaysia, and other similar platforms allows financial institutions that have a surplus of funds to buy commodities and sell commodities on the condition of deferred payment to institutions experiencing a deficit of available funds.

Al-Amine (2013a) stated that the market size of Commodity *Murabahah* transactions exceeded $1.2 billion and that the Commodity *Murabahah* is a widely used instrument for short-term liquidity management, particularly in Saudi Arabia, UAE, and other gulf countries (El-Gamal, 2006). Bahrain Financial Exchange established the *Bait al-Bursa* commodity trading platform (Al-Amine, 2013a). In recent years, Malaysia innovated the traditional Commodity *Murabahah* and formulated a Commodity *Murabahah* Program (CMP) in which transactions rely on Crude Palm Oil (CPO) contracts as the underlying assets (Sobol, 2013; Dusuki, 2007).

Sobol (2013) reiterated El-Gamal's (2006) assertion that Islamic financial institutions in Bahrain, Saudi Arabia, Qatar, Malaysia, Kuwait, and the United Arab Emirites frequently use Commodity Murabahah. Bank Negara Malaysia, The Central Bank of Malaysia, practices transactions of Commodity *Murabahah* between financial institutions and The Central Bank. Bank Negara Malaysia conducts Commodity *Murabahah* transactions with banks inside the country and with foreign banks including the Saudi Hollandi Bank and CIMB Bank Berhard. Al-Amine (2013a) stated that transactions on the basis of Commodity *Murabahah* recently began in the Malaysian market although, historically, the Malaysian market used instruments primarily based on the sale of debt, a practice that drew criticism from a majority of Islamic scholars.

According to Al-Amine (2013a:12), the use of Commodity *Murabahah* on an international level has brought several benefits. It is now relatively convenient for financial institutions to match "profiles of wholesale investments against projected deposit redemption" to generate additional returns from available short-term deposits. Commodity *Murabahah* facilitates diversification and enhancement of asset portfolios. However, the structure and mechanism of Commodity *Murabahah* historically failed to garner confidence from Muslims and a number of Islamic scholars it closely resembles that of conventional interest-based contracts (Al-Amine, 2013a).

3.7.2 Interbank Deposits on *Wakalah* Basis

Interbank deposits based on *Wakalah* are used as a liquidity management tool by Islamic banks and are a form of contract in which the principal places excess funds with an agent who invests those funds in a profitable business. In this arrangement, the agent charges a fee for services provided (Al-Amine, 2013a). Simply put, the principal and agent form an investment agency. Archer and Karim (2014) argued that Islamic banks might place funds with other banks on the basis of *Wakalah* or *Mudarabah* although in either situation the bank faces counterparty risk. Moreover, the placement of funds based on *Wakalah* or *Mudarabah* do not meet the high quality liquid assets (HQLA) requirements under Basel regulatory standards.

3.7.3 Short-term *Ijarah Sukuk* as a Money Market Instrument

In the view of Sobol (2013), short-term *Ijarah Sukuk* is another important liquidity management tool that is commonly used in countries like Bahrain, Brunei, Singapore, Malaysia and Pakistan. The Central Bank of Bahrain launched innovative *Shari'ah*-compliant tradable short-term *Ijarah Sukuk* to manage the liquidity needs of Islamic banks (Al-Amine, 2013a). This action was the first such experiment with *Shari'ah*-compliant tradable short-term *Ijarah Sukuk* in the Islamic financial industry. Recently The Central Bank of Bahrain developed all tenures of *Ijarah Sukuk, including* short-, medium- and long-term *Ijarah Sukuk*, and these instruments are issued on the behalf of the government of Bahrain (Al-Amine, 2013a). Malaysia has issued short- and medium-term *Ijarah Sukuk* for liquidity management, and the Kingdom of Brunei demonstrate its intentions of developing Islamic financial markets in the country (Al-Amine, 2013a) by issuing over B$4.151 billion worth of short-term *Ijarah Sukuk* by mid-2012.

Khalid (2015) argued that the use of *Sukuk* for medium- and long-term liquidity management brought to light several disadvantages including the fact that *Sukuk* faces higher market risk, has no secondary market, is regularly issued in only a few countries, and has a limited number of potential participants. These disadvantages make liquidity management difficult for Islamic banks that do issue *Sukuk*. Archer and Karim (2014) affirmed the views of Khalid (2015) by arguing that the issuance of globally recognized *Sukuk* is considerably small. However, Islamic banks still have an opportunity to invest excess funds in highly rated *Sukuk* (AAA) that are issued by the Islamic Development Bank and the International Finance Corporation (IFC).

Sobol (2013) stated that among Islamic scholars there is a lack of consensus about the compliance of *Ijarah Sukuk* to *Shari'ah* because the cash flows of rentals are benchmarked using the interbank rates established by the conventional banking industry rather than the value of underlying assets. Moreover, the secondary market for *Ijarah Sukuk* is still in the development phase and a shortage of participants is a major challenge.

3.7.4 Islamic Repo

Repos are, in fact, not financial instruments but are frequently used in money markets for liquidity management (Bacha & Mirakhor, 2013). A repo is a money market repurchase contract in which one party sells securities at an agreed upon price and is committed to repurchasing the same securities at a later date for a higher price (Hakim, 2007). The difference between selling price and repurchase price is the interest earned by the entity that buys such securities (Omar *et al.*, 2013). Repo transactions are also known as sale and buy-back agreements. Islamic repos are akin to conventional banking Repurchase Agreements (Repo) and the structure is based on Islamic law.

According to Al-Amine (2013a) the reasons for the rapid development of Islamic Repo include a number of benefits such as the availability of prompt liquidity, high turnover, and access to inexpensive funding. Malaysia pioneered the use of Islamic Repo instruments and The Central Bank of Malaysia uses a two party repo structure in which *Shari'ah*-compliant assets are sold to select banks for deferred payment. After the first transaction, the banks resell the purchased assets to the central bank on a cash basis. The Central Bank of Bahrain innovated Islamic Repo by incorporating a third party into the transaction (Al-Amine, 2013a).

A repo agreement entails two transactions. First, a financial institution in need of liquidity sells a security to a broker who then sells the security to The Central Bank of Bahrain. Second, the bank in need of funds makes a commitment to The Central Bank of Bahrain to buy the security at the time of maturity.

3.7.5 Way Forward for Liquidity Management

In order to overcome the daunting challenge of liquidity management, Khalid (2015) proposed two strategies. First, regulators and other relevant stakeholder should work to establish a dynamic liquidity management infrastructure including both primary and secondary markets. Second, establishing a standardized global regulatory and legal framework will help foster liquidity management.

Efforts have been made to address liquidity management issues but there are still hurdles and challenges including the lack of short-term instruments, limited numbers of banks in each participating country, and a small volume of transactions in local markets (Al-Amine, 2013a). Another important challenge that Islamic banks face is in achieving compliance with Basel III regulatory standards because Islamic banks cannot invest in interest-based instruments. Furthermore, the already issued *Sukuk* are not enough to meet the Basel III requirements (Al-Amine, 2013a). The business model of Islamic banks will be exposed to further liquidity risks, and it is paramount for a risk management framework to address symptoms and provide proper mitigation measures regarding hidden causes of liquidity risk (Ali, 2013). According to Al-Amine "greater convergence and harmonization of regulations and products will facilitate efficient and sustainable growth" (Al-Amine, 2013a:125).

3.8 Implications of Basel III for Islamic Banking

The recent global financial crisis that spanned from 2007 through 2009 compelled the banking industry to formulate new regulations, and in 2010 the Basel III frameworks was introduced (Shawamreh, 2013; Azeem *et al.*, 2015). The main purpose of the Basel III framework was to improve the capital requirements of financial institutions, protect investors and customers, and supports the financial stability of the global economy (Chia *et al.*, 2015). Wilson (2013) stated several reasons for the introduction of Basel III including limitations of Basel II, emergence of the global financial crisis in 2007, the burden on governments to rescue financial institutions, the absence of stress-testing, and reactive rather than proactive regulatory measures. Kennedy (2012) argued that a lack of sound corporate governance, business models based on achieving extraordinary profits, and the behavior of some market participants were behind the financial crisis and therefore it is unfair to fully blame a lack of effective regulations.

The Basel III framework's implementation is gradual and will be completed in 2019. The implementation of Basel III will require financial institutions to significantly revise and improve liquidity management, capital adequacy, and governance (Al-Hares *et al.*, 2013; Kennedy, 2012). The main purpose of Basel III was to foster capital adequacy, require stress testing, and improve the market liquidity of financial institutions (Chia *et al.*, 2015).

The Basel III regulatory framework enhanced the framework established by Basel II, most importantly in the area of liquidity management for meeting the Liquidity Coverage Ratio (LCR) and the Net Stable Funding Ratio (NSFR) (Wilson, 2013). Basel III required banks to have liquidity provisions equal to 30 days cash outflows, which would help ensure the availability of adequate liquidity. Other notable additions in Basel III included capital adequacy, leverage ratios, and counterparty credit risk (Kennedy, 2012). The Liquidity Coverage Ratio holds banks accountable for maintaining enough liquidity to effectively meet market shocks, and the Net Stable Funding Ratio requires banks to have access to long-term and structural funding profiles. This means that financial institutions are required to maintain stable funding equal to one year according to the composition and structure of the assets of the bank (BIS, 2014). This is also referred to as available stable funding.

Islamic banks are part of global financial system and are required to comply with the Basel III. Under the Basel III framework there is no distinction between conventional and Islamic banks (Alam, 2013). The following section provides an overview of the challenges faced by Islamic banks in light of Basel III.

3.8.1 Challenges Posed by Basel III to Islamic Banks

Following are the important challenges that Islamic banks are facing in light of the Basel III framework:

1) Islamic banks are facing one of the biggest challenges of managing liquidity risk due the underdevelopment of *Shari'ah*-compliant securities, which restrict the availability of short-term liquid instruments (Msatfa, 2012; Vizcaino, 2014b; Schoon, 2013). In the context of liquidity risk, Islamic banks are required to meet the Liquidity Coverage Ratio and are pushed to meet the high-quality liquid assets (HQLAs) requirements of Basel III. The banks should maintain the high-quality liquid assets so that they may withstand large volume cash outflows for up to 30 days. In order to accommodate the requirement for high-quality liquid assets, financial instruments and assets must represent low risk, highly tradability, low credit risk, and low market risk (Archer & Karim, 2014). The shallowness of the Islamic securities market makes it difficult for Islamic banks to meet the high-quality liquid assets requirements (Ozkan, 2015), which poses a significant challenge.

2) Kennedy (2012) argued that the fragmented structure of the Islamic financial institutions, along with a shortage of short-term liquidity instruments, presents an important challenge.
3) The main source of deposits in Islamic banks is deposits to profit-sharing investment accounts (PSIAs), which are generally perceived as volatile when compared to conventional deposits (Vizcaino, 2014b). According to Song and Oosthuizen (2014), Islamic banks are generally more solvent than conventional banks because profit-sharing investment accounts are quasi-liability deposits and holders of these deposits are expected to bear all losses on their investments unless there is strong evidence of negligence on the part of the bank. This transfer of risks to the depositor provides an additional buffer for Islamic banks.
4) Because Islamic banks use *Mudarabah* and *Musharakah* for investment purposes they face equity investment risk (Msatfa, 2012). Basel III also asserts that financial institutions should define capital requirements for counterparty credit risk. The World Islamic Banking Competitiveness Report 2013–14 released by Ernst and Young, an international consulting firm, showed that Islamic banks in Gulf Cooperation Council countries would suffer a reduction of about 3% in capital ratios if they did not engage in efficient capital planning.
5) Because of the lack of standardization and harmonization with *Shari'ah*-compliance practices Islamic banks face reputational risks (Msatfa, 2012). Therefore, the Basel Committee on Banking Supervision (BCBS) asserted that financial institutions must adopt uniform methods to manage the consequences of reputational risk.
6) Because of the investments in technologies for risk management Islamic banks are now vulnerable to operational risk, and the establishment of internal control systems is needed to ensure compliance with the proposed standards (Ozkan, 2015).
7) The Basel Committee on Banking Supervision emphasized the fact that banks should avoid holding equity positions in companies they finance (Schoon, 2013). This creates challenge for Islamic banks because *Mudarabah* and *Musharakah* transactions are conducted on the basis of profit sharing, which is considered equivalent to holding an equity position. The rationale of Basel Committee on Banking Supervision is that holding equity in a business that the bank has financed constitutes a conflict of interest.
8) Because investment activities are prone to market and counterparty risks Islamic banks that have big investment portfolios will especially experience the effects of Basel III (Msatfa, 2012). For example, risk is higher in business transactions that deal with lower-rated or unstable counterparties. On the other hand, a larger deposit base can protect retail Islamic banks from assuming higher levels of risk by spreading that risk among a large number of both low-risk and high-risk depositors.

3.8.2 Opportunities for Islamic Banks

Islamic banks are better positioned to cope with the requirements of Basel III because the majority of the Islamic banks belong to strong economies such as those in the Middle East and South East Asia (Vizcaino, 2014b). Kennedy (2012) asserted that Islamic banks are not posing systemic risk to the financial system for a number of reasons including the fact that their presence is still relatively small in comparison to conventional banks, and Islamic banks are engaged in limited cross-border dependencies and business transactions.

With the exception of a few large banks, Islamic banks are not a dominating force in the financial industry. It is worth mentioning that if assets of a bank exceed $100 billion that bank is considered as a systemic risk by the Basel Committee on Banking Supervision. Despite the growth of Islamic banking, it is expected that only a few Islamic banks have the potential of become a dominating force (Kennedy, 2012). Islamic banks avoid speculative business practices such as derivatives and, therefore, face comparatively fewer issues in fulfilling minimum capital standards when compared to conventional banks (Vizcaino, 2014b). Msatfa (2012) pointed out the fact that because of prohibitions on short selling activities Islamic banks face less market risk and, as a result, are minimally impacted by Basel III in this regard. However, Islamic banks may face high risk when using *Bay' Salam* and *Istisnah* instruments due to fluctuations in underlying prices of supporting commodities.

According to an empirical study conducted by Al-Hares *et al.* (2013), Islamic banks in Gulf Cooperation Council countries appear to be well capitalized and exhibit better CAR (19.92% vs. 14.4%) when compared to conventional banks. Therefore, Islamic banks are not required to find ways to rigorously increase capital. Other notable findings are: Islamic banks hold higher liquidity ratios, lower efficiency ratios, and higher solvency ratios when compared to conventional banks in the same regions.

It is also likely that Basel III requirements for increased capital and liquidity will affect banks in emerging economies, but Islamic banks in the Gulf Cooperation Council will not be affected to the same degree because these banks are already well capitalized (Msatfa, 2012). Song and Oosthuizen (2014) performed an empirical study to determine the impact of Basel III on the capital requirements of Islamic banks in 29 countries where a majority of the Islamic banks were operating. Song and Oosthuizen found that CAR for Islamic banks ranged from 8% to 12% and the majority of the Islamic banks were strongly positioned to meet the minimum capital adequacy requirements established by Basel III.

According to Bank Negara Malaysia (2013) Basel III regulations provide an exciting opportunity for the Islamic finance industry to develop new *Sukuk* structures that could meet capital adequacy requirements. In November 2012, Abu Dhabi Islamic Bank (ADIB) was the first Islamic institution to issue *Sukuk*, and it did so at a value of $1 billion. The issuance received an overwhelming market response and was 30 times over-subscribed. One order was received for $15.5 billion even though the profit rate of 6.375% offered was the lowest profit rate offered for this kind of instrument.

Basel III provides an opportunity for financial institutions to generate alternative sources of liquidity if they find it difficult to obtain financing through equity (Bank Negara Malaysia, 2013b). With the issuance of the Islamic Financial Services Board Exposure Draft 15 in November 2015 the Islamic Financial Services Board addressed the use of *Sukuk* for raising additional capital, and Islamic banks can now issue *Sukuk* to meet the regulatory minimum capital requirements of Basel III. However, Al-Amine (2013a) argued that because of the lack of *Sukuk* market liquidity in Islamic financial institutions might not find active *Sukuk* buyers when liquidity is needed.

The issuance of short-term *Sukuk* by the International Islamic Liquidity Management Corporation helps to increase the availability of short-term liquidity instruments for Islamic banks (Vizcaino, 2014b). In addition to this, Dubai is aspiring to list tradable *Sukuk* on its exchanges and is expected to achieve this in the near future.

3.8.3 Response of Supporting Islamic Institutions and Corporate Governance

Not until after 2019, when the Basel III regulations are fully enforced, will it be possible to comprehend all possible implications for Islamic banks. However, it is widely believed that capitalization and funding levels will be directly affected (Msatfa, 2012). The role of institutions supporting Islamic finance, including the International Islamic Liquidity Management Corporation and the Accounting and Auditing Organization of Islamic Financial Institutions, will be important in providing necessary guidance to the market, and these institutions have already taken various measures in this regard.

Basel III has implications for conventional banks to implement corporate governance standards and processes that currently only apply to Islamic banks (Msatfa, 2012). The new changes in the Basel framework place ultimate responsibility for business operations, formulation of risk strategy, financial soundness, and corporate governance on the board of directors. The board has a broad role in risk management for financial institutions. These amendments in the new framework also help Islamic banks improve oversight over the board of directors and senior management, ensure smooth operations, and enhance regulatory compliance.

The new Basel III framework also requires large Islamic banks to create an audit committee or similar department that will have the responsibility of supervising the accounting policies and practices of the bank (Msatfa, 2012). The objective of this requirement is to facilitate transparent financial reporting practices and impose a system of checks and balances on senior management. Auditors will be responsible for oversight related to compliance with *Shari'ah* rules and regulations. The establishment of a risk management committee on the highest level is also recommended and can ensure implementation and enforcement of risk management policies adopted by the bank.

Under the Basel III framework, financial institutions are required to implement sound stress-testing practices (Msatfa, 2012). Islamic banks are required to conduct several tests including scenario analysis and stress-testing in the context of qualitative and quantitative analysis. The requirement imposes a challenge on Islamic banks in light of new *Shari'ah*-compliant products and would require the identification of weaknesses present in unidentified risk concentrations.

Schoon (2013) stated that the Islamic Financial Services Board has had close collaboration with Basel Committee on Banking Supervision in recent years but is not expected to issue any revisions related to the regulatory treatment of *Mudarabah* and *Musharakah* transactions in the short-term. As was discussed in Chapter 2, *Mudarabah* and *Musharakah* transactions are generally capital intensive that require careful calculations of cost of capital at Islamic banks while dealing with clients and developing future transactions.

According to Athreya (2014), the response to the implementation of Basel III in Muslim countries, especially in the Middle East, varies. Banks in Qatar implemented a blend of Basel III and proposals issued by the Islamic Financial Services Board with anticipated improvement in the operational capabilities of Islamic banks in Qatar. The United Arab Emirates and Saudi Arabia decided to allow Islamic banks to implement both Basel III and proposals of Islamic Financial Services Board one at a time. In this way, Islamic banks in The United Arab Emirates and Saudi Arabia will have sufficient time to adjust their operations.

Azeem *et al.* (2015) stated that the majority of Islamic banks are small and will be less affected by the implementation of Basel III. Islamic banks in Malaysia are holding sufficient Liquidity Coverage Ratio (LCR). Kennedy (2012) concluded, "Basel III is unlikely to materially change the existing challenges faced by the Islamic banks."

3.8.4 Basel III and Islamic Finance Industry: Way Forward

Basel III will affect the liquidity risk management of Islamic banks. Islamic banks also face corporate governance issues presented by a lack of product standardization and challenges with ensuring *Shari'ah*-compliance. The Basel III framework provides an opportunity for the Islamic finance industry to examine such challenges and leverage industry strengths to further emerge as a stable and responsible financial system.

Islamic wealth management is a promising sector of the Islamic financial industry. The following section provides a discussion of wealth from an Islamic finance perspective.

3.9 Wealth Creation and Management in Islam

According to Ahmed (2013) there is no standard definition of wealth management, but the common focus of wealth management is on private banking for wealthier clients. Maude (2006:1) stated that the definition of wealth management is "financial services provided to wealthy clients, mainly individuals and their families."

The concept of wealth in Islam is different than the conventional concept of wealth, which aims to generate maximum short-term returns irrespective of the development and prosperity of overall society in the long term (Wouters, 2013). In the conventional western world, individuals view wealth as a personal accumulation of assets after taxes. Individuals believe that in paying taxes they have done their fiduciary duty and they rely on the government to deploy taxes collected to facilitate developmental activities for the benefit of society. Alternatively, the Islamic perspective on wealth management goes beyond the accumulation of financial resources and emphasizes the idea that development of community and taking care of the poor through compulsory payments of *Zakat* are important (Wouters, 2013). Therefore, in Islamic societies every individual has a responsibility to fulfil the needs of the community and to address the needs of the poor. According to Possumah and Ismail (2012), in capitalism wealth is considered a scare resource, individuals have absolute ownership and they have freedom to use assets for their own personal satisfaction. In Islam, wealth is viewed as gift of *Allah* that is bestowed upon individuals who are then entrusted to use those resources for the welfare of all human beings.

Shanmugam and Zahari (2009) stated that according to Islam *Allah* is the creator of the whole universe and therefore everything belongs to Him. However, human beings can earn wealth through hard work or inheritance. Money, which is a form of wealth, should be earned and spent by the Muslims in accordance with the principles established by Islam. Ariff and Mohamad (2013) stated that *Allah* owns all wealth, but acknowledged that human beings can earn wealth through effort in order to fulfil the needs of family and community. In addition to this, *Allah* has given wealth to individuals to perform good deeds on earth and on the day of judgement He will ask about the spending of wealth as is evidenced by the following verses of the Quran.

> "To *Allah* belongs the heritage of the heavens and the earth; and Allah is well-acquainted with all that ye do" (Quran 3:180).
> "And He has subjected to you, as from Him all that is in the heavens and on earth: behold, in that are signs indeed for those who reflect" (Quran 45:13).

Wouters (2013) cited four parameters that constitute a sustainable framework of wealth according to Islam. First, everything belongs to *Allah* and this principle changes the perspectives of human beings. Second, the role of a man is as the guardian of wealth entrusted by *Allah*. Therefore, man has limited ownership rights for the claim to wealth and the right to use and distribute wealth. Third, earning wealth is considered a form of worship and all activities for gaining wealth should fall within the rules imposed by Islam. Finally, wealth alone is neither good nor bad in and of itself, and the righteousness of wealth it depends entirely upon how it is employed by those who possess it.

3.9.1 Size of Global Islamic Wealth Management Industry

The Islamic Wealth Management Report (IWMR) that was issued in 2016 by Edbiz Consulting, a London based Islamic finance consulting firm, estimated the size of global Islamic wealth by the end of 2014 was $11.3 trillion, which is relatively small in comparison to the size of global wealth ($107.3 trillion). The Islamic Wealth Management Report (2016) further stated that the households of high net worth individuals (HNWIs) held about 30% or $3.35 trillion of the total Islamic wealth, whereas Muslim businesses, Islamic financial institutions, and majority of governments in OIC control the remaining 70%. Farooq (2014) stated that not all Muslim high net worth individuals (HNWIs) are interested in investing in *Shari'ah*-compliant wealth. Similarly, a recent global survey of knowledge, attitudes, and practices of the global wealth management industry (conducted by Edbiz Consulting) indicated that 18% (out of more than 50) industry practitioners and experts cited the difficulty and inconvenience of investing in *Shari'ah*-compliant products and services (Azmi, 2016).

Thomson Reuters released a 2015 Global Islamic Asset Management Outlook report revealing that the Islamic wealth management industry is growing rapidly and may benefit from various opportunities including digital wealth management, socially responsible clients, and growing retail and institutional demand. But the Islamic wealth management industry also faces challenges such as the limited availability of risk management products and evident liquidity risk that may hamper the future growth.

3.10 Concluding Remarks

Chapter 3 provided an overview of the broad topics of risk management, Islamic wealth creation, and wealth management as they pertain to Islamic banking and finance. With the growth and expansion of the Islamic financial industry into unfamiliar legal and regulatory jurisdictions the exhaustive risk management structures have become a necessity. Risk management for Islamic financial institutions, as was discussed in Chapter 3, has primarily focused on the gradual increased use of risk management tools such as derivatives.

Islamic financial institutions and market oversight bodies like the International Islamic Financial Markets are gradually gearing their efforts toward gaining a consensus about the *Shari'ah*-compliant use of derivatives. Islamic scholars have demonstrated resistance to endorsing the use of derivatives in Islamic finance transactions because many of them believe that derivatives rely on speculation, excess uncertainty, and gambling, all of which were heavily responsible for issues faced in the recent financial crisis.

The issue of liquidity risk management is one of the most critical challenges for Islamic financial institutions for a number of reasons including limited options of inter-bank and money market instruments, a shallow secondary market, and a limited number of market participants. Fragmented efforts have been made to address this issue through the establishment of the Liquidity Management Corporation (LMC) and the International Islamic Financial Markets (IIFM) in Bahrain, and the International Islamic Liquidity Management Corporation (IILM) and Islamic Financial Services Board (IFSB) in Malaysia. Islamic financial institutions, regulatory bodies, and other stakeholders must take coordinated measures to harmonize product structures, regulations, and practices, and to create a consensus among Islamic scholars.

The introduction of Basel III brings opportunities and challenges for Islamic banks. Islamic banks are more capable of meeting capital requirements, but are still facing major issues related to corporate governance, supervision, and liquidity risk management. Islamic banks are making efforts to align their business activities to meet requirement of Basel III, and in 2012 Abu Dhabi Islamic Bank (ADIB) issued the first *Sukuk* worth $1 billion. It is more important now than ever for Islamic supporting institutions, including the Accounting and Auditing Organization for Islamic Financial Institutions (AAOIFI) and the Islamic Financial Services Board, to engage with the Basel Committee on Banking Supervision in an effort to sort out convergence issues.

Finally, the Islamic wealth or asset management industry is still in the initial phases of growth, with assets much smaller in value than the conventional asset management industry. The limited number of *Shari'ah*-compliant financial tools and capital market instruments are the major reason for the underdevelopment of the Islamic wealth management sector. It is expected that this promising sector will boom when Islamic financial institutions gain ready access to tradable instruments. *Zakat*, *Sadaquah*, *Qard Hasan* and *Waqf* are relevant functioning examples of wealth management and distribution in Islam.

Chapter 4: Global Emergence of Islamic Finance in Western Europe: a Case Study of the United Kingdom

4.1 Introduction

The main purpose of Chapter 4 is to discuss the global emergence of Islamic finance from the Western European perspective. According to international consulting firm Ernest and Young (E&Y) (2016:2):

> "Islamic finance is one of the fastest growing areas of the global financial services industry. The spread of Islamic finance into Western markets demonstrates that it is now being viewed by investors, financial institutions and regulators as a viable alternative to conventional products."

The United Kingdom is the leading pioneer in promoting Islamic finance as an alternative to other financial models, and is considered a role model for doing so in other non-Muslim countries. In regards to Western Europe, London can be seen as the Islamic financial hub.

Chapter 4 also provides a detailed explanation of the evolution of Islamic finance in the United Kingdom, and provides an overview of the lessons that can be derived from the implementation of the United Kingdom's regulatory model. A comparison of Germany's financial regulatory model to the United Kingdom's regulatory model will be provided in an effort to draw meaningful conclusions that could be helpful for German regulators and financial institutions that wish to foster growth in Islamic banking and finance.

In summary, Chapter 4 provides an overview of the Islamic banking and finance industry, the evolution of Islamic finance in Europe, a case study of the United Kingdom's model for Islamic banking and finance in Europe, a comparative analysis of the financial regulatory models in the United Kingdom's and Germany, problems and challenges Islamic banking and finance is currently facing in the United Kingdom, and a chapter summary.

4.2 Brief Overview of Global Islamic Banking and Finance Industry

Belouafi and Chachi (2014:43) described the early development of Islamic finance as follows:

> "Islamic financial operations were known and practiced since the 7th century AD when the Prophet Mohammed (peace be upon him) prohibited some transactions involving *Riba* (interest), *Gharar* (deception), *Qimr* (gambling), *Mujazafah* (speculation), *Ihtikar*

(monopoly) and other similar transactions and allowed some other transactions such as *Murbaah* (Mark-up sale), *Mushrakah* (partnership), *Murabah* (sleeping partnership), *Muzraah* (Sharecropping) and similar transactions. Some of these operations were known to many earlier civilizations but they were developed further under the Islamic civilization."

There are mixed views about the contemporary development of Islamic finance. However, many scholars believe that the concept of Islamic banking first presented in the 1940s after a book by Anwar Iqbal Qureshi entitled *Islam and the Theory of Interest* (1946) and an article by Naeem Siddiqui entitled *Banking on Islamic Principles* (1948) were published (Belouafi & Chachi, 2014). Subsequently, some Muslim scholars and organizations have tried to put the theoretical concepts of Islamic banking into practice. One named example is that of Al-Naggar, who initiated the Mit-Ghamr Local Savings Bank (MGLSB) in Egypt in 1963. This model of banking was inspired by the model employed for German savings banks but was based on *Shari'ah* principles. Moreover, Tabung Haji in Malaysia (THM), also known as Pilgrims Fund Corporation, established a bank on the basis of *Shari'ah*.

4.2.1 Market Size of Global Islamic Finance Industry

Shari'ah-compliant assets were valued at around $2 trillion at the end of 2014, showing a growth of 12% compared to 2013, and were projected to reach more than $2.2 trillion by the end of 2015 and exceed $3 trillion by 2018 (TheCityUK, 2015). *Shari'ah*-compliant assets experienced annual growth of 20% from 2007 to 2014, and the size of global *Shari'ah*-compliant assets has tripled since the start of the financial crisis in 2007.

As shown in Figure 3, by the end of 2014, the Gulf Cooperation Council region recorded the majority share of Islamic financial assets at 38%, while regions of the Middle East and North Africa (MENA) recorded 35% and the Asian region recorded 22%. This report also revealed that *Shari'ah*-compliant banking is still underdeveloped despite the strong growth of Islamic finance. At the present time, 80% of the Muslim population has no access to *Shari'ah*-compliant banking. From Figure 3, it can be concluded that assets of the Islamic financial industry have shown consistent growth since 2006. However, Islamic financial assets have grown even more rapidly in recent years, beginning in 2012. The main reason for the higher rate of growth is a global recognition of the viability of Islamic banking and finance.

Islamic finance encompasses a broad range of services including Islamic banking, which accounts for 79% of global Islamic financial assets. In addition to this, *Sukuk* bonds have a market share of 16% of total assets (TheCityUK, 2015). Islamic funds and *Takaful* have a market share of 4% and 1%, respectively (These Islamic financial services will be briefly discussed in the following sections).

Figure 3: Global Assets of Islamic Finance and Islamic Finance by Region

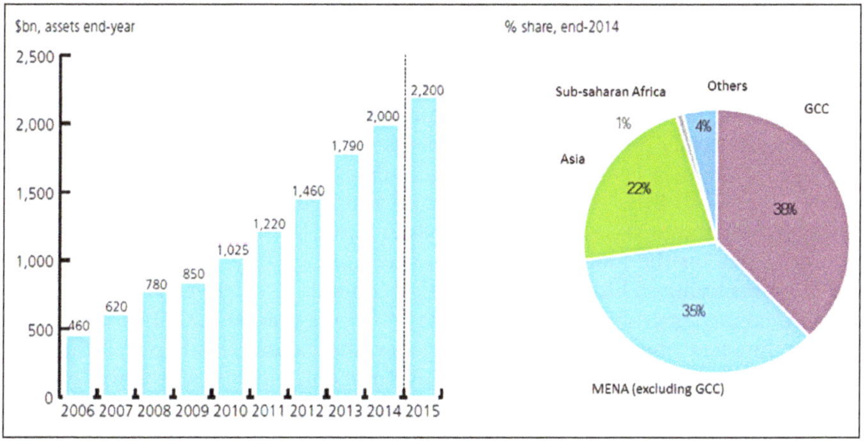

Source: TheCityUK (2015)

4.3 Evolution of Islamic Finance in Europe

Islamic finance in Europe evolved during the 1980s when the first Commodity *Murabahah* was introduced on the London market. The Islamic insurance (*Takaful*) was established in Luxembourg, and Al-Baraka International was established in the United Kingdom (Belouafi & Belabes, 2010).

Alrifai (2015) believed that the first Islamic financial institutions were established in Switzerland and Luxembourg not because of a driving demand but because financial groups in the Middle East were looking to diversify their assets in offshore jurisdictions. *Takaful* SA was the first Islamic financial institution established in Luxembourg in the 1980s, and the Dar al-Mal al-Islami (DMI) group established Faisal Private Bank, a private bank in Geneva, Switzerland.

Islamic finance is as an alternative value proposition and has proven a viable system in the global financial landscape due to financial inclusion, commercial drive, and internationalisation (Grewal, 2013). Grewal (2013) stated these following points as main drivers of Islamic finance in Europe:

- After the global financial crisis and the Euro-zone sovereign debt crisis, more people are now looking into Islamic finance as a safer alternative
- Growing demand of *Shari'ah*-compliant products
- The increasing awareness of Islamic finance as another, more ethical form of investment
- Abundance of liquidity from oil-producing nations that have affluent individuals with vested interests in Europe
- Rapid growth of the global *Sukuk* market

- The expected decline in cost brought about by economies of scale will push for a comprehensive *Sukuk* market in Europe
- Regulatory support, which includes tax and legislative changes to accommodate the growth in Islamic finance

Flaunet (2014) identified five distinctive market characteristics that are favourable to sustain a steady growth of Islamic finance products. They are a) encouraging demographics, b) a favourable economic momentum, c) *Shari'ah*-friendly legal environments, d) little competition, and e) strong demand. Europe has a large untapped customer base of more than 20 million Muslim residents. European countries are on the lookout for new sources of liquidity. Higher saving rates for Muslims living in Europe and growing economic ties between European and Muslim countries are signs of favourable economic momentum. This makes the Islamic financial model attractive, and governments and regulatory authorities in many countries are supporting its development. However, Islamic banking products are not widely available, even in the face of strong demand and a growing need for such services. Many financial institutions in Europe offer Socially Responsible Investments (SRIs).

Certain countries have a strong culture of ethical investments. For example, France and the United Kingdom are leading countries with the highest volume of Assets under Management (AuM), and France and Belgium have more than two hundred Socially Responsible Investments (SRIs) funds. Germany is fourth in both Socially Responsible Investments retail funds and in number of funds. As was discussed in Chapter 2 section 2.5.7, the Islamic banking and finance system is a financial system based on ethical principles. The strong ethical investment cultures in countries like France and Germany are favourable for *Shari'ah*-compliant products and services. Therefore, it could be possible that non-Muslims who are inclined toward ethical investments may think to use Islamic banking and finance in this regard.

Since 2000 there has been significant growth in the number of Islamic financial institutions in Western European countries. By the end of 2013, the United Kingdom had the highest number of Islamic financial institutions (22), followed by Switzerland (4), France (3), and Germany, Ireland and Luxembourg (1 each). It can be concluded that flexibility in regulations and openness toward Islamic banking and finance have better supported the development of Islamic financial institutions in the United Kingdom, when compared to that in Germany. Sections 4.6 and 4.7, which follow, will explain this topic in detail.

4.4 Islamic Banking and Finance and the United Kingdom

The First International Conference on Islamic Economics was held in 1976 in Jeddah, Saudi Arabia. The outcome of the conference helped in the establishment of the Islamic Foundation in Leicester, United Kingdom and paved the way for an early start of Islamic financial activities in the United Kingdom (Belouafi & Chachi,

2014). The Islamic Foundation introduced the Islamic Economic Unit to undertake research into Islamic banking and finance. Mohammad (2015:119) reckoned that the United Kingdom has the "largest Islamic banking sector outside the Middle East and Asia." The United Kingdom is now the leading Islamic financial hub in Europe.

Figure 4 highlights some of the key features of the United Kingdom's Islamic finance industry. For example, the regulatory frameworks and tax laws were specifically designed to cater to the needs of Islamic banking and finance in the United Kingdom. These initiatives paved the way for the issuance of the UK's first sovereign *Sukuk* in 2014. Another feature of the UK's Islamic finance industry is the presence of technical expertise in the areas of secondary market liquidity management and corporate financing and financial engineering (with more than 200 international law firms). A large number of financial institutions prefer to issue *Sukuk* on the London Stock Exchange (LSE). For example, more than $51 billon was raised through the issuance of *Sukuk* on LSE by the end of November 2015. As can be seen in Figure 4, all major accounting and consulting firms have dedicated departments for Islamic finance in the UK. Moreover, more than 70 universities and four professional institutions provide Islamic banking and finance education for local and international students. Finally, Islamic finance has been used to finance the development of the UK's infrastructure, and it is expected that Islamic finance will play a significant role in this regard in the future. Thus, from Figure 4, it can be concluded that the UK has the necessary expertise to develop the Islamic financial industry and present London as one of the leading global Islamic financial hubs.

Figure 4: Key Features of the United Kingdom's Islamic Finance Industry

1	The UK has created one of the most attractive regulatory and tax systems for Islamic finance anywhere in the world, and the success of the UK's sovereign *Sukuk* in 2014 was a significant milestone in the development of the UK and the global Islamic finance industry.
2	Over twenty banks, of which five are fully Sharia compliant, are located in the UK. This is substantially more than in any other Western country. Also, many foreign banks access Islamic finance through the London markets or London based teams for specific initiatives (treasury, trade finance, property finance, agency desks for corporate financing/lending).
3	The depth and breadth of London's capital markets provides companies and issuers of financial products with access to a wide pool of investors and secondary market liquidity.
4	The London Stock Exchange (LSE) is a key global venue for the issuance of *Sukuk*. To date over $51bn has been raised through 57 issues. Four ETFs and two ETPs are also quoted on the LSE. The LSE also launched its Islamic Finance Market Index in 2013.

5	In 2014, the UK Government announced that UK Export Finance (UKEF) was planning to provide *Shari'ah*-compliant support for British exporters. Shortly afterwards, UKEF underwrote its first Islamic bond, providing cover for a $916m *Sukuk* issued by Dubai's Emirates Airline.
6	London is home to over 200 international law firms. Approximately 25 of these firms have established dedicated Islamic finance units. The majority of Islamic contracts governed by English law.
7	The UK's largest accounting, consulting, and professional service firms all have Islamic finance departments providing trusted advisory services to UK and international clients.
8	Qualifications in Islamic finance offered by four professional institutes and nearly 70 universities and business schools.
9	Use of Islamic finance for major infrastructure projects in London and across the UK. Current trends suggest that the role of Islamic finance in funding infrastructure development will continue to grow in the years ahead.

Source: Adapted from TheCityUK (2015)

In 2013 the Islamic Bank of Britain (IBB) conducted a survey of 300 Muslims and non-Muslims in the United Kingdom about consumers' attitudes and understanding of Islamic finance (Choudhury, 2014:24). The results of the survey showed that 66% of the respondents believe that "*Shari'ah*-compliant finance is appropriate in a modern Western society such as the United Kingdom." Furthermore, 81% of Muslim and non-Muslim customers of The Islamic Bank of Britain were willing to use *Shari'ah*-compliant finance again in the future. At the time of the survey, 36% of the Muslim population in the United Kingdom used *Shari'ah*-compliant finance. However, it must be noted that 9% of the 36% used it "very often." The survey also showed that 45% of Muslims who were currently not using Islamic financial products were "considering doing so in the future."

4.5 Size of Islamic Finance Market in the UK

The United Kingdom has been one of the most important destinations of Islamic finance outside of the Muslim world since the introduction of Islamic products worldwide. A supportive regulatory and financial environment and key government policy initiatives made the United Kingdom the "leading Western center for Islamic finance" (TheCityUK, 2015:7). TheCityUK's (2015) report highlighted distinctive features of Islamic finance in the United Kingdom, such as the assets of Islamic service providers, which equalled $4.5 billion by the end of 2014.

The United Kingdom is home to twice the number of Islamic institutions as the United States or any other Western country. Most importantly, the recent ICD Thomson Reuters Islamic Finance Development report assigned the United Kingdom an index value of 16.2, which is 5.9 points above the global average of 10.3.

ICD Thomson Reuters Islamic Finance Development annual report categorizes different countries on the basis of growth in different sub-sectors of Islamic finance, knowledge about Islamic finance, governance level, corporate social resonsibility (CSR) and awareness. The United Kingdom as having a clear advantage in areas such as knowledge (22.1), governance (16.7), CSR (23.3), and awareness (13.8) amongst the Western countries. Meanwhile, Germany has only secured an index value of 0.3, and is well behind in other indicators (as compared to the United Kingdom).

Islamic finance now plays a pivotal role in the economic development of the United Kingdom and has been used for infrastructure development projects such as "The Shard, Battersea Power Station regeneration, London Gateway, the Olympic Village and redevelopment of Chelsea Barracks" (TheCityUK, 2015:5). Furthermore, Gatehouse Bank PLC, a fully *Shari'ah*-compliant bank, which started its operations in 2008, has already invested £700 million for the construction of more than 6,500 homes in the United Kingdom.

In order to gain a comprehensive overview of the size of the Islamic finance market in the United Kingdom, the following section outlines the different segments of Islamic financial services.

4.5.1 Islamic Banking

There are number of Islamic banks operating in the United Kingdom. In addition to five full-fledged Islamic banks, several conventional banks have established Islamic banking windows. Islamic Bank of Britain PLC has now been renamed Al-Rayan Bank PLC. Founded in 2004, this was the first *Shari'ah*-compliant bank opened in the United Kingdom. All prominent conventional banks, such as Barclays, BNP Paribas, Citi Group, Deutsche Bank, HSBC, Standard Chartered, and UBS, have established dedicated Islamic banking windows in order to cater to their Muslim clients. It can also be concluded that the Islamic banking windows and full-fledged Islamic banks are highly competitive because the local Muslim population is small (approximately 3 million).

Table 4 provides a brief overview of the full-fledge Islamic banks operating in the United Kingdom, their date of inception, and the range of business activities at each. Al Rayan Bank PLC was acquired by Qatar's Masraf Al Rayan in 2014 and is the only retail Islamic bank that has five branches across the United Kingdom. All other banks are wholesale investment banks that are engaged in capital market, real estate, wealth management, and treasury business. The The European Islamic Investment Bank (EIIB) was established in 2005 and offers investment banking services to its customers. In 2007, the Bank of London and the Middle East (BLME) were established with the primary goal of offering wealth management services, including private banking and asset management, to High Net Worth Individuals (HNWIs). Islamic banking continued to grow in the UK, and in 2008 two new banks were established (Qatar Islamic Bank UK (QIB UK) and Gatehouse Bank PLC). Both banks deal in wholesale investment banking activities but the Gatehouse Bank PLC also manages real estate portfolios of its clients in the US and in the UK. It is worth mentioning that in 2012 the Gatehouse Bank PLC issued the first *Sukuk Al-Ijarah* that was backed by real estate assets. In 2013, the Abu Dhabi Islamic Bank UK was established by the Abu Dhabi Islamic banking group in order to cater to the financial needs of its customers in the UK. In short, it can be concluded that the Islamic banking market in the UK has shown steady growth since the establishment of the first full-fledged Islamic bank in 2004, growth that no other European country's Islamic banking market has yet been able to match.

Table 4: Full-fledged Islamic Banks in the United Kingdom

Name of Institution	Inception Date	Nature of Work and Activities
Al Rayan Bank PLC (former Islamic Bank of Britain-IBB)	2004	Engages in retail banking and the only Islamic bank with a high street presence – having five branches and around 50,000 customers. The bank offers a wide range of *Shari'ah*-compliant financial products.
European Islamic Investment Bank (EIIB)	2005	Engaging in wholesale investment banking and offers its customers *Shari-'ia*-compliant Treasury and capital markets, asset management, private banking, trade finance, correspondent banking, and advisory and corporate financial services. EIIB is headquartered in London.
The Bank of London and The Middle East (BLME)	2007	Engages as an independent wholesale *Shari'ah*-compliant bank based in London. Its offering spans corporate banking, treasury, and wealth management comprised of private banking and asset management.
Qatar Islamic Bank UK (QIB UK) (European Finance Hose)	2008	Engages as a wholesale Islamic investment bank. It provides *Shari'ah*-compliant investment banking services including trade finance, private equity, and asset management to clients ranging from high net worth individuals to sovereign wealth funds and other institutional investors.
Gatehouse Bank PLC	2008	Engages as a wholesale investment bank operating in capital markets, real estate, asset financing, treasury, and *Shari'ah* advisory services. The bank manages $1.7bn in real estate assets in the US and UK. In December 2012 the bank issued the UK's first ever real estate backed sterling *Sukuk Al-ljarah.*
Abu Dhabi Islamic Bank UK (ADIB-UK)	2013	Engages as a wholesale bank that is already operating a large branch network in Egypt and is in the process of extending operations to several markets across the Middle East and beyond. ADIB UK limited was established to bring the bank's services to clients in the UK.

Source: Adapted from Belouafi and Chachi (2014)

4.5.2 *Sukuk*

By the end of 2014 more than 57 *Sukuk* bonds had been issued in the London Stock Exchange (LSE) with a value of $51 billion (TheCityUK, 2015). This makes the London Stock Exchange one of the leading global stock exchanges for the issuance of *Sukuk* bonds. GE Capital issued the first *Sukuk* in 2009 and became the first United States corporation to list *Sukuk* on the London Stock Exchange. In 2010, International Innovative Technologies (IIT), a corporation in the United Kingdom, issued the first corporate *Sukuk* in the history of the United Kingdom. In 2007, 12 *Sukuk* had been issued with a total worth of £11 billion. Between 2008 and 2011, the size and volume of *Sukuk* trades have declined in the global economic slowdown. Apart from the corporate *Sukuk* issued, the British govenerment issued a five year sovereign *Sukuk* bond worth £200 million in 2014. This *Sukuk* issuance was oversubscribed when the British government received orders totalling £2.3 billion.

The volume of *Sukuk* listed on the London Stock Exchange declined from 2012 to 2013. Two main factors contributed to this trend. First, many international investors from the South East Asia region preferred to issue *Sukuk* in Malaysia, rather than in the UK. Second, some investors also decided to issue *Sukuk* in the Irish Stock Exchange and, therefore, offered fewer *Sukuk* on the London Stock Exchange, thus the volume declined.

4.5.3 Islamic Funds

The United Kingdom is known for its traditional role of fund management through recent decades, but in the past few years the United Kingdom's fund management industry has advanced even further. On behalf of its overseas clients, the United Kingdom fund management industry manages funds worth more than £2.2 trillion, which is significant given the fact that 40% of the asset management firms in London belong to overseas investors. The United Kingdom holds almost $600 million in net Islamic fund assets and seven unique *Shari'ah*-compliant Exchange Traded Funds (ETFs). In addition to this, two *Shari'ah*-compliant Exchange Traded Products (ETPs) are listed on the London Stock Exchange (TheCityUK, 2015:13).

After discussing the growth of different segments of Islamic financial industry it is important to identify and describe the key drivers of the financial segments in the United Kingdom. The following section provides insights into the factors behind the development of Islamic finance in the United Kingdom.

4.6 Driving Factors behind the Development and Growth of Islamic Finance in the UK

The unprecedented growth and development of Islamic finance in the United Kingdom can be exemplary for other non-Muslim countries. A mix of political, economic, regulatory, and demand factors have enabled London (in particular) and the United Kingdom (in general) to be viewed as the Islamic financial hub and role model in Western Europe. Table 5 presents a brief overview of some of these factors.

Table 5: Factors Behind the Development of Islamic Finance in the UK

Political Factors: i. The strategic vision of the UK government is supported by all key stakeholders ii. The official policies of attracting inward foreign investments and eliminating domestic financial exclusions by the UK government iii. "Our commitment to help London lead the way in Islamic finance across the world" (David Cameron, WIEF 2013) iv. The development of Islamic finance has enjoyed cross-party support over the past decade. There have been two key policy objectives: first, to establish and maintain London as Europe's gateway to international Islamic finance; and second, to ensure that no party in the UK is denied access to competitively priced financial products on account of their faith	***Economic Factors:*** i. The excess liquidity in the Gulf and London's attractiveness as a financial market ii. Most of the Muslim countries follow the "Common Law" and the relevant professional expertise is available in the UK iii. Strong growth of OIC (Organization of Islamic Countries) countries (fueled by Oil prices) iv. The industry is becoming more standardized and convergent (e.g., common accounting and auditing standards AAOIFI) v. Potential for large capital inflows into City of London due to the size of the global market, which will strengthen the UK as a financial center vi. Economic liberalism during the 1980s paved the way for private ownership, liberal norms, and deregulation of the financial system
Regulatory Environment Factors: i. The Financial Services Authority (FSA) policy of providing a "Level Playing Field" (no favors, no discrimination) to all financial institutions ii. Timely and pragmatic tax reforms to accommodate the nature of Shari'ah-compliant products iii. The existing regulatory and legal frameworks did not hinder the establishment of Islamic financial institutions or windows iv. The whole Islamic financial sector operates under a single piece of legislation (Financial Services & Market Act 2000) v. Initiatives to ensure consistent regulatory treatment of Islamic finance with its statutory objectives and principles	***Demand/Muslim Population Factors:*** i. Commitment from retail customers ii. More Islamic financial services products being developed *iii.* Resurgence of Muslim cultural values *iv.* Enabling more access to financial services for UK's 2–3 million Muslims *v.* Proactive role by Muslim community organizations such as Islamic Foundation, Muslim Council of Britain and Islamic Finance Council (IFC)

Source: Adapted from Raza (2010); Choudhury (2014); Flaunet (2014); Belouafi and Chachi (2014) and UKifs (2013)

According to Chase (2012), Western Europe has 31 Islamic financial institutions. However, the distribution of these institutions is not even. For instance, out of the 18 states in Western Europe, only a few countries have Islamic institutions: the United Kingdom, France, Switzerland, Germany, Ireland, and Luxembourg. As mentioned earlier, out of all of these countries the United Kingdom is home to 22 of the 31 institutions. This raises the question, "Does openness to regulatory reforms and institutional flexibility have a positive impact on the development of Islamic finance in the United Kingdom?" To answer this question we can refer to Table 5 in section 4.6, which provides a holistic picture and explains what led to the emergence of the United Kingdom as an Islamic financial hub.

As far as political factors are concerned, four main sources play an important role. First, the United Kingdom's government developed a long-term vision to foster Islamic finance within the country, and stakeholders supported that vision. Second, the United Kingdom's government pursued the goal of financial inclusion for both internal and external investors, thus attracting foreign direct investment (FDI). Third, a speech given by Prime Minister David Cameron at the World Islamic Economic Forum (WIFE) in 2013 further strengthened the confidence of investors. Fourth, and finally, the government decided to build up the role of London as a European gateway for Islamic finance.

Chase (2012) argued that three separate factors have helped in the recognition of London as an Islamic financial hub and spurred growth of Islamic finance: legal reforms, implementation, enforcement, and a general openness to alternative finance. Moreover, The Global Financial Centers in the Index 18 report published by The Z/Yen Group (2015) reasserted the aforementioned arguments by stating that London has become the world's leading financial center, with New York ranked second and Frankfurt ranked 14th.

As far as economic factors are concerned (please see Table 5), London has provided an excellent investment platform for the excess liquidity of the Gulf States that primarily resulted from higher oil prices. Another important factor, which the United Kingdom shares with other countries, is the existence of common law. Liberal economic policies adopted by the government during the 1980s and the availability of professional expertise such as consultancy firms were driving factors for the growth and development of Islamic finance in the United Kingdom.

The third dimension in the robust development of Islamic finance in the United Kingdom is the regulatory environment, as depicted in Table 5, The Financial Services Authority (FSA) policy for creating a 'level playing field' under the supervision of a single financial sector regulator following the Financial Services and Market Act (FSMA) of 2000.

The fourth dimension of growth in Islamic finance in the United Kingdom is demand, as related to Muslim population factors, also pictured in Table 5. Since the evolution of Islamic finance in the United Kingdom, Muslim organizations such as Islamic Foundation, Islamic Finance Council (IFC), and the Muslim Council of Britain have created awareness among the United Kingdom's Muslim population. These efforts have played an important role in the resurgence of Muslim cultural values. Parallel to these developments, the Islamic financial institutions have developed innovative financial products to cater the demand.

A number of factors influence the decision of a non-Muslim country to become a global leader in Islamic finance. The following four are the most important factors as argued by Dar (2015).

First, financial and regulatory authorities perceived a demand from the local Muslim population for Islamic financial products in the United Kingdom. The government recognized that there was need to offer Islamic financial products and services to the Muslim minority. The government, which is predominately non-Muslim, believed in financial inclusion and therefore allowed (and encouraged) Islamic banking offering *Shari'ah*-compliant products and services.

Second, individuals like Andrew Buxton (a former Chairman of Barclays Bank), Iqbal Khan (Chief Executive Officer, *HSBC Amanah* Finance UK), Richard Thomas (CEO of Gatehouse Bank) and other members of the 2000 working committee formed by the government worked to identify the key barriers to the development of Islamic finance. These individuals convinced authorities to allow Islamic banking into the United Kingdom (Dar, 2015).

Third, academics like Simon Archer (University of Surrey), Professor Rodney Wilson (Durham University), and Professor John Presley (Loughborough University) played an important role in making sure that Islamic banking and finance was recognized as a viable option for a number of universities in the United Kingdom. The aforementioned academics played an instrumental role in creating awareness for Islamic banking and finance in British academia and indirectly influenced the policy makers (Dar, 2015).

Fourth, and finally, the government adopted the idea of using Islamic finance to bridge the gap between the West and the Muslim population.

These four factors led the United Kingdom to decide to enter into, and eventually become an important player in Islamic banking and finance. Since 2000, there exists in the United Kingdom a complete platform for Islamic banking and financial services on the retail and wholesale side of investment banking, fund management, insurance, and Islamic finance indices. In 2004, the United Kingdom witnessed the establishment of the first fully-fledged retail bank, The Islamic Bank of Britain. In 2005, the first wholesale *Shari'ah*-compliant bank, The European Islamic Investment Bank, was launched (Dar, 2015). Given the positive developments in Islamic banking and finance in the country, the United Kingdom provides an example of successful engagement with Islamic finance for the benefit of the nation and its people.

4.7 Comparative Analysis of the UK and German Regulatory and Supervisory Model

Conducting a comparative analysis between the regulatory and supervisory models of the United Kingdom and Germany requires insight into the regulatory events (phases) that shaped the development of Islamic finance in the United Kingdom.

4.7.1 Regulatory Phases in the UK

Islamic banking products first launched in the United Kingdom in the 1980s, Figure 5 shows the various phases of development and growth for Islamic finance in the United Kingdom. Phase 1 represents activities that occurred prior to 1995, and the most notable of which was the permission to establish the Al-Baraka Bank was granted by the Bank of England (BOE) in 1983 (Belouafi & Chachi, 2014). Al-Baraka Bank established two more branches in London in 1988 and 1989. Later, in 1991, a fourth branch opened in Birmingham. Al-Baraka Bank was the only bank that provided Islamic banking services in accordance with the 1987 Banking Act in the United Kingdom. In the first phase, the growth of Islamic banking products was slow and the Al-Baraka Bank failed to expand and increase its presence. It was during this time that Al-Baraka Bank established itself as an investmnet company rather than a banking insitution.

Figure 5: Summary of the Regulatory Phases in the United Kingdom

Phase 1: Before 1995 (No Action)
✓ International commodity Murabaha operations ✓ Al-Baraka International (1983–1993) ✓ No discussion at the regulatory level about the issue ✓ Same regulation; neither special provision nor minimal changes for Islamic products have been introduced ✓ Islamic modes bear higher costs (e.g., Charge of double SDLT on property transfer)
Phase 2: Before 1995–2003 (Action)
• Sir Edward George speech at the Islamic Foundation in Sept 1995 • The FSA establishment in 1997 • Government consults Muslim community about the introduction and development of Islamic finance in 1999 • Bank of England (BOE) recognition of the potential of Islamic finance growth in the UK in 1999 • High-level working group formation in 2000 to identify barriers facing Islamic finance development • Sir Howard Davies, FSA Chairman speeches 2002 (Markfield-UK) and 2003 (Bahrain) • First changes in the Finance Act 2003 • Attendance of various activities about Isalmic finance by UK officials

Phase 3: After 2003 (Pro-Action)
❖ Further changes in Finance Acts of subsequent years ❖ Gordon Brown delivers budget speech in 2006 and promotes London as leading international finance center ❖ Mr. Brown pledges, at the Islamic Finance and Trade Conference in June 2006, to support the growth of Islamic finance ❖ Islamic Finance summit was held at 11 Downing street in April 2007 and the Islamic Finance Experts Group (IFEG) established ❖ FSA document,*Islamic Regulation and Challenges*, released in the UK in November 2007 ❖ Government documents, *Perspective of the Development of Islamic Finance in the UK*, are released in Decmber 2008

Source: Adapted from Belouafi and Chachi (2014)

Phase 2 occurred between 1995 and 2003, as can be seen in Figure 5, and established the framework we see in the Islamic finance industry in the United Kingdom today. During this period the British government and financial institutions took several important steps. Most importantly, the Financial Services Authority (FSA) was established as a single regulator with oversight for the financial market. In 2000, the Bank of England formed a special committee tasked with documenting critical barriers for the development of Islamic finance in the United Kingdom and proposing solutions for overcoming the barriers. The developments of Phase 2 lead to the passage of the Finance Act of 2003.

Phase 3 continued the momentum experienced in Phase 2 and introduced positive regulatory changes since the passage of the Finance Act of 2003 (please see Figure 5). In 2006, Gordon Brown, former Prime Minister of the United Kingdom, sent positive signals when he pledged to promote London as a leading international Islamic finance center in his budget speech. In April of 2007, the Islamic Finance Experts Group (IFEG) was established at the Islamic Finance summit, which was held at Downing Street. In November 2007 the Financial Services Authority issued a report *Islamic Finance in the UK: Regulation and Challenges*, which outlined several different regulatory initiatives and challenges faced by the Islamic finance industry in the United Kingdom.

4.7.2 Islamic Finance Taxation Changes in the UK

Taxation is one of the important elements of the United Kingdom's regulatory framework, but taxation of Islamic finance is considered an obstacle in Western countries. This is because transactions based on Islamic financial instruments are subject to taxes (Choudhury, 2014). Keeping this hurdle in mind, the government of the United Kingdom has taken various steps to create a level playing field for Islamic finance.

As Figure 6 shows, major changes have been implemented through financial regulation since 2003. The most important of these may be the Finance Act of 2003, which provided relief from the Double Stamp Duty Land Tax (SDLT) on two main Islamic finance instruments: home finance tools *Murabahah* and *Ijarah*. The Finance Act of 2006 extended this relief to property finance. The Finance Act of 2007 applied a tax structure for the *Sukuk* bond that more similarly aligned with that of conventional bonds.

In 2008 and 2009, as shown in Figure 6, further amendments were introduced in the Finance Acts. The main area of focus was the exception of stamp duty and stamp duty reserve tax for *Sukuk*. These changes led the growth of *Sukuk* issuance in the UK during the subsequent years. Moreover, in 2009 insurance companies were redefined as financial institution. In 2010, through the Statutory Instrument number 814, it was ensured that the *Sukuk* Alternative Finance Investment Bonds (AFIBs) benefited from the Stamp Duty Land Tax (SDLT) exceptions. In 2011, the Finance Act of 2011 was synchronised with the Income Tax Act of 2007 for better treatment of SDLT for financial institutions. Finally, through the Finance Act of 2013, further tax relief was provided to financial institutions. Thus, from Figure 6, it can be deduced that since 2003 the UK authorities have introduced consecutive tax relief initiatives to provide Islamic financial institutions a level playing field.

Figure 6: Timeline for Islamic Finance Taxation Changes in the United Kingdom

Timeline	Major Changes
2003	• Finance Act 2003: Relief from Double Stamp Duty Land Tax (SDLT) on Home Finance *Murabahah* and *Ijara* Products
2005	• Finance Act 2005:Alternative Finance Arrangements: ✓ Profit Share Return (*Mudarabah*) ✓ Alternative Finance Return (*Murabahah*) • Extending (SDLT) exemption to include *Musharakah* home finance products
2006	• VAT treatment of Islamic Financial Products (*Murabahah, Mudarabah, Musharakah, Wakalah* and *Ijara*) • Finance Act 2006: Extend (SDLT) relief on property finance to all entities, including companies, clubs and LLPs. • Taxation of *Wakalah* based deposits
2007	• Finance Act 2007 introduced legislation provisions allowing *Sukuk* to be taxed similar to conventional bonds. • Introduced further amendments to the SDLT relief
2008	• The Finance Act 2008 added amendments for Stamp Duty and Stamp Duty Reserve Tax for *Sukuk* • Gave power to Treasury to raise funds using *Sukuk* • Introduced anti-avoidance measures on alternative property finance transaction

Timeline	Major Changes
2009	• The Finance Act 2009 introduced provisions to exempt land that is used for *Sukuk* purposes from (SDLT). • The Statutory Instrument No 2568, 2009 extended the definition of financial institution under the alternative finance arrangement to include Insurance Company
2010	• The Statutory Instrument No 814, 2010 amended the rules on anti-avoidance to ensure that the SDLT relief available for *Sukuk* Alternative Finance Investment Bonds (AFIBs).
2011	• Sch.21 Finance Act 2011 replaced the definition of a Financial Institution for SDLT purposes with the definition used in the Income Tax Act 2007
2013	• Finance Act 2013 section 157 and schedule 40 set out relaxation of alternative finance structures, from the strict position of imposing the Annual Tax on Enveloped Dwellings and the 15% SDLT rate

Source: Adapted from Choudhury (2014)

Mentioned above are changes in tax laws that made Islamic finance an attractive value proposition and a *friendly investent choice* in the United Kingdom (Choudhury, 2014:36). Governmental and financial institutions tried to follow the principle of *no obstacles and no special favors* in all forms of finance, including Islamic finance.

King (2015) conducted an interview with Choudhury, the CEO of Al Rayan Bank PLC, who described the regulatory environment in the United Kingdom as follows:

> "The UK to my mind is possibly one of the best jurisdictions in the world – including the Islamic world – in terms of *Shari'ah*-compliant finance. The environment is good because the regulator and the government are very supportive of positioning the UK as a place to do business."

Choudhury then further added his opinion about the regulatory approach by stating:

> "I think what really stands out in terms of the UK approach is the commitment to providing a regulatory level playing field for sharia-compliant finance to benefit its citizens, including *Shari'ah*-compliant student finance and removal of double stamp duty on Islamically financed real estate transactions, for instance. This helps to build community cohesion and financial inclusiveness. A number of other European jurisdictions support Islamic finance at the wholesale level but they aren't doing it for their people."

4.7.3 Regulatory and Supervisory Developments in the UK

This section provides an overview of the regulatory and supervisory models governing financial institutions in the United Kingdom and Germany (please see Figure 7). Eleven individual regulatory bodies merged in 1997 to form the Financial Services Authority. Abolishment of the Double Stamp Tax Duty in 2003 was a significant change in finance regulation in the United Kingdom. The Islamic Bank of Britain PLC was opened in 2004 in the United Kingdom, but since then Islamic banking and finance has expanded in the country and currently six full-fledge Islamic banks, including one retail bank, are operating. In 2014 the government undertook an unprecedented initiative and issued the first £200 million sovereign *Sukuk*, becoming the first non-Muslim government to issue such a *Sukuk*.

The Financial Services Authority imposed five requirements for legal registration of a foreign bank in the United Kingdom and made compliance compulsory for all firms seeking authorization to operate in the country (please see Figure 7). The first requirement stated that firms must have the right legal status for the activities it wishes to undertake, as European directives impose certain restrictions on the official use of the term *bank* in labelling a financial institution. The second requirement mandated that all firms incorporated in the United Kingdom must have a headquarters with active management functions located in the United Kingdom. The third requirement established an expectation that all banks operating in the United Kingdom would be subject to the authority and supervision of the Financial Services Authority without interference. The fourth requirement stated that all firms must maintain sufficient financial and non-financial resources for proposed activities. The fifth and final requirement is described as the *fit and proper* requirement insists on transparency for all conduct and operations of a firm.

Figure 7: United Kingdom and German Regulatory and Supervisory Models

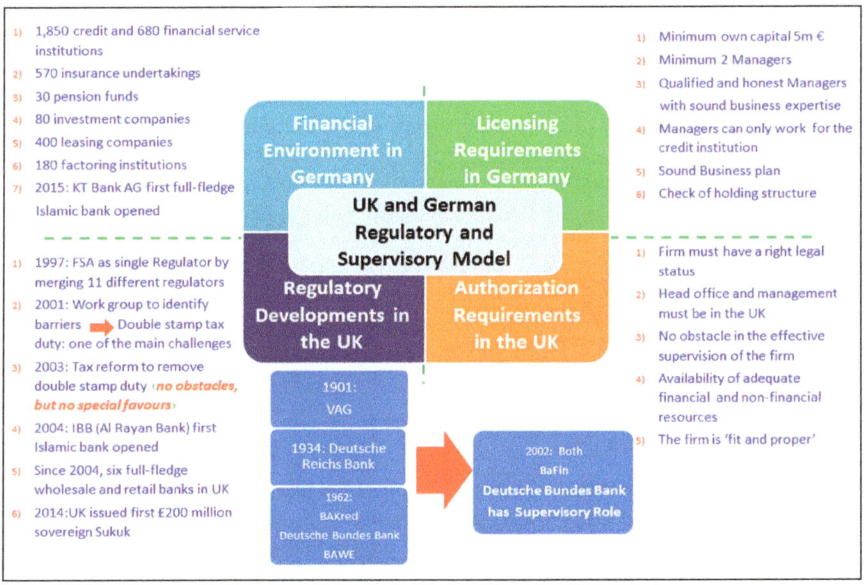

Source: Based on Expert Interviews (2014) and FSA (2007)

4.7.4 Regulatory and Supervisory Developments in Germany

The financial environment in Germany is composed of a large number of credit (1,850) and financial (680) service institutions (please see Figure 7 above). BaFin, a German Financial Services Authority formulated six basic requirements for the issuance of a banking license: a minimum capital of €5 million, at least two qualified managers, honest managers with sound business background, managers who work only for the bank, a sound business plan, and transparency into the structure of the bank.

As far as Islamic finance is concerned, Germany was the first Western country to benefit from an Islamic capital market. The German state of Saxony-Anhalt issued a five year €100 million asset-backed *Sukuk* in 2004. However, the largest development in the German market was the opening of KT Bank AG in July 2015. KT Bank AG was the first full-fledged Islamic bank in the country. According to Flaunet (2014:9), the prospects for Islamic finance in Germany are promising because Germany is the largest economy in Europe, and because Germany has strong economic ties with a number of Islamic countries, such as Turkey. Germany also has "strong demand for alternative sources of funding."

The German banking regulatory and supervisory model has evolved slowly and gradually. In 1901, the Insurance Supervision Act (*Versicherungsaufsichtsgesetz*–VAG) passed, but the Great Depression of the 1930s caused tremendous economic and financial disruption for highly industrialized nations and the German government decided to establish a dedicated banking supervision department. This responsibility was given to the Deutsche Reichsbank (J Engels 2014, Personal Communication, 15, December). After the Second World War, as a part of economic reconstruction activities, a decision was made to restructure the nation-wide banking regulatory system. In 1962, the Federal Banking Supervisory Office (Bundesaufsichtsamt für das Kreditwesen – *BAKred*) was created and charged with the responsibility of partnering with Deutsche Bundesbank to provide supervision of the banking industry. In 1995, the Securities Trading Supervisory Office (Bundesaufsichtsamt für den Wertpapierhandel – BAWe) was established with the objective of supervising the trading and investment sector. The two (*BAKred,* BAWe) regulatory and supervisory bodies operated under the Ministry of Finance (MoF). In 2002, BaFin was created and emerged as an independent judicial organization that cooperates with the Deutsche Bundesbank on all supervisory matters related to the financial industry (please see Figure 7 above). A major development in regulation occurred with the issuance of a full-fledged banking license by the BaFin to the KT Bank AG in 2015 (KT Bank AG, 2015).

During an interview on 15 December 2014, German senior financial advisor J Engels stated his understanding of the rationale of the fragmented supervision of German financial system as:

> "Each country has an individual development, individual traditions and individual mentalities. In Germany, the financial services market is, with around 1.900 banks to supervise and (since 1998) also with 650 financial services institutions very fragmented. So, it was according the individual German experience a very helpful to share this task between old BAKred/ today's BaFin and Deutsche Bundesbank."

4.8 Islamic Banking Problems and Challenges in the UK Market

The Islamic banking industry in the United Kingdom still faces many challenges despite all the past and recent progress. Choudhury (2014) identified the three most eminent challenges as: consumer education and awareness, liquidity management, and the development of frameworks and standards. The shortage of liquidity management instruments is one of the more important challenges as the inability to adequately manage liquidity negatively influences the earnings of the Islamic banks.

According to Raza (2010), a complete understanding of *Shari'ah* principles by financial regulators, consumers, and professionals is quite important, particularly for the growth of new Islamic markets. Many consumers and professionals still face a dilemma concerning whether or not the Islamic window or the fully-fledged Islamic institution are appropriate models for Islamic banking. Both models have many advantages and disadvantages. Many customers might still perceive the Islamic banking window as less trustworthy even though it may be the most efficient route for entering into a new market with minimum funding and fewer capacity challenges. On the other hand, establishing a full-fledged Islamic bank brings challenges in the form of capacity issues, substantial setup costs, high overhead costs, a higher degree of regulatory supervision and monitoring.

In an interview with King (2015) Choudhury, CEO of Al Rayan Bank PLC, described the most important challenge faced by the first *Shari'ah*-compliant bank in the United Kingdom as:

> "Awareness of Islamic finance, even among the UK's Muslim community, was low. This meant that we had to work hard to build relationships and educate people to build up our profile."

Another significant challenge for Islamic banks operating in non-Muslim environments is the use of Islamic terminology in bank names. For instance, Islamic Bank of Britain PLC rebranded itself Al Rayan Bank PLC to appeal to a wider customer base. This change was accompanied by a savings account promotion. Following the rebranding and promotion efforts the bank experienced a 55% increase in savings account applications from non-Muslims (Vizcaino, 2014a). The bank also witnessed significant success while marketing Islamic products in Scotland when it avoided using Arabic naming conventions and terminology.

4.9 Concluding Remarks

The United Kingdom provides an environment where Islamic banking thrives even though there is a small population so only about 3 million Muslims. Any country that would like to play a future role in the advancement of Islamic banking to reap the benefits of reaching a wider market could emulate the United Kingdom's model for Islamic banking and finance (Dar, 2015).

Political and regulatory factors have played an instrumental role in the unprecedented growth of Islamic banking in the United Kingdom and the development of the largest Islamic banking sector outside the Middle East and Asia. The robust development of Islamic finance in the United Kingdom is a result of the openness of the financial sector to new ideas and regulations. The most important lesson that could be applied in other countries that aspire to become Islamic financial hubs is to see Islamic finance as an opportunity rather than a threat. The identification of key regulatory hurdles and step-by-step solutions as pursued by the United Kingdom's regulatory bodies presents an effective mechanism for other countries. However, the United Kingdom's Islamic financial model should not be adopted without consideration for local business and economic environments, as every country has a unique culture, financial environment, and growth potential.

The most important prerequisite to developing Islamic finance in other countries, particularly in Western countries, is the creation of awareness through the education of customers, regulators, and other relevant segments of society about key products and benefits available in Islamic finance. Another lesson that could be learned from the United Kingdom's experience with Islamic banking is the importance of human capital in facilitating growth. The United Kingdom leveraged expertise through human capital provided by leading financial consultancy groups and trained staff from top ranked British universities such as University of Durham, Markfield Institute of Higher Education, University of Bolton, and Aston University.

Another significant influence on the growth of Islamic finance in the United Kingdom was the inclusion of wholesale and investment banking. Germany has not embraced wholesale and investment banking to the degree to which the United Kingdom has. Slower development of Islamic financial services in Germany can be tied to a lack of a proactive approach to political and regulatory approach, unlike that taken in the United Kingdom.

The following chapter provides an overview of the German financial system and the initiatives taken by financial institutions in regard to Islamic banking and finance in Germany.

Chapter 5: Overview of the German Financial System and Islamic Banking in Germany

5.1 Introduction

There has been relatively little research exploring the nuances of the German financial system in the context of Islamic banking. The aim of this chapter is to provide a brief overview of the key aspects of the German financial system and to describe developments concerning Islamic banking. Chapter 5 provides a history of Muslims in Germany, including statistics about the current population and the role of the government in bridging gaps between Muslims and the state, and provides a timeline of the evolution of some Islamic banking and finance products in Germany. Chapter 5 also describes the role of the German banking supervisory authority (BaFin), the prevailing financial environment, the banking supervision mechanisms, the licensing procedure for Islamic financial institutions, the existing market players in the Islamic banking industry, and various initiatives taken to introduce *Shari'ah*-compliant financial products and services. Finally, Chapter 5 provides a discussion of the causes for low market demand of Islamic banking products in Germany and a chapter summary.

5.2 Muslim Population in Germany

The Ottoman Empire established its first interaction with the West to learning new military skills. Subsequently many Muslim countries were subjugated by Western powers during the 18th and 19th centuries (MacEoin, 2009). This close interaction between Western and Islamic powers brought new insights for Muslims in the areas of commerce, culture, democracy, and education.

In Europe, after the Second World War, many countries faced of shortage of labor. To overcome this problem many Muslims were welcomed by Europe, Germany in particular, as guest workers during the 1960s (Schirrmacher, 2007). The majority of the workers in Germany had Turkish origins and many workers in the United Kingdom came from Southeast Asian countries such as India and Pakistan.

According to a 2015 report published by the Pew Research Center, a public opinion polling organization, Germany had 4.76 million Muslims, which constituted about 5.8% of the 82 million people living in Germany. Germany is home to the largest population of Muslims living in Europe. According to Kern (2016), by the end of 2015 Germany's Muslim population reached six million. France also has a significantly large Muslim population of 4.71 million, which constitute about 7.5% of the country's total population. The United Kingdom and Italy are home to more than two million Muslims.

5.3 Government Initiatives

Many Muslims came to Germany during the 1960s as guest workers and gradually chose Germany as their country of permanent residence (Schirrmacher, 2007). The government unintentionally ignored this development until terrorists attacked the United States on 11 September 2001. In 2006 a major initiative was taken by the Federal Ministry of Interior to establish and organize the German Conference of Islam (Deutsche Islam Konferenz DIK) in Berlin (Farhoush & Schmidt, 2011). The primary purpose of this initiative was to establish close contact at the highest government level with the Muslim population and to understand Muslim social behavior, views, and concerns pertaining to German law and the government.

A representative nationwide study emerged from this conference. The initiative, which launched in 2007, had the objective of gaining insight into Muslims lifestyle, beliefs, attitudes and values. More than 6,000 participants with more than 49 countries of origin were selected to participate in the study (Farhoush & Schmidt, 2011). The results showed that the Muslim population is heterogeneous and their opinions about the religious matters vary from country to country.

5.4 Evolution of Islamic Finance in Germany

There have been many attempts to bring Islamic banking and finance products to Muslims living in Germany. The first such initiative was spearheaded by the Commerzbank group in 1999 when it launched the Al-Sukoor European Equity. Figure 8 shows the major developments related to Germany's Islamic banking and finance industry since 1999. Another development was the issuance of a €141 million asset-backed *Sukuk* bond by the German federal state, Saxony-Anhalt in 2004. Two major German banks, Commerzbank and Deutsche Bank, also launched *Shari'ah*-compliant products, but the initiatives were not successful and were discontinued in 2005 because they garnered inadequate demand.

Figure 8: Major Developments Related to Islamic Banking and Finance in Germany

Timeline	Major Developments
1999	• Launch of Al-Sukoor European Equity Fund by Commerzbank Group for middle Eastern institutional investors
2000	• Al-Sukoor European Equity Fund was made accessible to German private investors in 2000
2004	• Issuance of €141 million asset-backed *Sukuk* bond by the German federal state of Saxony-Anhalt • Opening of Kuveyt Turk participation bank representative office in Mannheim

Timeline	Major Developments
2005	• Deutsche Bank AG issued Shari'ah compliant Islamic Equity Builder Certificates at Frankfurt Börse • According to EU Prospectus Directive (date: 1st July 2005) a European prospect for listed companies is possible. When accepted in one EU country this licensed prospect can be used in all other EU countries. • Al-Sukoor European Equity was closed down in 2005 due to a lack of demand when it could only manage to raise € 4 million of assets
2007	• Deutsche Bank Group issued the first *Shar'iah* compliant hedge fund. However, it drew a lot of criticism from religious scholars because it was linked to a non-*Shar'iah*-compliant instrument.
2008	• First IIR Islamic Finance & Real Estate Forum held in Frankfurt/M on 4–5 November 2008
2009	• First Islamic Finance conference organized by BaFin in Frankfurt in October 2009 • Discussion on Islamic banking and finance in Baden-Württemberg parliament
2010	• Kuveyt Turk participation bank obtained limited banking license • Decision to open four Islamic Theology centers by the Federal Ministry of Education and Research at four universities located in Münster/Osnabrück, Tübingen, Frankfurt/Giessen and Nuremberg-Erlangen
2011–2012	• Application of a full-fledged banking license by Kuveyt Turk participation bank to BaFin • Second Islamic Finance conference organized by BaFin in Frankfurt • Issuance of QES *Shari'ah* compliant Islamic finance certificate by Landes Bank Berlin AG • Asset Management CIMB Principal Islamic Asset Management issues Shari'ah compliant investment fund in Germany
2013	• Shut down of QES Islamic finance certificate by Landes Bank Berlin AG due to lack of demand
2015	• Issuance of a full-fledge banking license to KT Bank AG by the BaFin in March 2015 • Start of operations of KT Bank AG in Frankfurt in July 2015

Source: Ahmad *et al.*, 2014; BMBF, 2015; BaFin, 2015; Siadat, 2013; Colditz, 2009; J Engels (2014, personal communication. 15 December); N Siegfried (2015, personal communication. 28 May); Gassner, 2003a, Deutsche Bank AG (2007); Farhoush and Schmidt (2011) and KT Bank AG (2015)

In 2007, the Deutsche Bank AG released the first *Shari'ah*-compliant hedge fund (see Figure 8 above), but many Islamic scholars criticized the structure because it was the structure linked to non-*Shari'ah*-compliant instruments. Academic institutions and industry players also contributed to the evolution of Islamic banking and finance in Germany. The first IIR Islamic Finance and Real Estate Forum was held in Frankfurt in 2008 followed by two conferences organized in Frankfurt by BaFin in 2009 and 2012 to engage the banking industry in a discussion of new opportunities arising from Islamic finance in Germany. The Kuveyt Türk Katılım Bankası A.Ş submitted its application for a full-fledge bank license and was approved in March 2015. The purpose behind these major developments was to explain how small and isolated initiatives paved the way in creating awareness among industry players.

5.5 The Role of BaFin Regarding Islamic Finance in Germany

Bundesaufsichtsamt für Finanzdienstleistungen (BaFin) which is also known as German Banking Supervisory Authority organized the first Islamic finance conference on 29 October 2009 in Frankfurt am Main. The conference was considered a signal from the highest German authority to facilitate Islamic finance activities in the country (IslamicFinance.de, 2012). The main point on the agenda for the event was to review the progress of Islamic banking and finance in different regions (including Europe), and to discuss regulatory and legal challenges faced by Islamic banks operation or seeking approval to operate in Germany. Keeping in mind the positive response from the market players, Bafin decided to organize another conference on 10 May 2012 to discuss *Shari'ah*-compliant capital market products such as *Shari'ah*-compliant funds, Islamic investments, private equity funds, and *Sukuk*. The conference also focused on the various challenges associated with product structure and development.

5.6 Overview of the German Financial Environment and Banking Supervision Mechanism

BaFin is the main actor in the field of supervision of financial services in Germany. Based on the section seven of the German Banking Act, BaFin co-operates deeply with the Deutsche Bundesbank on the day-to-day supervision of banks. During a personal communication on December 2014 Mr J Engels stated that BaFin has more than 2,400 employees in Frankfurt and Bonn offices and it is responsible for the supervision of a large number of institutions:

- 1,850 credit institutions
- 680 financial service institutions
- 570 insurance undertakings
- 30 pension funds

- 80 investment companies
- 400 leasing companies
- 180 factoring institutions

5.6.1 Foreign Banks from Muslim Countries Operating in Germany

According to Burghardt and Fuß (2004), there are more than 13 banks that are owned by Muslim countries and operating in Germany. ABC International Bank, located in Frankfurt, was the only bank that engaged Islamic banking products on the behalf of his client. ABC International Bank carried out a project finance deal for a client based in Jordan even though the bank did not possess an Islamic banking licence in Germany and the transaction of project finance was completed with the help of ABC Bahrain (Burghardt & Fuß, 2004). Banks other than ABC International Bank are primarily engaged in the business of import and export finance. For instance, the branch of the National Bank of Pakistan (NBP) located in Frankfurt am Main primarily processes remittances, provides trade related services to German and Pakistani companies, and provides support in bilateral transactions. The KT Bank AG is the only bank that possesses a full-fledge banking license to operate in Germany, and it can offer a wide variety of Islamic products and services.

Apart from Turkey, no other European country has an immigrant's population that would provide the optimal target group to which Islamic banking could be targeted. For this reason, many European banks have shown little to no interest in pursuing Islamic banking opportunities.

5.6.2 German Banking System

The term *bank* is used in Germany to describe only those financial institutions that engage in a wide range of activities including, but not limited to, commercial and investment banking, insurance and brokerage services, and payment services. (Biswas & Löchel, 2001). The German banking system is a three-pillar banking system that includes private banks, cooperative banks, and public banks.

The German banking system can be broadly categorized into universal and special banks according to the nature of business conducted. Universal banks are those institutions that cover a broad range of banking activities including issuing credit, granting loans, accepting deposits, offering fund management, engaging in underwriting, and providing investment banking. Commercial and saving banks and credit cooperatives are considered universal banks. Special banks are composed of mortgage banks, building and loan organizations, banks with special functions or that other specialized financial services or products; such as investment companies.

The German banking structure, which has more than 2000 financial institutions including large banks like the Deutsche Bank AG and the Commerzbank AG. Germany has 180 regional commercial and private banks and 430 saving banks and Land banks. Co-operative banks play a major role in the German financial industry, with more than 1100 institutions nationwide. In addition, there are more than 130 representative offices of various international banks located in Germany (J Engels, 2014, Personal Communication, 15 December). The German banking system comprises of a large number of financial institutions. Among these participants more than 70 are foreign banks, 13 of which were from Muslim countries.

5.6.3 Licensing of Islamic Financial Institutes According to the German and European Banking Law

Three types of financial and business entities fall with the scope of the German Credit Act (Kreditwesengesetz), which was implemented in 2002 (Gassner, 2004). The first type includes credit institutions, but only those credit institutions that are permitted to include in *Bank* the institution name pursuant to the § 1 German Credit Act. Engels (2010:181) outlined the definition of credit institutions as follows: "Credit institutions are enterprises engaged in banking transactions." There are nine kinds of banking transactions identified by the § 1 German Credit Act. These transactions are:

- Accepting the deposit business
- Advancing the credit
- The discount business
- The securities business
- The safe-custody business
- The investment fund business
- The revolving credit business
- The guarantee business
- The giro account business

Before discussing the licensing requirements it is important to analyse whether Islamic financial institutions fall under the definition of applicable to a credit institution as defined by the German and European banking law. Article 1 of Directive 77/780/EEC and Article 1 of Directive 2000/12/EC issued the European Commission (EC) defined a credit institution as "an enterprise which is engaged both in deposit and credit business" (Engels, 2010:182). These two definitions imply that German law has a wider scope for defining a credit institution when compared to the European banking law that limits the scope only those institutions that simply accept deposits and advance credit. The German banking law does not require that a credit institution fit the description of the above mentioned businesses types. It is possible that a bank can engage in only some of the activities.

Engels (2010) further maintained that Islamic financial institutions may be able to take part in five different business activities according to the § 1 German Credit Act such as accepting deposits, granting loans, performing securities, providing safe-custody, and engaging in giro business. Therefore, Islamic banks can be considered credit institutions and they can use the word *bank* in the institution's name once they have been given permission under German and European law.

There are four main avenues for establishing an Islamic financial institute in Germany:

A. Establishment of a new bank
B. Acquisition of a bank or transformation of an existing non-Islamic bank into Islamic
C. Establishment of a bank by using the European Passport option
D. Opening an Islamic banking window

In an interview on 15 December 2014, Mr J Engels, Senior Policy Officer of BaFin, stated the below mentioned criteria that BaFin has formulated for establishing a credit institution. The criteria is pertinent in the case of Option **A**, and these requirements are standard for Islamic and conventional financial institutions:

- Minimum requirement of capital (€5 Million)
- Minimum requirement of two managers
- Managers must be qualified and honest
- Managers can only work for the credit institution
- Verification of ownership
- Verification of holding structure
- No verification required on markets (we do not make analysis regarding market i.e., how many banks are there or is there any overbanking or not)

Mr J Engels (2014) further stated that:

> "Anyone wishing to conduct banking business or e-money business or to provide financial services or payment services in Germany requires written authorisation. Authorisation to conduct banking business is granted by the European Central Bank (ECB) in consultation with BaFin pursuant to sections 32 and 33 of the Banking Act (Kreditwesengesetz – KWG) in conjunction with Article 4(1) of the SSM (Single Supervisory Mechanism) Regulation. Authorization to provide financial services is still granted by BaFin (sections 32 and 33 of the KWG)."

According to Grieser (2008), in the case of option **B**, individuals and organizations must immediately inform the BaFin and the Deutsche Bandesbank regarding the acquisition of a bank, as per the section 2c paragraph 1 of the German Banking Act. The BaFin has a right to reject the application if the acquisition is not in compliance with the prescribed rules. Moreover, the financial institution must fulfil obligations regarding deposit participation funds, organizational duties, and restructuring the institution according to the requirements of the Accounting and Auditing Organization for Islamic Financial Institutions (AAOIFI).

Mr. J Engels explained the procedure for Option **C** in his interview on 15 December 2014, stating that "since 1993 under the European passport, a license of one bank is valid in other 28 EU countries." If a bank or financial institution wants to provide services in an additional member state of the European Union (EU) or European Economic Area (EEA) the institution must apply for a notification with its home supervisory authority. For example, a bank with a license to operate in the United Kingdom can ask the United Kingdom authority to notify the German authority (BaFin) that the bank wants to provide services in the German market. He further stated, "If the home authority does not see any legal problems it will forward the notification to the host authority and – to stick with our example – after a period of 3 months at the longest the UK bank can then start business in Germany."

With Option **D**, any existing conventional banking can open a dedicated Islamic banking branch fully compliant with the rules of *Shari'ah*. There have been many banks in the United Kingdom and many Muslim countries where non-Islamic banks have introduced special branches to cater the demand of their Muslim customers. However, in this scenario, the bank must fulfill the legal provisions prior to offering *Shari'ah*-compliant products.

5.7 Market Players in Islamic Banking in Germany

Germany has a universal banking system comprised of a large number of banks ranging from small domestic banks to large international banks. Some banks and insurance companies have already addressed the special financial needs of Muslim customers (Farhoush & Schmidt, 2011). For instance, HypoVereinsbank (HVB) with the help of YapiKredi, offered targeted financial services to Muslims of Turkish origin, and Helvetia, a German insurance company, introduced hotline in Turkish to advice its clients. Allianz, one of the biggest German insurance companies in Europe provides Turkish-speaking staff to serve the Turkish target group. These examples show that market players consider Muslims, and especially Turkish-Muslims, valuable customers and an important demographic segment of the market. According to Farhoush and Schmidt (2011), there are not many financial institutions that could offer broad range of *Shari'ah*-compliant products and services to Muslims living in Germany. Among large number of mutual fund managers there are only two companies, Allianz Global Investors and Alliance Unit Trust Management, whose products are accessible for German investors who prefer *Shari'ah*-compliant financial products. Thus, there is shortage of *Shari'ah*-compliant products available to Muslims in Germany.

The following section explores the some of the initiatives pursued by conventional banks in the field of Islamic banking and finance, and provides an overview of the new establishment of *Shari'ah*-compliant KT Bank AG in Germany.

5.7.1 KT Bank AG (Kuveyt Turk)

Kuveyt Türk bank opened its representative office in Germany in 2004 and in 2010 received a limited banking permit to engage in remittances transfers (Uğurlu Soylu, 2014, Personal Communication 15 December). In October 2012, Kuveyt Türk Katılım Bankası A.Ş applied to the BaFin for a full-fledge banking license, which was granted in March 2015. In March 2015, KT Bank AG became the first bank in Germany to obtain a full-fledge banking license to offer financial products and services on the basis of Islamic economic principles from BaFin. With the new license, Kuveyt Türk Katılım Bankası A.Ş was able to engage in the business of accepting deposits and lending credit. KT Bank AG started its operations in July 2015 and has opened branches in Berlin, Frankfurt am Main, and Mannheim. KT Bank AG is owned by the Kuveyt Türk Participation Bank A.Ş., Istanbul, and is offering *Shari'ah*-compliant products in Germany (KT Bank AG, 2015).

5.7.2 Landesbank Berlin AG

Landesbank Berlin AG is the subsidiary of Landesbank Berlin Holding AG (LBBH). It is considered a universal bank and has business operations ranging saving banking facilities to credit card business conducted in strategic alliance with credit issuing companies (Landesbank Berlin AG, 2014). Landesbank Berlin issued the QES *Shari'ah*-compliant Islamic finance certificate in 2011 and was awarded a *Shari'ah*-compliance certificate by the Central Council of Muslims in Germany (ZMD) (N Siegfried 2015, Personal Communication, 28 May). Central Council of Muslims in Germany is a recognized *Shari'ah* supervisory board that verifies *Shari'ah*-compliance of financial products. These certificates were registered on a number of stock exchanges, including those in Frankfurt am Main, Stuttgart, and Berlin, at a starting price of 100 Euro. Despite the good performance history of the certificate it was closed down in 2013 when it only managed to generate few million euros (N Siegfried 2015, Personal Communication, 28 May). The primary reason for termination of this offer was lack of demand from the market. At the end of 2013 the value of the QES *Shari'ah*-compliant Islamic finance certificate was about €130. The certificate gained €30 value within three years. From this information, it can be concluded that the certificate showed strong growth, but the customer base was not large enough.

5.7.3 Deutsche Bank AG

Deutsche Bank AG is one of the largest German banks to recognize the Turkish community as a potential target group and founded the first *Bankamiz* branches in Germany, a dedicated branch for Turkish speaking clients (Farhoush & Schmidt, 2011). The main purpose of these branches is to offer free remittances facilities to Turkey and to provide consulting services in Turkish (language) to its Turkish customers in Germany. The Deutsche Bank AG (2015) website stated that:

> "On the Islamic capital markets side, Deutsche Bank has been honored to work with our sovereign, quasi- sovereign and private clients such as the State of Qatar, Saudi Aramco, Saudi Electricity Company, Khazanah, Dubai Islamic Bank, Banque Saudi Fransi, Dar Al Arkan Real Estate Development Company and many others to arrange and book-run landmark *Sukuk* transactions enabling them efficient and swift access the Islamic capital markets to achieve their funding objectives."

In the view of Abdel-Khaleq (2015), Deutsche Bank AG has, in cooperation with National Commercial Bank (NCB) Saudi Arabia, played an instrumental role in the structuring of *Shari'ah*-compliant investment funds. The structuring of *Shari'ah*-compliant funds was done under the supervision of leading *Shari'ah* scholars during 1990s. The NCB offered this fund in Saudi Arabia and the first subscription amounted to US $275 million.

Keeping in view global demand of Islamic finance in particular jurisdictions, the Deutsche Bank AG launched 'five DWS Noor Islamic Funds' in Dubai and Bahrain, which were made available to individual and institutional clients with a minimum subscription of US$ 1,000 transacted through the Deutsche Asset and Wealth Management (AWM) division (Deutsche Bank AG, 2006). The Deutsche Asset and Wealth Management is among the top ten asset managers worldwide and managed assets worth of €1.159 billion as of March 2015, and has operations in more than forty countries (Deutsche Asset and Wealth Management, 2015).

Deutsche Bank AG has been one of the more proactive banks in the global Islamic financial market, and the above stated examples show that Deutsche bank AG has the expertise needed to structure and offer relevant products in the German market.

5.7.4 Commerzbank AG

Commerzbank AG is recognized internationally as one of the leading banks for private and corporate customers and has presence in more than 50 countries, including Germany. In 2014 Commerzbank AG generated a gross income of €9 billion and employed more than 52,000 workers (Commerzbank AG, Annual report 2014). According to Geyer (2002), Commerzbank group issued the Al-Sukoor European Equity Fund through its subsidiary Commerz International Capital Management (CICM) in 1999 with the aim of attracting Middle Eastern institutional investors. The launch was supervised by a *Shari'ah* supervisory board comprised of five Islamic scholars. In 2000, the Al-Sukoor European Equity Fund was made available to the German private investors, and was managed strictly according to *Shari'ah* rules. However, the fund only managed to generate €4 million in assets and was closed down in 2005 (Geyer, 2002; Aichbichler, 2009).

Chahboune and El-Mogddedi (2008) pointed to three main reasons for the failure of the Al-Sukoor European Equity Fund. First, it was not properly marketed to clients in the private sector. Second, the target groups in Middle Eastern countries were institutional clients in equity finance when the highest potential in those countries was in real estate. Third, the events of September 11 2001 (terrorist attacks perpetrated on the United States) had negative implications of the world financial market that also affected the fund.

Despite this setback, the Commerzbank AG continued to maintain an interest in the field of Islamic finance and has since established offices in Dubai, Cairo, Beirut, Istanbul, Tripolis, Kuala Lumpur, and Singapore. Commerzbank AG (2015) satisfied the needs of its customers in Middle East, Malaysia, and in Turkey with interest-free services and states its expertise as:

"Commerzbank Financial Institutions is currently developing further Islamic Banking techniques, allowing our clients to structure their business in a *Shari'ah*-compliant way."

In 2012, Commerzbank AG performed the role of Joint Lead Manager (JLM) for the Kuveyt Turk Participation bank, the second largest bank of Turkey, and successfully raised $350 million by issuing the *Sukuk Al Iijara* (Commerzbank AG, 2012). Commerzbank AG gained a competitive advantage with its presence in leading financial centers and leveraged that advantage to organize road shows for investors in Kuala Lumpur, Dubai, Abu Dhabi, London, and Zurich. In summary, the successful completion of the Kuveyt Turk transaction underlined the expertise of the Commerzbank AG. Despite this, Commerzbank AG has shifted its focus to international Islamic banking and finance projects because it experienced a lack of demand for products offered in Germany and decided to strengthen its position globally.

5.7.5 Targo Bank AG & Co. KGaA

Targobank AG is another internationally prominent bank operating in Germany. With more than 7000 employees working in 363 branches in 200 cities Targobank AG has 4 million banking customers (Targobank AG, 2015). Stumpfegger (2015) argued that Targobank AG is also trying to attract the Turkish community by offering different products and services in the Turkish language. Targobank AG has introduced 149 *Targobank Bankadas* branches in Germany at which Turkish customers can receive consultation services pertaining to giro accounts, saving accounts, real estate financing, and business loans in Turkish (Disimino & Hähn, 2015). Customer service lines offer call center extensions that direct calls to Turkish-speaking customer service agents.

5.8 Other Islamic Banking and Finance Initiatives in Germany

According to Farhoush and Mahlknecht (2013), Islamic banking and finance dates back to the 1990s when several Turkish companies, namely Kombassan Holding, Jet-Pa, Yibitas Holding, and Yimpas Holding, offered Islamic financial products to local Muslims predominately from Turkish origins. The Islamic holdings of these companies offered high returns on investment and were able to attract 200,000 to 300,000 Muslims customers mainly through mosques; thus, offerings of Islamic financial products by Turkish holdings were considered the first Islamic banking and finance initiative in Germany.

According to Gassner (2004), a *mega financial scandal* known as the *Turkish Holdings* took place in Germany when a large number of Turkish mosque organizations pooled the resources of their members for investments in Turkey. More than €5 billion was lost by inexperience of investors and this caused widespread distrust among Muslims. Contrary to this, Farhoush and Mahlknecht (2013) argued that the estimated loss caused by Turkish holdings to Muslims living in Germany ranged €5 to €50 billion. Thus, Turkish people witnessed negative experience when they used Islamic financial products and the event raised many questions about the regulations addressing financial investments. This was specifically important to Muslim investors who lost their funds because these investments were made without authentic supervision of a *Shari'ah* board and without taking into account the applicable German laws (Gassner, 2004).

Al Sukoor and the UBS (Lux) Islamic fund, which were launched and marketed in Germany by two different firms, were other Islamic finance initiatives (Gassner, 2003a). The Al Sukoor fund was initiated by the Commerzbank group, the largest bank in Germany, to sell products to potential investors living in Germany. The UBS (Lux) Islamic fund, which later on renamed as the Noriba Global Equity Fund, was exclusively target to Middle Eastern investors. These funds were stock market funds with long-term maturities and were suitable for those investors who were interested in long-term investments in real estate. Many Muslims living in Germany were already familiar with the Islamic banking and finance products through these initiatives.

According to Farhoush and Schmidt (2011), various organizations in Germany, in addition to financial institutions, have tried to design marketing campaigns to address the specific needs of Muslims. The largest telecommunication company, E-plus, introduced services in the Turkish language and provided special mobile services between Germany and Turkey. In Muslim majority areas, such as Ruhr and Berlin, various initiatives were taken with consideration for Muslim customs and traditions. For example, adjustments have been made in old home facilities and funeral laws. Some swimming pools have also introduced specific timings for Muslim women and even some special TV programs are also available.

The Bankamiz and YapiKredi were two early initiatives in the arena of Islamic banking in Germany, but these initiatives failed to attract the attention of a large enough segment of the Muslim population. Two reasons were suspected for having played an important role in this failure (Farhoush & Schmidt, 2011): the Turkish community was heavily exploited in the case of Turkish holdings and the marketing campaigns were not effective. To encourage various companies to offer Islamic products in Germany, the Deutsche Börse, a leading stock exchange, approved different Exchange Trade Funds (ETFs): db x-trackers S&P Europe 350 Shari'ah ETF but the fate of such initiative was also similar to earlier mentioned examples (Farhoush & Schmidt, 2011).

5.9 Why Low Demand of Islamic Banking and Finance Products?

Although various initiatives have been undertaken to address the needs of Muslim customers through the introduction of *Shari'ah*-compliant or *Shari'ah* board approved products, improved customer service, and education about available products, the response to these initiatives have been underwhelming. According to Colditz (2009), four key factors have contributed to Germany's experience with low demand for *Shari'ah*-compliant products and services. First, the majority of the overall Muslim population is using conventional banking products and are well integrated into the conventional financial system. Second, the Turkish population is the largest Muslim minority demographic among Muslims living in Germany and Turkish Muslims exhibits more secular characteristics than do their Muslim counterparts of other national heritage and have a low demand for Islamic products and services. Third, most of the Muslims living in Germany practice separation of private life and religion, which might be another factor of low demand. Fourth, as many banks are already providing cheap banking products, such as home finance, business loans, and car financing, the cost of doing business with an Islamic bank would be higher than doing business with a conventional counterpart. This represents a disadvantage for potential Muslim customers and could discourage them from using products offered by Islamic banks (Colditz, 2009). There are several other causes of low demand for Islamic banking and financial products in Germany including low incomes among the Muslim population and the low number of Muslim women participating in the labor force (Schönenbach, 2012).

Farhoush and Mahlknecht (2013) outlined the five main reasons for low demand for Islamic banking and financial products in Germany including a) lack of awareness about retail financial products, b) poor marketing, c) lack of credibility among financial institutions offering Islamic products and services, d) lack of supporting institutions that could increase awareness about Islamic banking and finance, and e) a scattered Muslim population in Germany, which makes it difficult to offer products and services. The topic of inadequate demand for Islamic banking and finance will also be discussed in detail in Chapter 8.

5.10 Concluding Remarks

As the preceding discussion has highlighted, the German government and its relevant authorities have taken measures to integrate Muslims into mainstream society since the arrival of foreign guest workers in the 1960s. Germany has more than 4.76 million Muslim residents, which does not take into account the number of asylum seekers presently entering Germany from Muslim countries such as Syria, Iraq, and Afghanistan. Different avenues could be available for entering the Islamic banking industry including the establishment of a new bank, acquisition of an existing non-Islamic bank, conversion of an existing bank into an Islamic bank, or use of the European passport option. Opening a *Shari'ah*-compliant Islamic banking window if a full-fledge bank is not possible.

The Islamic financial industry is not a new to German financial institutions, and several German banks such as the Deutsche Bank AG and the Commerzbank AG have been key players in promoting the use of Islamic banking products in global financial markets. The available evidence seems to suggest that the Muslim population demonstrates low demand for *Shari'ah*-compliant products. There could be multiple factors behind the low demand including a shallow range of products and services, low levels of awareness among consumers about *Shari'ah*-compliant financial products, inadequate marketing strategies, a lack of a full-fledge bank until 2015, and mistrust in Islamic financial products because of Turkish holdings scandal.

Chapter 6 provides a review of existing literature to highlight important studies in the area of Islamic banking and finance in Germany.

Chapter 6: Review of Existing Literature

6.1 Introduction

Before providing a detailed overview of the methodologies and theoretical foundation for this study, it is important to provide an overview of the previous research with regard to Muslim consumer behaviors and attitudes toward Islamic banking and finance in Germany. This literature review will discuss prominent research trends and evaluate the strengths and weaknesses of the existing literature. Regarding the scholarly literature in Germany, the topic of Islamic banking and finance has been approached from many different perspectives and researchers have used different tools, including thematic, quantitative, and qualitative methods, to draw conclusions about the potential of Islamic banking products. The available literature suggests that in the early 2000s non-academic also began paying attention to the topic of Islamic banking and finance, but from 2010 onward more scientific studies were performed.

Chapter 6 includes a review of different studies investigating the banking behaviors of immigrants in Germany, and contains an overview of a number of studies in the area of Islamic banking, Islamic insurance, and quantification of the potential of Islamic banking and finance. Chapter 6 also provides an overview of past studies and the relevance or significance of those studies to this study, and concludes with a chapter summary.

6.2 Studies about Immigrants and their Banking Behavior

In 2005, with a special focus on Turkish immigrants in Germany, Gleisner *et al.* (2010) studied immigrants' banking behaviors and consumption choices as they related to bank nationality. This study used a quantitative survey and a sample size of 1006 participants in Rhine-Main and Berlin metropolitan area (which includes cities such as Frankfurt, Wiesbaden, Offenbach, Mainz, Darmstadt, Berlin, and Brandenburg). The main objective of this study was to analyze immigrants' bank selection criteria in the context of home nation banks (banks from Turkey) and host or third nation banks (German banks or international banks). Thus, a broader aim of this study was to analyze the implications of globalization on the retail banking industry and to determine whether non-domestic banks operating in foreign countries gain an advantage in the local market when compared to domestic banks.

Gleisner *et al.* (2010) found that only 9% of the respondents (from a sample of 584) were customers of a home nation bank, and the remaining 91% of the respondents were customers of host or third nation banks. The study also found that some 60% of the customers of home nation banks sent remittances to their countries of origin compared to 40% of the customers of host or third nation banks (Gleisner *et al.*, 2010). The findings of this study also showed a trend for product differentiation as a main cause for consumers selecting a home nation bank. An increased integration of Turkish immigrants into German society may decrease their tendency to select products and services of the home nation banks (Gleisner *et al.*, 2010). From the Islamic banking and finance perspective and in the context of Germany, it can be inferred from this study that an Islamic bank with suitable products may be in a better position to attract Muslim consumers. For example, if a Turkish owned bank offered attractive financial products to Muslims living in a Turkish community in Germany it can be inferred from this study that Muslims in that community would prefer to do business with the Turkish bank rather than the local bank.

Recently, a study for the Deutsche Bank AG placed a special focus on the customers of *Bankamiz*[7] branches when conducting a study that investigated the relationship of customers from Turkish origin with banking products in Germany (Heinen *et al.*, 2015). The main purpose of this study was to investigate the untapped business potential of serving consumers with a migrant background. The study was a significant undertaking for business considerations because more than 16.5 million people live in Germany. Heinen *et al.* (2015) used data collected in interviews with the customer advisors of the *Bankamiz* branches in Germany, in conjunction with data provided by the Deutsche Bank, to make a comparison of the attitudes between customers of *Bankamiz* branches and retail customers of the Deutsche Bank.

This study revealed that customers with a Turkish migrant background seemed to be very cautious when selecting financial investment products, and first generation Turks tended to opt for less risky banking products (such as current accounts). Moreover, 73.6% the customers of *Bankamiz* branches were using current accounts and payment processing services, 36.8% were using savings products (which includes savings books and special savings plans), and 22.2% were using pensions, including insurance (Heinen *et al.*, 2015).

The findings relevant to this study were those that indicated good growth potential for the use of financial products among migrant-origin customers in Germany (Heinen *et al.*, 2015). The studies conducted by Gleisner *et al.* (2015) and Heinen *et al.* (2015) both targeted the Turkish community residing in Germany. Regarding research methodologies, the study by Gleisner *et al.* (2010) was structured, scientific and used a large sample size of 1006 Turkish respondents. The study by Heinen *et al.* (2015) was based on the interviews conducted with advisors of the *Bankamiz* branches and information provided by the Deutsche Bank. Therefore, the scope of the Heinen *et al.* (2015) study is further limited to the segment of Turkish Muslim population banking at *Bankamiz* branches and by the fact that there is no informa-

7 *Bankamiz* is a customer interface of Deutsche Bank for people of Turkish descent living in Germany. Based on the shop in shop concept, it operates in regions and cities with a high density of ethnic Turks, employing advisors who are also of Turkish origin. Since *Bankamiz* was established in 2006, Deutsche Bank has significantly increased its market share among this target group. The aim is to have 60 branches with a total of 70 *Bankamiz* advisors in Germany by the end of 2015. (This information is adapted from Heinen *et al.*, 2015).

tion available about sample size. However, the study conducted by Heinen *et al.* (2015) is contemporary and provides more recent insights when compared to the study conducted by Gleisner *et al.* (2010).

Hayen *et al.* (2005) investigated the relationship between Turkish migrants and financial services in Germany in a project sponsored by the German Federal Ministry of Food, Agriculture, and Consumer Protection (BMLV). The aim of the study was to analyze the preferences of migrants with Turkish backgrounds regarding financial products. For this purpose, Hayen *et al.* (2005) used a sample of 1002 respondents (the total population size was 8000 but only 1199 respondents agreed for interview, and 197 interviewees terminated the call before interview completion) and data were collected through telephone interviews between July 2005 and August 2005. A standard questionnaire, which was prepared in both German and Turkish, was used for each interview. The average duration of the telephonic interviews was approximately 25 minutes.

Hayen's (2005) study ascertained that 67.9% of the respondents from Turkish origin invested in real estate in Turkey, whereas only 22.1% had invested in real estates in Germany. At the time of the study, significantly fewer respondents were benefiting from the financial products offered by local financial institutions. Only 19.4% had a savings account, 9.2% had life insurance services, 6.2% had building savings scheme contracts, and 4.8% had private pension schemes (Hayen *et al.*, 2005).

The studies by Gleisner *et al.* (2010) and Hayen *et al.* (2005) were conducted in 2005. Their data indicate a low penetration of the Turkish migrant population was participating in the German financial system. The Heinen *et al.* (2015) study differs when compared with the study of Hayen *et al.* (2005) in that Hayen *et al.* (2005) concluded that 22.1% Turkish respondents had invested in real estate in Germany, but Heinen *et al.* (2015) revealed that migrants have shown good interest in financial products in Germany. This difference in findings might have been caused by a gap in time between the two studies. Another reason might be that Heinen *et al.* (2015) studied only Turkish customers of *Bankamiz* branches whereas Hayen *et al.* (2005) studied a broader demographic and used a randomly selected sample.

6.3 Studies about Islamic Finance in Germany

The topic of Islamic finance is broad and includes many subtopics including, but not limited to, Islamic banking, Islamic insurance, and Islamic capital markets (Ebert & Thießen, 2010). Islamic banking officially started in Germany in 2015 with the establishment of KT Bank AG and past literature on Islamic banking and finance, particularly in mainstream scientific journals, is limited if not non-existent. The potential for Islamic banking and finance in Germany is reliant on the existence of a larger Turkish Muslim minority population, few research studies have analyzed the banking behavior of the Turkish community with regard to local German banks and foreign international banks, independently of their relation with Islamic banking and finance (Schuster, 2013; Farhoush & Schmidt, 2011; and Heinen *et al.*, 2015). Past studies provide background and insights about the Turkish community that might be of importance to this study, which aims to explore the perceptions of Muslims living in Germany toward Islamic banking and finance. The available literature pertinent to Islamic banking and finance can be divided into different sections and themes as discussed below.

6.3.1 Muslim Consumers Behavior toward Islamic Banking and Finance Products

The most significant research to consider in regard to this study was conducted by Farhoush and Schmidt (2011) and analyzed the implications of countries of origin toward buying behaviors involved in purchasing Islamic banking and finance products in Germany. The study was conducted by using a standard questionnaire comprised of 50 quantitative questions and three qualitative questions. The survey was completed online with the help of Islamic institutes located in Germany. The final sample size was 373 (A total 781 people opened and viewed the questionnaire, but 408 people left it incomplete). Generally, the participants of this survey were those people who had memberships with the collaborating Islamic institutes.

The findings of this study indicated that 70% of the respondents consider themselves very religious practicing Muslims, and that the majority of the respondents have basic knowledge about banking products including real estate, mutual funds, and stocks. The overwhelming majority of the 70% who considered themselves very religious stated that conformity with the Islamic rules prohibiting the use of interest and speculation was very important to them (Farhoush & Schmidt, 2011). When asked about the market potential for *Shari'ah*-compliant products and services in Germany, 75% of the respondents expressed a willingness to use *Shari'ah*-compliant savings accounts, 73.4% expressed willingness to use loans and real estate financing or mortgage financing, and 52% were willing to use mutual funds. A majority of the respondents desired loans and financing to buy homes, and over 50% wished for retirement savings and insurance products. This study also found that over 50% of the respondents have no issues with using banking products from conventional banks provided they are *Shari'ah*-compliant and approved by a respected institution.

As was mentioned, the study mainly addressed the topic of Islamic banking and finance through the perspective of the respondents' countries of origin. The findings revealed that 23.4% of the respondents cited that they want to stay in Germany, and that the second and third generations of foreign workers (predominantly of Turkish origin) wanted to live in Germany. Second and third generation workers expressed high demand for personal loans, mortgages, and investments (Farhoush & Schmidt, 2011).

Between October 2008 and February 2009, Alexander *et al.* (2010) conducted a study in Germany to investigate the potential of Islamic banking products in the German market. The study focused on Muslim immigrants, mainly those of Turkish and Arabic origins. The study employed a quantitative survey and qualitative interviews for data collection. The quantitative survey was conducted with a sample size of 111 spanning six cities including Berlin, Freiburg, Stuttgart, Göttingen, Hannover, and Leipzig. The standard quantitative questionnaire was created with the help of finance and banking department of Technical University Chemnitz, and specific questions were designed to gain information about Muslim consumers' preferences while keeping in mind intercultural background of the respondents. Prior to distribution the questionnaires were translated into the Arabic and Turkish languages.

The survey results revealed that 54% of respondents were using EC-cards, 16% were using credit cards, and 14% were using savings accounts from traditional banks. Alternatively, 84% of the respondents demonstrated an interest in Islamic banking products: 23% of respondents said they were aware of *Qard Hasan* and 18% of respondents expressed awareness about *Mudarabah*. Furthermore, 29% indicated that they were very religious, and 61% believed that *Riba* is prohibited and compliance to this rule was important to them. Gassner (2003a) pointed to results of a Zentrum für Türkeistudien (Zft), the Center for Turkish Studies that indicated 23.2% of the Turkish population living in Germany considered interest (*Riba*) unacceptable on religious grounds.

Other research tool used by Alexander *et al.* (2010) included qualitative interviews of four Muslim umbrella organizations, which were performed in Leipzig, Berlin, Hannover, and Frankfurt am Main, and group interviews with the Department of the Islamic Studies at the University of Leipzig, and association of Arab Student and Academics (Vereines arabisher Studenten und Akademiker or VASA). The main findings of the qualitative research were: a) the respondents are skeptical about Islamic financial products because of bad experiences with past products, especially respondents of the older generation and b) the respondents demonstrated a basic level of interest in Islamic financial products (Alexander *et al.*, 2010).

Yildiz (2014) employed a qualitative research method for his study titled *Islamic Banking in Germany: Challenges for Implementation in a Conventional Financial System,* which took place between November 2011 and November 2012. The main focus of this study was to examine the implementation of Islamic banking in the German financial environment. This qualitative study involved ten expert interviewees from Germany, but the profiles of these interviewees were kept anonymous. One interviewee was selected from the German regulatory authority and Islamic bank (Kuveyt Türk Katılım Bankası A.Ş), one from the Association of German banks, and one from the Association of Foreign Banks in Germany. Three interviewees were chosen from different financial institutions in Germany, and three interviewees were researchers, two university professors and one professional from a research institute (Yildiz, 2014).

The key findings of this study were that Islamic banking in Germany would face challenges including integration in a conventional environment, compliance with the regulatory hurdles, and a lack of demand of Islamic financial products (lack of demand was the result of image issues caused by the Turkish holdings scandal that took place between 1995 and 2002. In the scandal a large number of Turkish Muslims lost cumulative savings of about $ 25 billion.) (Yildiz, 2014). Yildiz further argued that in the United Kingdom's Islamic banking was signaled by the famous conventional banks such as the HSBC Bank PLC, Lloyds Bank PLC and others that showed interest in Islamic banking in the United Kingdom. However, in Germany, a similar situation does not exist for the[8] Kuveyt Türk Katılım Bankası A.Ş. In addition to this, several government ministries in the United Kingdom made regulatory and legal changes to facilitate Islamic banking, and Islamic banking was embraced with an open attitude and supported by top political leadership in the United Kingdom (Yildiz, 2014).

Yildiz (2014) also concluded that Islamic banking was being acknowledged as an alternative financial system in Germany, but pointed out that there is a big difference between the United Kingdom and German regulatory approaches toward the matter of Islamic banking as an alternative. In the United Kingdom, the Prime Minister supported Islamic banking and encouraged investors in London to participate in the market. In Germany, the same level of political support was not present and there were no conferences held on this topic post the 2012 BaFin conference.

The studies of Farhoush and Schmidt (2011) and Alexander *et al.* (2010) (discussed in more detail above) reported almost identical percentages of the respondents who believed that compliance with *Riba* is important and necessary. However, Alexander *et al.* (2010) showed comparatively higher numbers of respondents who expressed interest in Islamic banking and finance than did Farhoush and Schmidt (2011) (84% vs. 75%). The difference may be a consequence of the fact that Alexander *et al.* (2010) used a relatively small sample size of 111 and the study was mainly conducted in Berlin, Freiburg, Göttingen, Hannover, and Leipzig, but Farhoush and Schmidt (2011) used a larger sample size of 347 and data was collected through an online survey.

Similar to the studies of Farhoush and Schmidt (2011) and Alexander *et al.* (2010), The Institute of Islamic Banking and Finance (IFIBAF), an Islamic financial consulting firm based in Frankfurt, conducted a survey in Germany (2010; cited in Casper, 2014) to find out the potential of Islamic banking products and services in the market. This study was based on a random sample of 1000 respondents and findings showed that 63.5% of the respondents had already heard about Islamic banking, 72% showed interest in Islamic financial products, 17% had no interest in Islamic financial products, and 60% were interested in buying Islamic products from well-recognized Islamic banks. Moreover, 90% of respondents indicated that they would welcome the establishment of an Islamic bank in Germany, and an estimated savings potential of interviewed respondents was approximately €22–38 billion, with indicated potential annual savings of about €2.2 billion (Casper, 2014; El-Mogaddedi, 2010).

The findings of the Institute of Islamic Banking and Finance study (2010) somewhat closely resembled the findings presented by Farhoush and Schmidt (2011) and Alexander *et al.* (2010) and supported the assertion that 63.5% of the respondents had already heard about Islamic banking and finance, while 72% of the respondents would have liked to use Islamic banking products and services. Moreover, these studies were conducted in a similar time period.

8 Yildiz used the word „Hayal Bank“ for Kuveyt Türk Katılım Bankası A.Ş

The Institute of Islamic Banking and Finance study (2010) differs in two ways from the study of Farhoush and Schmidt (2011). First, Farhoush and Schmidt (2011) included Muslims and non-Muslims in their study, albeit few non-Muslims and sample size was smaller compared to that used in the Institute of Islamic Banking and Finance study (347 vs. 1000). Second, the Institute of Islamic Banking and Finance study (2010) was more general and business oriented in nature, and the study conducted by Farhoush and Schmidt (2011) limited its scope to studying Islamic banking through the lens of countries of origin, which narrowed the focus and further limited the population under study.

An earlier study, conducted by Wackerbeck and Heimer (2006; cited in Wurst, 2011) examined the awareness of Muslim customers about Islamic banking products in Germany. Wackerbeck and Heimer (2006; cited in Wurst, 2011) reported that only 51% of the Muslim respondents knew about Islamic banking products, and only 4% were currently using such products. A majority of the respondents were using the services of conventional banks because Islamic banking products were not available to them. Mortgage products were highly desired products by two-thirds of the respondents (Wurst, 2011).

Ernst *et al.* (2013) cited an empirical study from 2006 that found that two-thirds of the respondents ranked real estate financing as the most desired product. Furthermore, Ernst *et al.* (2013) stated that according to another study conducted in Germany in 2009 approximately 43% of the Muslim respondents expressed demand for Islamic insurance and approximately 40% expressed demand for both investment funds and consumer financing. The main drawback, which stems from the studies conducted by Wackerbeck and Heimer (2006) and the studies cited by Ernst *et al.* (2013), is that there is a lack of key information like population sample and data analysis methodologies.

6.3.2 Quantification of the Potential of Islamic Banking and Finance

Researchers and institutions have conducted investigations aimed at quantifying the potential of Islamic banking and finance. According to Gassner (2003b and 2004) and Colditz (2009), Germany is home to more than 600,000 Muslim households. This number includes approximately 553,000 salaried employees who are part of the German social insurance contribution system, and another 55,000 (estimated) that are self-employed. Furthermore, these households have €15 to 25 billion in assets deposited with German financial institutions. The average Muslim household income amounts to €1,769 per month, which is substantially lower than the average German household income of €2,733.

Gassner (2003b and 2004) further asserted that the savings rate of Muslim households is comparatively double that of the average German household, and argued that the reason behind this was that a vast majority of Muslims had not used banking products that provide alternatives to savings accounts. Despite the fact that the average German household contributed a lower percentage of their incomes to savings they spent €459 per month, which is more than the €371 an average Turkish Muslim household spent on financial services per month. Furthermore, Gassner (2003b and 2004) also derived an estimated Muslim household yearly demand of €2.7 billion in financial services and estimated that Muslims living in Germany have a collective annual income of around €13 billion.

The Deutsch-Emiratische Industrie-und Handelskammer conducted a study in 2010 examining the potential of Islamic banking in Germany. The findings suggested that the wealth of Muslims ranged from €18 to €25 billion, and that Muslims exhibited a higher savings rate of 18% compared to the 10% savings rate of other Germans. This study highlighted the fact that 72% of the respondents were keen to know about Islamic banking products, and 60% of the respondents expressed a willingness to invest in *Shari'ah*-compliant products if offered by a German bank. However, 94% of the respondents expressed interest if a standalone Islamic bank offered the same products. (This may be indicative of the findings within the study that indicated 74% of the respondents self-identified as religious, which indicated a preference for *Shari'ah*-compliant banking options.) Three of the most desired products were mortgage finance (62%), insurance products (43%), and investment funds (42%).

Similar to the study of the Deutsch-Emiratische Industrie-und Handelskammer (2010) and Gassner (2003b, 2004), the strategy-consulting firm, Booz & Company (2008; cited in PwC, 2008) which was based in Munich, also explored the potential of Islamic banking and finance in Germany. The study reported that the German market had a potential of €1.2 billion per annum for Islamic banking and finance products, although no more than 5% German Muslims were using Islamic financial products and services (PwC, 2008). The study showed that almost 60% of the respondents were interested in Islamic banking products and services, and the most popular products were home financing, consumer loans, and insurance products (PwC, 2008; Farhoush & Schmidt, 2011). The study also stated that the German financial institutions had not shown interest in the local market because of regulatory challenges. However, different German banks were already working in Muslim countries, such as Indonesia and Saudi Arabia, in the area of Islamic banking and finance.

Gassner and Wieners (2009) reported additional findings of the Booz & company study of 2008 indicating that:

- 57% of the Muslim respondents preferred their current financial service providers to be Islamic banks
- 29% cited non-Islamic banks and 26% cited banks interdependent of financial intermediaries

On the question of different factors influencing purchasing behavior:

- 62% indicated that the certification of Islamic products is compulsory
- 49% preferred consultation in their native language
- 43% preferred that the consultant be Muslim (Gassner & Wieners, 2009).

Despite sincere efforts to find the original study of the Booz & Company, the literature finds only a few studies that have referred to the findings of the study. Nevertheless, the available evidence suggests some mixed views about the potential of Islamic banking and finance. For example, the Deutsch-Emiratische Industrie-und Handelskammer (2010) study demonstrated that the wealth of Muslims was €18 to 25 billion, whereas the research of Booz & Company (2008) predicted the potential of Islamic financial products in Germany was an estimated €1.2 billion per annum. Most importantly, neither study provided further information about methods of data collection and calculations used to drive the aforementioned wealth potential.

Braham's (2012; cited in Schuster, 2013) study approaches the topic of Islamic banking and finance from savings and income perspective of the Muslims. The study stated that there were 2.70 million Muslims of Turkish origin comprising 72,000 households in Germany, and that the average gross household income was €1,917 per month (lower than the one of German households as of €2,596). Moreover, Turkish households exhibited higher savings of €402 per month compared to the nationwide average of €259 per month. These findings point to the fact that addressing the banking concerns and needs of the Turkish community in Germany is an attractive business proposition. In addition, the study determined that the investment potential for insurance products is about €3.47 billion and approximately €25 billion is deposited in German banks. Furthermore, there were 71,000 Turkish enterprises and self-employed individuals represented a collective of almost €10.80 billion in investment potential (Schuster, 2013).

6.3.3 Muslim Consumers Behavior toward Islamic Insurance Products

Evens (2014) examined the potential of *Shari'ah*-compliant insurance products in Germany from a marketing perspective. This study was conducted between February 2012 and June 2012 and used a sample size of 412. A standard questionnaire was used to assess the interest of the Muslim respondents in Islamic insurance products, consumer expectations from an Islamic insurance provider, and consumer preferences concerning product pricing. The questionnaires were translated into the Turkish and Arabic languages. Questionnaires in the Turkish language were distributed in four mosques in Frankfurt am Main, to Turkish Muslims in Germany who were referred to the study, and online. The majority of the data were collected through mosques and personal references. About 50% of the respondents were from Turkish origin, and more than one-third were from Arabic origin. The study findings revealed that 62% of the respondents indicated a willingness to buy Islamic insurance products whereas 32% answered 'maybe' (Evens, 2014). Of the respondents 71% desired car insurance and 36% desired private insurance or legal coverage insurance, respectively (Evens, 2014).

Wackerbeck and Kearney (2006 and 2004; cited in Evens, 2014) investigated the market potential of Islamic insurance products in Germany. Wackerbeck used a sample size of 200 Muslims who were asked about their opinions regarding desired Islamic insurance products in Hessen and Rheinland-Pfalz regions. This study found that 25% of the respondents expressed a strong interest; while 18% showed little interest in such products and services (Evens, 2014). Kearney (2004; cited in Evens, 2014) reported that the German market had a potential for achieving €1 billion annually. It is worth noting that both studies were not available in literature; and thus, it was not possible to comment on the research methodologies (Evens, 2014).

The recent study presented by Evens (2014) was more comprehensives compared to the studies of Wackerbeck and Kearney; however, it lacked two important elements that a contemporary study should incorporate. First, the respondents' data were interpreted only through descriptive statistics and there were no in-depth efforts to investigate the interdependencies and correlations of the different data sets. Second, the qualitative interviews were discussed and interpreted without creating themes, commonalities, and dissension on specific issues.

According to Schönenbach (2012), Germany had a population of 4.3 million Muslims and the majority of them (2.7 million) were of Turkish origins. Muslims living in Germany were not affluent, which could have been attributed (in part) to the lower average level of education within the Muslim population (predominately among those from Turkish origin) and low labor force participation by Muslim women (Schönenbach, 2012). Schönenbach further argued that several attempts had been made in the past to introduce *Shari'ah*-compliant products, like the *Meridio fund* (issued by Meridio Asset Management Inc. based in Cologne in 2010) and *Al-Sukoor fund* (issued in 2005), but these products were not well-received and the relative poverty of the German Muslims might have been the main reason for failure with these initiatives (Schönenbach, 2012).

Haug *et al.* (2009) conducted a study titled *Muslim Life in Germany* which was published by the German Federal Office for Migration and Refugees (BAMF) in relation to the German Islam Conference held in 2009. The study found that 20% of Muslims living in German households relied on the public welfare system to survive, which was mainly a consequence of higher unemployment rates among Muslims in Germany, even though approximately 80% of Muslim households in Germany had partial or full income through jobs or businesses (Haug *et al.*, 2009; Schönenbach, 2012). The studies of Schönenbach and Haug *et al.* contradicted other studies, including those from Braham (2012), Booz & Company (2008), the Deutsch-Emiratische Industrie und Handelskammer (2010), and the IFIBAF (2010), which demonstrated very high savings and investment potential.

6.4 Discussion about Existing Studies and our Proposed Study

The previous section provided an overview of various studies investigating the potential of Islamic banking and finance in Germany. Review of the literature revealed a gap in the existing research left by the existence of little to no research designed to provide a comparative analysis of Islamic finance in Germany and the United Kingdom. The current research aimed to address the gap discovered in the existing literature and to do a thorough theoretical mixed methods study involving both quantitative and qualitative research methodologies.

Past studies reviewed in the previous sections were relevant to the study of Islamic banking and finance and were scientifically performed. However, a number of them did not provide sufficient information about sample size, time period, or applied data collection methods. The current study possesses a number of distinctive features compared with the study performed by Farhoush and Schmidt (2011) and Alexander *et al.* (2010). For example, the samples was distributed over 9 major German cities with large Muslim populations including Berlin, Hamburg, Duisburg, Essen, Duesseldorf, Munich, Frankfurt am Main, Cologne and Bochum, thus a higher sample size of 402 is used. There are two other important differentiating factors. First, this study took into account the knowledge, attitude and perceptions of general Muslim populace toward Islamic financial products and services and investigates the Muslim umbrella organizations in Germany. The study then compared the results with general Muslim respondents. Second, this study aimed to do qualitative interviews with different leading market experts from Germany, the United Kingdom, and Saudi Arabia to seek evidence from the supply side for meaningful insights (an element not currently available in literature or available as quantitative data). Among other factors compared to studies from Farhoush and Schmidt (2011) and Alexander *et al.* (2010), this study was contemporary in nature and was carried out post-establishment of the first *Shari'ah*-compliant Islamic bank in Germany.

Two other studies from Evens (2014) and Yildiz (2014) were relevant to the broader topic of Islamic banking and finance. However, Evens (2014) approached Islamic insurance topic from only the marketing perspective. Therefore, the current study took a broader focus and used different data sets to analyze the retail Islamic banking and finance market in Germany. On the other hand, Yildiz's (2014) study only relied on ten qualitative interviewees and the scope of the study was restricted to the examination of the co-existence of Islamic banking system in a secular conventional system. The current study embraced a broader scope because it focused on retail Islamic banking in Germany (targeting general public retail consumers and Muslim umbrella organizations) and examined the reasons for the success of the Islamic banking in the United Kingdom. This study also examined the important success determinants for Islamic banking in the German market. Moreover, the current study was a mixed methods study.

In the review of literature citing empirical studies relevant to Islamic banking and finance in Germany reviewed only a few studies explaining research methodologies and data analysis techniques. Studies by Farhoush and Schmidt (2011), Alexander *et al.* (2010), Evens (2014) and Yildiz (2014) were the exceptions. The shortcomings of Farhoush and Schmidt's (2011) study were that they conducted pilot interviews only in the German city of Cologne and respondents were asked specific qualitative questions about the demand of Islamic mortgage products. Farhoush and Schmidt validated the study based only on responses collected in this manner. It would have been appropriate to diversify the respondents of the pilot study for additional meaningful insights. Moreover, the study only incorporated three qualitative questions, which is a far lower number than other studies relevant to Islamic banking and finance conducted in different countries (Rahman,2012; Almutairi, 2010 and

Hasan, 2011). Alternatively, the current study uses well-balanced quantitative and qualitative techniques to thoroughly address the research topic.

As highlighted above, few studies have explored the success factors of Islamic banking in Germany although the need is evident in view of the formal start of Islamic banking in Germany. Therefore, the proposed study focuses on Islamic banking in the context of the United Kingdom's experience with Islamic banking since the establishment of the first *Shari'ah*-compliant bank in the United Kingdom in 2004. Moreover, in the absence of scientific and well-established studies, limited literature on Islamic banking in Germany suggests that the known facts need to be further investigated and analyzed.

The existing literature shows that no study has identified the different challenges that Islamic banking may face in secular environments where conventional banking has deep roots and a long history of financial intermediation. The findings from previous studies on Islamic banking are inconclusive in this regard and varying data exists on the level of awareness about the Muslims about Islamic banking (Wackerbeck & Heimer, 2006; cited in Wurst, 2011; IFIBAF, 2010; cited in Casper, 2014 and Ernst *et al.*, 2013). In addition, past studies do not contain up-to-date information as they were conducted in 2006, 2008, and 2009 (Wackerbeck & Heimer, cited in Wurst, 2011; Booz & Company, cited in PwC, 2008 and Haug *et al.*,2009). It has been widely acknowledged that there is demand for Islamic financial products in Germany despite failed attempts to reach the interested demographic (Farhoush & Schmidt, 2011; Casper, 2014; El-Mogaddedi, 2010 and PwC, 2008). The aim of this study was to analyze the perceptions of Muslims in Germany toward Islamic banking and finance and to determine the success factors of Islamic banking in Germany and the United Kingdom.

6.5 Concluding Remarks

Based on the discussion above, it can be concluded that the topic of Islamic banking and finance has recently gained attention in some academic circles in Germany. However, at present, different researchers have examined the German market with a special focus on the Turkish community and their findings show mixed results concerning the level of awareness, market potential, and the willingness of the Muslims to buy *Shari'ah*-compliant products and services. The available literature revealed that almost all of the discussed studies were conducted prior to the establishment of the first *Shari'ah*-compliant KT Bank AG in 2015. Most importantly, no previous study has addressed issues such as the challenges associated with Islamic banking in Germany and the European Union, the perceptions of Muslim umbrella organizations, and the future of Islamic banking in Germany. The current study aimed to close the gap identified in the literature by thoroughly analyzing the German retail Islamic banking and finance market.

The following chapter provides a review of the theoretical framework and research methodologies applicable to this study.

Chapter 7: Theoretical Framework and Research Methodology

7.1 Introduction

The purpose of Chapter 7 is to establish the theoretical framework and research methodology that provide the foundation of the current study. Chapter 7 provides an explanation of the research methodology consistent with the specific rules and course of action required to carry out this study, and an overview of quantitative and qualitative research methodologies and the relevance of each to this study. Chapter 7 also provides a theoretical framework based on the Theory of Planned Behavior (TPB), followed by an overview of the conceptual model. Various methods of data collection, questionnaire design, and the practical steps applied to data collection, as well as a discussion of the different analysis techniques of quantitative and qualitative data will also be provided in Chapter 7, which will conclude with a chapter summary.

7.2 Research Methodology

The word *methodology* indicates different methods and principles employed for the purposes of conducting scientific research (Saunders *et al.*, 2012). Gould and Kolb (1964:425) asserted the definition of methodology as "the systematic and logical study of the principles guiding scientific and philosophical investigation." The methodology applied to any given scientific research project depends upon the nature and complexity of the research questions. Therefore, a research question should be concisely addressed to draw conclusions by employing the appropriate research methods. According to Williams (2007), research methodology is a prescribed course of action taken by the researcher to conduct a research project. Furthermore, Blaug (1992: xii) defined methodology as:

> "... a study of the relationship between theoretical concepts and warranted conclusions about the real word; in particular, methodology is that branch of economics where we examine the ways in which economists justify theories and the reasons they offer for preferring one theory over another; methodology is both a descript discipline – 'this is what economist do' – and a prescriptive one – 'this is what economist should do to advance economics'."

7.3 Methods Used in this Research

There are two main empirical research types in social sciences: quantitative and qualitative (Saunders *et al.*, 2012). Because the framework for this study aimed to conduct an analysis of the knowledge, attitudes, and practices of consumers concerning retail banking products, and to assess the barriers to Islamic banking in Germany both quantitative and qualitative approaches are applicable and have been applied in this study. The rationale of conducting a mixed-methods study that included a combination of qualitative and quantitative research was to improve validity and accuracy of the results. Using a combination of the two also provided triangulation of the data (Abdullah, 2007). Saunders *et al.* (2012) argued that a good research uses combination of quantitative and qualitative methods. As such, using either method alone would not have been sufficient to gather information to address the research questions proposed by this study. The logic applied to including a qualitative approach was that it is the appropriate methodology to gain full understanding of the topic and key insights from the perspective of industry leaders and experts. Likewise, the logic applied to including a quantitative approach was that the quantitative approach is appropriate to addressing the hypotheses proposed by this study.

7.3.1 Quantitative Approach

In a quantitative approach, a researcher identifies suitable variables, finds suitable testing instruments, and applies the appropriate statistical measures (Malhotra & Birks, 2006). Kothari (1990) stated that the quantitative approach is used to generate data in quantitative form, which can then be analyzed in a rigid fashion using quantitative analysis. This approach is also known as deductive and requires that a lot of attention be placed on procedures and methodology (Saunders *et al.*, 2012).

7.3.2 Qualitative Approach

According to Malhotra and Birks (2006) a qualitative research approach is exploratory in nature and is usually undertaken with small samples for the purpose of understanding and highlighting new insights to address research questions. The qualitative research approach is an inductive method through which the researcher leverages tools that enable the collection of rich data describing attitudes, perceptions, or experience relevant to answering the research questions. Such tools include case studies, focused group discussions, and semi-structured interviews. Qualitative research leverages in-depth interviews with open-ended questions to collect richer information through which to answer the research question(s) because the researcher has the opportunity to ask follow-up questions intended to get the interviewee to clarify or expand upon on an answer already given (Folkestad 2008; Leedy & Ormand, 2010).

7.4 Theoretical Framework: Theory of Planned Behavior

The theoretical framework of a study establishes the guidelines for conducting research and identifying variables, statistical relationships to be examined, tools for data collection, and scientific approaches to data analysis and interpretation. The Theory of Planned Behavior provides a theoretical framework for the current study.

All human actions are guided by certain attitudes and intentions. Figure 9 depicts three variables that influence the intention to engage in a particular behavior: attitude toward the behavior, subjective norms (social context or influence), and perceived behavioral control. Alam *et al.* (2012:1032) concluded that "the more favorable the attitude and subjective norm and the greater the perceived control, the stronger the person's intention to perform the behavior in question. Given a sufficient degree of actual control over the behavior, people are expected to carry out their intentions when opportunity arises. Intention is, thus, assumed to be the immediate antecedent of behavior." Thus, from Figure 9, the conclusion can be made that customer behavior is based on intention. Intention is influenced by a number of factors including social context, religious obligations, and personal observations.

Figure 9: Theory of Planned Behavior (TPB)

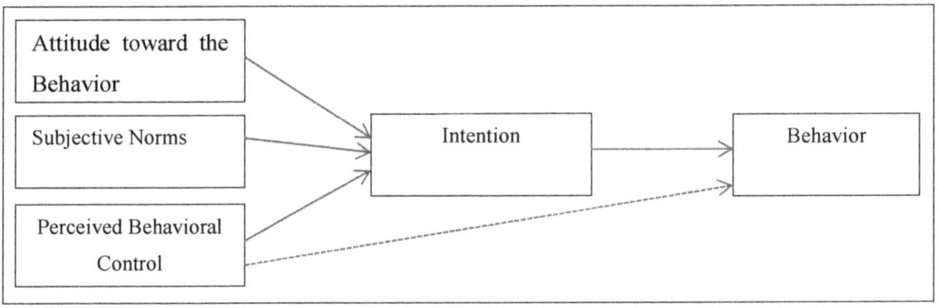

Source: Adapted from Ajzen (1991)

The Theory of Planned Behavior is an extended form of the Theory of Reasoned Action (TRA), which was originally developed by Fishbein and Ajzen in 1975 and revisited by Ajzen and Fishbein in 1980 (Ajzen,1991). The perceived behavioral control dimension is an addition to the original Theory of Planned Behavior introduced in 1975. Theory of Reasoned Action states that a consumer has different alternatives, choices, and decision to make when opting to purchase a particular product or service, and is based on the relationship of these alternatives with the intentions of the individual. As earlier mentioned, the Theory of Reasoned Actions has been used in various studies; however, many researchers have also used an updated version of the theory, the Theory of Planned Behavior for example, which is also supported by empirical evidence in the areas of consumption and psychology (*Alam et al.*, 2012). Therefore, the scope of the Theory of Reasoned Action is not limited to the aforementioned fields but extends to the increased popularity of organic foods, consumption of halal foods, and even online purchasing behavior. Many researchers, including Newas (2014) and Gait (2009), have used the Theory of Theory of Reasoned Actions in the area of consumer decision making.

7.5 Proposed Conceptual Framework for this Study

As mentioned earlier the theoretical framework for the current study is based on the Theory of Planned Behavior. Figure 10 presents a proposed conceptual framework for this study. This model is based on different factors including:

- Knowledge and awareness level
- Perceptions of consumers
- Willingness to switch (toward Islamic banking)
- Relevance of Islamic products
- Religious obligations
- Benefits of Islamic finance for Muslims

For the purposes of this study, the level of knowledge, awareness, and perceptions of consumers refers to that of only Muslims living in Germany and assumes that participants have some information and familiarity and possess, at a minimum, a theoretical awareness of and familiarity with the existence of Islamic banking and finance. The factors identified by the Theory of Planned Behavior contribute to a particular attitude about the adoption of Islamic banking products and whether Muslims living in Germany perceive such products as a good value proposition so that they are willing to switch to Islamic banking products once relevant products are offered to them. As can be seen in Figure 10, religious obligation is another factor that affects the choices of individuals and the degree of religious obligation indicates the level of intended compliance with the basic Islamic principles (Amin *et al.*, 2011).

Figure 10: Proposed Conceptual Framework

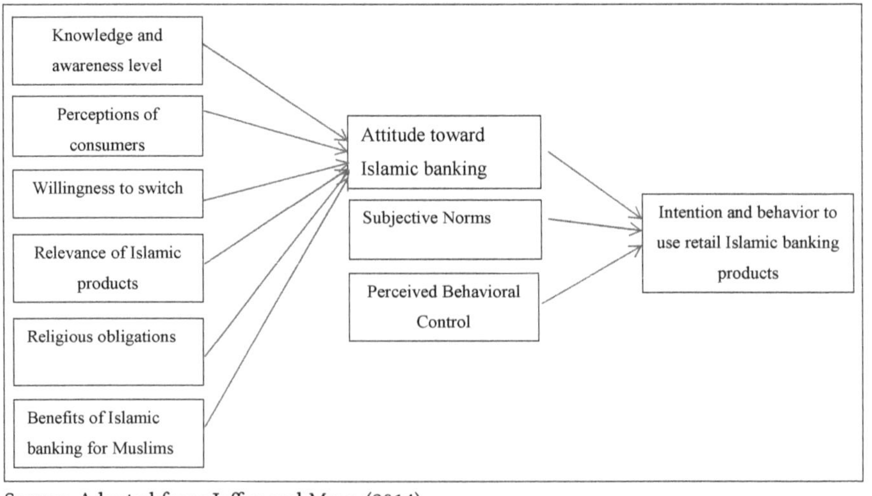

Source: Adapted from Jaffar and Musa (2014)

The theoretical framework (please see Figure 10) outlined for the current study assumes that degree of religious obligation is directly connected with the use of (or willingness to use) Islamic retail banking products. The theoretical framework also assumes that the use of Islamic banking products will bring benefits for Muslims, individually and collectively, by providing them with attractive alternative products that could provide them with religious satisfaction and enable compliance to the Islamic principles they value. The theoretical framework will also provide an opportunity to those Muslims who are not currently using financial products because of their beliefs.

7.6 Methods of Data Collection

Questionnaires will be used for both quantitative and qualitative data collection.

7.6.1 Population and Sampling

For the purpose of this study, total population of Muslims living in Germany is identified as the population. Sekaran (2003:266) stated that population is the total collective of any given variable from which a smaller segment (sample) is drawn for the purposes of conducting research, and defines sampling as "a subgroup or subset of the population. By studying the sample, the researcher would be able to draw conclusions that would be generalizable to the population of interest."

Three different techniques were used to gather data for this study. The data gathering process for retail banking consumers commenced at the end of May 2015 and lasted until the end of July 2015. Data collection for semi-structured interviews began on 15 December 2014 and continued until the end of June 2015. Moreover, the data collection from Muslim organizations in Germany began in June 2015 and ended in July 2015.

7.6.2 Sample Size for Retail Banking Survey

The following calculation, adapted from Abduh and Omar (2012) and Isreal (1992), was used to calculate appropriate sample for this study:

$$n_0 = \frac{z^2pq}{e^2}$$

Where:

$n0$ = sample size
Z = Z-value of α (α in this study is corresponds to 1.96 at 95% confidence level)
P = Variability (value of variability in this study is 0.5 and this is safest possible assumption at 95 per cent confidence level)
q = 1-p
e = chances of error or sampling error tolerated in this study is 0.05

Therefore, sample size is equal to

$$n_0 = \frac{z^2pq}{e^2} = \frac{(1.96)^2(0.5)(0.5)}{(0.05)^2}$$

$$=385$$

The sample of consumers was calculated using a 95% confidence level. Therefore, the intention was to gather minimum data of 385 respondents. However, the actual sample size was 402.

7.6.3 Pilot Study

Before taking steps to conduct the field survey, a pilot study of the questionnaire was completed with a sample size of 25 respondents, which corresponds about 6 per cent of the total sample size used in this study. The purpose of the pilot study was to ensure that the respondents understood the purpose, content, and sequence of the questions in questionnaire. After the pilot study concluded a few adjustments were made on the basis of recommendations given by respondents, and were implemented to improve the questionnaire by making the questions more meaningful and systematic.

7.6.4 Sample Size for Muslim Umbrella Organizations Survey

For the purpose of the current study, Muslim umbrella organizations in Germany were considered a population from which a sample was selected. A questionnaire was designed to seek required information. Based on the information availability about the organizations (name, address, phone, and email) a total of 40 organizations were selected. These organizations have a nationwide footprint and represent a variety of ethnic groups.

The questionnaire for Muslim organizations consisted of eight questions ranging from general awareness to product relevant questions.

7.6.5 Sample Size for Semi-Structured Interviews

As semi-structured interviews are normally considered appropriate to address highly specialized research questions interviewees were selected using purposeful sampling in which participants were selected based on their potential for possessing expert knowledge and information on the subject matter under investigation (Marshall, 1996). However, there is no prescribed rule regarding the number of interviews required to satisfy the research. For instance, Mason (2010) stated that average PhD theses employed approximately thirty-one interviews but the larger sample size is not the guarantee to achieve stated objectives and even with minimum interview sample such as three it could be possible to draw desired conclusions. Therefore, in order to comprehensively address the research questions and hypothesis, the researcher decided to conduct 15 semi-structured interviews but interviewing concluded with the 13th interview. The interviewees were chosen from four countries Germany, the United Kingdom, Turkey, and Saudi Arabia and came from the Islamic banking, regulatory, legal and corporate environment. After each interview, a text transcript of the interview was prepared and sent to the interviewee for review and confirmation.

7.7 Questionnaire Design

The retail banking questionnaire was divided into five parts and posed a total of 22 questions. Part one was designed to garner general banking and finance information from the respondent and consisted of two questions. The second part aimed to gather information regarding the perceptions of consumers about Islamic banking and had nine questions. The purpose of the third part was to ascertain information about consumers' willingness to switch to Islamic banking and consisted of three questions. The fourth part concerned the relevance of Islamic products and services for consumers and consisted of one question. The fifth and final part was designed to collect demographic and personal information and consisted of seven questions.

A seven-point Likert scale was used in the questionnaire. Malhotra and Birks (2006) stated that a seven-point Likert scale was suitable for those surveys that seek to find consumer attitude and perceptions toward products and services by measuring broad generalizations. Hence, for this questionnaire, scale one (1) indicates very strongly disagree whereas scale seven (7) very strongly agree for the eight questions. There were also five multiple-choice questions where respondents had the option to select more than one answer. Including eight scale questions there were 22 questions, a total of seventeen questions were single choices could be selected.

However, in the Muslim umbrella organizations questionnaire, two questions were multiple choice and the remaining four questions required respondents to select a single answer. Respondents were also provided with blank space to add further comments or answers if the choice they preferred was not included in the available list. Therefore, both questionnaires were constructed using simple, closed-ended questions.

7.7.1. Translation of the Questionnaires

Retail banking and Muslim organization questionnaires were translated from English to German by an individual with competencies in both the German and English languages. However, the retail banking questionnaire was also translated into Turkish to increase the response rate. To ensure the reliability and validity of the both questionnaires, the translated questionnaires were reviewed and verified by full-time university professors with a proficient command of the German, English, and Turkish languages. Suggestions provided by these experts were applied accordingly.

7.7.2 Validity and Reliability of the Instrument

Validity and reliability are two key considerations researchers must consider when conducting scientific research. In the pilot study, both aspects were addressed and attention was paid to whether respondents from various educational and occupational backgrounds had any issues concerning the questionnaire design, language, or sequence of questions. Cronbach's Alpha, which is also known as Alpha coefficient, is used to measure the reliability of the scale, which is also called an internal consistency of the scale in this study (Sekaran, 2003). This measure reveals how closely different items in a questionnaire correlate with other items in the questionnaire. If the value of Cronbach's Alpha is greater than 0.7 it means that the scale has high level of reliability (Gait, 2009). Alternatively, Malhotra and Birks (2006) suggested that any value of Cronbach's Alpha below 0.6 shows lack of consistency and reliability. The value of Cronbach's Alpha calculated for this study is above 0.7, which means that the scale revealed a high level of reliability.

7.7.3 Advantages and Disadvantages of Questionnaire Method

A self-administered questionnaire serves multiple objectives. It is flexible enough to gather a desired set of data and allows the researcher the liberty of selecting the best-suited variables. It also provides an option for data collection that is relatively inexpensive and less time consuming when compared with many other methods available such as focused group interviews. A questionnaire with simple, easy to understand questions can improve the accuracy of research. However, such a questionnaire could be misleading if the structure of the questionnaire is inappropriate or reflects researcher bias or the content is difficult for respondents to comprehend. To validate the questionnaire and mitigate bias, an independent third party reviewed the questions.

7.7.4 Advantages and Disadvantages of Semi-Structured Interviews

The fundamental advantage of data collection through semi-structured interviews is extraction of detail information, which may not be possible through other methods such as field surveys. Furthermore, in-depth interviews allow the researcher to ask some unstructured questions relating to the some other aspect of the topic not directly addressed by a response to the original, structured questions.

Woods (2011) has highlighted some disadvantages of semi-structured interviews such as it can be time-intensive, spontaneous questions asked may be difficult to quantify and analyze, and the ability of the interviewer to conduct an interview in a proper way and without an element of bias. The interview questions must also be clear and free of researcher bias so as not to lead the respondent to a specific answer.

7.7.5 Research Ethics

For this study primary data collection through expert interviews and field surveys was carried out, therefore ethical considerations were very important while dealing with study participants. First, participants were assured of confidentially and an authorization letter from the university was provided so participants could understand the purpose of the study. For expert interviews, proper steps were taken prior to meet or telephone such as contacting them on email and fixing appointments.

7.8 Practical Steps of Conducting the Field Survey

As already discussed, More than 4.76 million Muslims living Germany. The majority of the almost 5 million Muslim residents lived in the provinces of North Rhine-Westphalia and Hessen. Keeping in mind the largest Muslim populations, Berlin, Hamburg, Duisburg, Essen, Duesseldorf, Munich, Frankfurt am Main, Cologne, and Bochum were selected as geographic locations in which to engage in data collection. Moreover, careful consideration was taken to ensure that the respondents were selected randomly. Locations that would provide the maximum chances to find Muslims in each city were selected for the purposes of conducting random samplings from those populations:

i. Mosques
ii. Turkish kebab shops and Muslim restaurants
iii. Grocery shops
iv. Muslim community organizations
v. Muslim concentrated areas

A self-administered questionnaire was prepared and distributed to the respondents in the above-mentioned locations along with the authorization letter stating the purpose of the study, which was issued by the university. In the early phase of data collection, a low response rate from the field survey resulted in the decision to expand the sample size. To increase the response rate the same questionnaire was also created online in English and German. A pre-test was made to ensure the validity and reliability of the online instrument. There were two main reasons to create the questionnaires online. The aim was to reach the maximum number of potential participants in other cities apart from above stated cities and to reach those people who were not willing to fill the questionnaire out on a paper-based form and preferred an online option. The link for the retail banking questionnaire was randomly sent through e-mail to organizations (including cultural organizations) and various people living in Germany (200 questionnaires were filled on paper and 250 were filled online). On the other hand, the link of questionnaire about Muslim organizations was sent only to Muslim umbrella organizations (for instance, *Islamrat für die BRD*, *Ditib* and *Islamische Glaubensgemeinschaft Baden-Württemberg*). Six hundred retail banking questionnaires were distributed and 450 responses were received. Among 600 returned survey forms 402 were usable forms, thus providing a 67% response rate.

40 Muslim umbrella organizations were contacted but only 8 organizations filled the questionnaires, returning a 20% response rate. For qualitative research, 24 experts were contacted and 15 agreed to take part in the interviews. However, two interviews were unusable for analysis and were not included in the data for this study.

7.9 Data Analysis Methodology

Different analysis techniques for quantitative and qualitative data are discussed in detail in the following section.

7.9.1 Analysis of Quantitative Data

After the data collection phase, the next step was to analyze the data to draw meaningful conclusions. As this study combined quantitative and qualitative research techniques different analysis tools and methods were applied to each set of data. For retail banking and Muslim organizations questionnaire the latest version (22) of Statistical Package for Social Sciences (SPSS) software was used. Use of this software is common practice in academic research in social sciences (Bryman & Cramer, 2001). Depending on the nature and format of the questions answered the appropriate statistical techniques applied for data analysis. Such techniques ranged from basic descriptive statistics to inferential statistics of more complexity and include Analysis of Variance (ANOVA) and correlation analysis. The use of descriptive statistics involves the use of measures such as mean, median, percentage, and frequency, and the application of tables and graphs. First, all the survey responses were transcribed in an Excel sheet and then coded before being loaded into the SPSS program.

Different quantitative and qualitative methods have been applied in past research, by various researchers, depending upon the aim of the study, the nature of questionnaire employed, and the sample size used in the study. This study employed descriptive analysis, which was one method used by Rosenblatt *et al.* (1988), Turnbull and Gibbs (1989), Laroche (1993), Yavas and Kaynak (1993), Owusu-Frimpong (1999), Omer (1992), Naser, Jamal and Al-Khatib (1999), Hamid, Nordin Zainuddin, Jahya and Ramayah (2004) and Okumus (2005). This study also applied ANOVA as one of the analysis techniques. ANOVA was used by Gerrard and Cunningham (2001). Descriptive statistics provide results that are easily explained and understood. These techniques were best suited to this study because one of the fundamental research questions sought to investigate the knowledge, attitude and perceptions of consumers as relevant to Islamic banking.

7.9.2 Analysis of Semi-Structured Interviews

In academic literature there are varieties of methods used to analyze the qualitative data. For instance, Saunders *et al.* (2012) suggest a three step processes to analyze the data, which was designed by Miles and Huberman (1994). The first step was data reduction in which a researcher tries to discard irrelevant data gathered from different sources like interview transcripts, observations, and field notes. Developing a good display of data and, for this purpose, different techniques could be used was the second step. For example, one might develop mind mapping, tables, graphs, and networks to display data. The third step was drawing conclusions and developing a summary on the basis of data reduction and display.

Folkestad (2008) suggested that a *quote-research method* is also widely used in social sciences. It is particularly useful when a researcher is not systematizing transcripts.

Woods (2011) mentioned different approaches for qualitative data analysis such as:

- Thematic analysis (also called content analysis)
- Discourse analysis
- Grounded theory

In thematic or content analysis the researcher analyzes interviews by making two important decisions (Woods, 2011). First, the decision must be made to identify themes by reading the data obtained through interviews and grouping similar themes into similar categories. Different categories of data are made on the basis of different codes generated by the researcher as they identify keywords, paragraphs, and unique aspects. Second, a decision must be made to analyze the interviewee independently or use cross-case analysis. The aim of thematic analysis is to reduce large text into meaningful information. Alhojailan (2012:40) explains thematic analysis as:

> "Thematic Analysis is considered the most appropriate for any study that seeks to discover using interpretations. It provides a systematic element to data analysis. It allows the researcher to associate an analysis of the frequency of a theme with one of the whole content."

Braun and Clarke (2006) suggested six phases in thematic analysis of qualitative data. The first phase dealt with understanding the data, which included transcription and the identification of important ideas. In the second phase, important codes were generated from the initial data. In the third phase, the researcher identified common themes. And in the fourth phase, themes were reviewed and compared with the earlier generated codes. In the fifth phase, suitable descriptions were assigned to each theme. Finally, in phase six, a report was prepared to articulate the important essence of the qualitative analysis.

The second approach to analyzing qualitative data is discourse analysis. This method seems similar to thematic analysis up to but not including the theme development stage. With this method the researcher asks additional questions, such as why themes are expressed or grouped in a particular pattern. The third possible approach to analysis of qualitative data is the grounded theory approach. The main feature of grounded theory is that data analysis is carried out parallel to data collection phase

(Alhojailan, 2012). Thus, this method is not suitable in those researches where the goal of researcher is to conduct comparative analysis of different sets of data.

Mainly thematic and content analysis approaches were leveraged for qualitative analysis in this study, and were applied by using inductive processes. Inductive processes require one to analyze all the answers obtained and then try to merge or combine meaningful units or codes to reduce data. Karim and Affif (2006) and Gait and Worthington (2008) used this method in their researches exploring Islamic finance. This method is suitable to this study because of the nature of the data. Therefore, it was easy to generate codes by analyzing the answers and developing important themes. Grounded theory is not appropriate to this study because the aim of this research is to compare findings of expert interviews, retail banking survey, and responses of Muslim umbrella organizations, which is only possible after the collection of data is complete. The discourse analysis approach is also not appropriate because the aim of the current study is to analyze the responses of respondents by developing themes and categories. The objective is not to analyze why the responding experts provided certain statements.

Three data collection methodologies were used. The three methods generated a minimum 47 questions. In order to achieve the research objectives, 30 data collection questions were aligned specifically with the research questions. Among the 30 data collection questions in this subset, 13 questions were included in the consumer retail banking survey, 11 questions were included in the qualitative interview protocol, and 6 questions were included in the Muslim umbrella organizations survey. Thus, it can be concluded that all three data collection methodologies had a fair representation in the greater collection of the questions designed to collect data for this study.

7.10 Concluding Remarks

In summary, this research uses the Theory of Planned Behavior as a foundation for the theoretical framework. A conceptual framework was developed based on the nature of the research questions and the design of the questionnaires. This mixed-methods study employed both quantitative and qualitative research approaches and leveraged three different and unique questionnaires. The first two questionnaires, used for consumer retail banking and Muslim umbrella organizations, were designed to gather quantitative data for quantitative analysis. Expert interviews are based on semi-structured questions and provided data for qualitative analysis.

Chapter 7 provided a discussion of the practical steps taken to collect data based on techniques applied by a variety of researchers to analyze data in past studies. The current study uses descriptive and inferential statistical for quantitative data analysis, and thematic and cluster analysis were applied in qualitative analysis.

Chapter 8 provides a detailed discussion of the empirical analysis of the quantitative data that was collected in the survey responses from retail Islamic banking consumers and Muslim umbrella organizations.

Chapter 8: Empirical Analysis of the Qualitative Data

8.1 Introduction

The purpose of this chapter is to analyze the qualitative data that was gathered through semi-structured interviews to answer the research questions formulated in Chapter 1. As discussed in Chapter 7, a thematic content analysis technique was used to interpret the data collected in 13 semi-structured interviews. This chapter is divided into three main parts and each part deals with a specific research question. In order to better understand the opinions of industry practitioners, responses were grouped into different clusters on the basis of consensus and disagreement in responses to particular issues, and were presented in tabular form.

Following are the 3 research questions that will be answered in this chapter:

4. What are the success factors for Islamic banking and finance in non-Islamic states that have a substantial Muslim population, specifically Germany and the United Kingdom?
5. What challenges are to be expected for Islamic banking in Germany and in the European Union?
6. What will the future of Islamic banking look like in Germany and in the European Union?

Chapter 8 is structured as follows: Part 1 deals with research question 1. In search for a comprehensive answer to the research question several questions were asked of the interviewees. Therefore, Part 1 is further divided into sub sections. Part 2 provides answers to Research Question 2 and addresses the topic of the challenges of Islamic banking in Germany and the European Union. This part also contains several sub sections. Finally, Part 3 discusses the prospects of success of Islamic banking in European countries including Germany, and has five sub sections.

Before a discussion of the research questions and an analysis of the data collected in the interviews, section 8.2 provides profile of the interviewees.

8.2 Profiling of the Interviewees

Thirteen experts and practitioners agreed to take part in the qualitative study (as can be seen in appendix, Table 8.2). These interviewees belonged to diverse sectors of the financial industry and included bankers, corporate leaders, investment professionals, academics, and consultants. Seven interviewees belonged to the banking industry:

- Mr. Uğurlu Soylu (Kuveyt Türk Katılım Bankası A.Ş.)
- Dr. Johannes Engels (BaFin)

- Dr.Muhammad Umer Chapra (Islamic Development Bank)
- Prof. Dr. Abdul Ghafar Ismail (Islamic Development Bank)
- Dr. Nikolaus Siegfried (Slower Capital, Landesbank Berlin AG)
- Dr. Zamir Iqbal (The World Bank Global Islamic Finance Development Center)
- Dr. Fabian Gleisner (Commerz Business Consulting, Commerzbank AG)

Three were from the corporate sector:

- Mr. Andreas Ernst (Enercon GmbH)
- Mr. Waheed Qasir (Maxim Corporate Finance LLP)
- Mrs. Nafisa Chaudhry (FMF Islamic Banking)

One was from the consultancy industry: Prof.Dr. Humayon Dar (Edbiz Corporation), and one each was from academia: Prof. Dr. Volker Nienhaus[9] (International Center for Islamic Finance) and Mr. Miryusup Abdullaev[10] (Deutsche Börse Group, in the stock market). Eight interviewees were from Germany, two were from the United Kingdom, one was from Turkey, and two were from Saudi Arabia. In addition to this, nine interviewees were in top management positions that included titles such as managing director, CEO, president, or business unit head. Specific details about industry, position, and country of each interview participant can be seen in the appendix for Table 8.2.

Part 1: Research Question 1
What are the success factors for Islamic banking and finance in non-Islamic states that have a substantial Muslim population, specifically Germany and the United Kingdom?

The findings of this study showed that the success factors for Islamic banking and finance in the United Kingdom are: the proactive roles of the government and its institutions, availability of the *Shari'ah*-sensitive consumers, presence of sound infrastructure and position of the United Kingdom as a global international financial intermediation center. The findings of this study revealed that the success factors for Islamic banking and finance in Germany are: presence of largest Muslim population, demand for *Shari'ah*-compliant products and services (especially in the Turkish community), quality and pricing of Islamic products, growing awareness about Islamic finance in Germany, and the value proposition of Islamic finance as an ethical finance option.

---

9 Nienhaus stated that "You may reproduce this email plus the transcribed answers to your questions as a bundle in an appendix of your thesis, but not the answers alone. The answers alone would not reproduce my reaction to your questionnaire in an appropriate manner" (replied via email on 18.01.2016).

10 It should be remembered that the views expressed by these interviewees especially Mr. Miryusup Abdullaev are their personal views and therefore does not represent the official policies of their respective institutions.

The following sections provide an overview of the data analyzed to draw this conclusion. In total 13 interviewees were asked six questions to address Research Question 1.

8.3 Key Reasons of Islamic Banking Success in the United Kingdom

The purpose of the interviews was to ask the practitioners to identify what they believed to be the key factors that played an important role in the development and success of the Islamic financial industry in the United Kingdom. Of the 13 participants surveyed for this study only 9 responded to the question about key reasons of Islamic banking success in the UK, which were grouped into two clusters on the basis of commonalities and differences.

Six out of nine interviewees expressed a perception that the success of Islamic banking and finance in the United Kingdom was fostered by such factors as: Islamic finance occurs in a risk-sharing system, and the United Kingdom took a proactive approach to regulatory flexibility. These are grouped in Cluster 1. Some interviewees, like Waheed Qasir who was President of Maxim Corporate Finance LLP UK, were among early advocates for Islamic finance in the United Kingdom and helped spur initiatives to create awareness in the Muslim community. Mr. Qasir, was on committees set up by the United Kingdom's government to propose solutions concerning various regulatory hurdles, including the issue of the double stamp duty tax.

Therefore, two themes were developed on the basis of views expressed in Cluster 1. First, the success of Islamic banking in the United Kingdom resulted from strong political will, the proactive role of the government, and support provided by financial institutions such as the Bank of England. Second, the recent financial crisis highlighted the weaknesses of the conventional financial system and many people in the government and the financial industry considered Islamic finance a valuable financial model.

Three interviewees out of nine are grouped in Cluster 2 because their views about the factors promoting the success of Islamic banking in the United Kingdom differed from those views expressed in Cluster 1. The three interviewees stated that Muslims in the United Kingdom, particularly those from the Indian sub-continent, have a higher tendency to prefer *Shari'ah*-compliant products than do Muslims living in Germany (mainly those Muslims from Turkish origin). A relevant factor may be that the three interviewees who represent the views in Cluster 2 were Germans and living and working in Germany, and two of them (Nafisa Chaudhry and Dr. Nikolaus Siegfried) had practical experience dealing with Islamic banking and finance products. Therefore, we can conclude that this is an important factor even though the demand exhibited by the Muslim community in the United Kingdom indicates that the preference for *Shari'ah*-compliant products and services is not a key driver for the success of Islamic banking.

8.4 Important Drivers for the Development of Islamic Banking in Europe

In order to answer Research Question 1, stated earlier in Part 1, the interviewees were further asked to name important drivers for the development of Islamic banking in Europe. Of the 13 participants surveyed for this study ten interviewees expressed their opinions about different factors that might play a significant role for the development of Islamic banking products and services in Germany and the European Union. The answers are grouped into two main clusters on the basis of similarities and differences concerning key underlying factors.

In Cluster 1, seven interviewees cited a number of factors ranging from the availability of sufficient human capital to the flexibility in the regulators' approach toward Islamic finance and creating an enabling environment. From these answers, three themes were generated. First, availability of sound infrastructure and policy were the key factors in the success of Islamic banking in the United Kingdom. Second, the United Kingdom and other European countries took advantage of their strategic positions to convince investors to invest in *Shari'ah*-compliant products and services. Finally, many interviewees believed that the success of Islamic banking in the United Kingdom was primarily due to the demand for Islamic banking and finance products. Therefore, these interviewees also believed that effective promotion of the Islamic banking industry contributed in the success of in Islamic banking the United Kingdom.

Alternatively, three interviewees held a different point of view and are grouped in Cluster 2. For example, Dr.Muhammad Umer Chapra, an eminent Islamic economist and the advisor to The Islamic Development Bank (IDB) based in Jeddah, stated that Islamic banking and finance has emerged as a viable alternative to conventional banking, especially after the recent financial crisis. Chapra also pointed out that different terms such as *risk-sharing finance*, *participating finance*, or *ethical banking* apply when describing or naming Islamic banking and finance products and institutions. His underlying message was to use neutral names in the European Union to avoid misconceptions about Islamic finance. Hence, according to Chapra, unique features of the Islamic financial system are driving forces in the development of Islamic finance in the European Union.

Nafisa Chaudhry, who was associated with FMF Islamic finance in Germany and now works as a freelance consultant, stated that the scope of Islamic banking and finance should be broader and should include the ethical perspective of banking to attract non-Muslims. Finally, Dr. Zamir Iqbal, Head of The World Bank Global Islamic Finance Development Center (GIFDC) based in Istanbul, argued that financial literacy of relevant stakeholders is a key factor. The inherent features of Islamic finance such as the prohibition of interest and the avoidance of excessive debt, *Gharar*, and uncertainty are important drivers for the development of Islamic banking in Europe.

8.5 Role and Influence of Religion and Countries of Origin on Islamic Banking

As the research question stated in Part 1 was concerned with the success factors for Islamic banking and finance in non-Muslim states like the United Kingdom and Germany, the interviewees were asked whether religion and countries of origin also constituted important success factors. In Islamic financial circles it has been debated that Muslims living in the United Kingdom exhibit a special interest in Islamic banking while Muslims in other European countries have shown low interest. Therefore, interviewees were asked whether or not they thought that the difference in demand patterns for Islamic banking products and services in the United Kingdom compared to Germany could be ascribable to the users' countries of origin. Of the 13 participants surveyed for this study, ten interviewees responded to this question and those responses were grouped into three clusters.

Half (50%) of the interviewees (5 of 10) showed consensus as all stated that the countries of origin for Muslims living in either Germany or the United Kingdom do play an important role in the level of demand for Islamic banking and finance products seen in each country. Therefore, these opinions were grouped in Cluster 1. Furthermore, two themes were developed. First, demography and religious characteristics of Muslims in the United Kingdom are behind the demand of Islamic products. Second, the Turkish community in Germany exhibits low demand of Islamic banking, an argument is strongly expressed by Dr. Nikolaus Siegfried, a former Senior Analyst at Landesbank Berlin AG, who was part of a team that issued the QES *Shari'ah*-compliant Islamic finance certificate in Germany in 2011, which was later terminated by the bank due to low demand from consumers.

Two interviewees disagreed with the statements mentioned in Cluster 1 and argued that consumers' awareness is more important than consumers' country of origin. These insights are grouped in Cluster 2. It should be noted that both interviewees (Prof Dr. Abdul Ghafar Ismail, Head of the Research Division at IDB and Dr. Zamir Iqbal head at GIFDC) did not have a deep understanding of Germany's or the United Kingdom's financial environment. However, both shared key insights about the global Islamic finance industry and are well respected in the field due to important contributions each has made to the body of literature discussing Islamic banking and finance.

Three out of 10 interviewees were grouped into Cluster 3 because of the different perspective they held from the rest of the interviewees in Cluster 1 and Cluster 2. Prof. Dr. Volker Nienhaus, adjunct professor at the International Center for Islamic Finance (INCEIF), was not sure whether country of origin contributed to higher demand in the United Kingdom. However, the rest of the interviewees stated that demand for Islamic products depends primarily on the quality and pricing of products. It is worth noting that Mr. Waheed Qasir runs a company in the United Kingdom that deals with Islamic banking and finance, and Mrs. Nafisa Chaudhry has worked at FMF Islamic Banking in Germany. Therefore, both possess insights and experience that frame key insights into the intricacies of their respective Islamic financial markets.

8.6 Retail and Wholesale Islamic Banking Potential in Germany

For a more in-depth discussion of the success factors of Islamic banking and finance in Germany, interviewees were asked to examine the potential for retail and wholesale Islamic banking. As far as the retail and wholesale Islamic banking potential in Germany is concerned, the opinions of twelve interviewees out of 13 (1 interviewee did not commented on the question) are grouped into three clusters.

The overwhelming majority (8 of 12) of the interviewees stated that Germany has huge market potential, as shown in Cluster 1. Among the eight interviewees who argued that Islamic banking and finance has good prospects in Germany, five were from Germany and most of them had worked in Germany. Uğurlu Soylu, Managing Director of Kuveyt Türk Katılım Bankası A.Ş. (at the time of this interview, Kuveyt Türk had applied for full banking license and received the full-bank status in March 2015 and renamed the bank as KT Bank AG), stated that some studies have shown that as such they expect that consumers will demand products such as loans, savings accounts, and business financing products. Dr. Fabian Gleisner, Consultant at Commerz Business Consulting-Commerzbank AG, pointed out that Islamic finance has "large potential" in Germany because of two factors: the Turkish community, which has access to information through Turkish media; and "Islamic finance is an interesting value proposition" for consumers in general.

Contrary to the majority of Cluster 1 interviewees, two (out of twelve) of the interviewees from Cluster 2 stated that the German market has low or limited potential for Islamic finance and presented different arguments to support their assessments. Dr. Nikolaus Siegfried cited the example of the failed attempt made by Landesbank Berlin AG to introduce a *Shari'ah*-compliant investment certificate in 2011. Prof. Dr. Humayon Dar, Chairman, President and CEO of Edbiz Corporation (an Islamic finance consulting company based in London) pointed to four reasons for little or no demand. Three of the reasons are relevant to the German and European financial environment: 1) Turkish Muslims living in Germany are engaged in low value businesses such as food delivery and restaurants, 2) Turkish Muslims are not well informed about Islamic banking because Islamic banks in Turkey have only 5% market share, and 3) pricing of Islamic financial products is very important for Muslims in Europe, but Islamic financial products are expensive compared to conventional counterparts. The fourth and final reason mentioned was that many Muslims in the European Union lack awareness about *Riba*.

Two (out of twelve) of the interviewees that are grouped in Cluster 3 stated that they do not know what the potential of Islamic finance is in Germany. However,

Dr. Zamir Iqbal pointed out that the commencement of operations at the Turk Kuwait bank (KT Bank AG) indicates reasonable potential.

8.7 Appropriate Islamic Banking Models for the German Market

Chapter 2 provided an overview the various models through which Islamic banking can be introduced. To address assumptions about the existing models interviewees were asked to describe an appropriate model for Germany. Two questions dealt with the issue of selecting an appropriate Islamic banking model for the German market. The focus was on exploring the viability of different models including the establishment of full-fledged Islamic banks, cooperative institutes, credit unions, or Islamic windows at conventional banks. The second question sought an answer to whether the United Kingdom's model of Islamic banking can be implemented in Germany, as discussed in section 8.8. The analysis of data collected for the first two questions also provided evidence to further answer Research Question 1.

Of the 13 participants surveyed for this study, 10 commented on an appropriate Islamic banking model for the German market. The comments are grouped into three clusters.

Six interviewees (60%) argued that more than one model could be suitable for Germany. However, whether or not a model is appropriate depends upon several factors including the level of demand for Islamic financial products and services. It should be noted that some of the interviewees from Germany, namely Nafisa Chaudhry and Miryusup Abdullaev, argued that it would be better to offer Islamic banking products through small institutions to assess whether the market has sufficient potential. Results from such pilot tests would either justify or nullify the perceived need for a full-fledge Islamic bank in the same region.

Contrary to Cluster 1, three interviewees (out of ten) stated that it would be better to offer Islamic financial products and services through a large full-fledge Islamic bank. For example, Dr. Nikolaus Siegfried asserted that cooperatives and community saving experiences were not successful in Germany mainly because there were only a few participants. However, he also stressed that there is lack of demand in Germany. All three interviewees in Cluster 2 were from Germany and two of them work in the banking industry.

Contrary to perceptions expressed by nine of the interviewees, Prof. Dr. Humayon Dar was the only person who suggested that the core markets for Islamic finance are in the Middle East and Far East. Prof. Dr. Dar strongly argued that Islamic banking has little potential in the United Kingdom and Germany, as is depicted in Cluster 3, and supported this claim by stating that in both countries the Muslim population is small. Furthermore, Prof. Dr. Dar pointed out the example of five Islamic investment banks that are currently operating in the United Kingdom but are not "providing real services to Muslims."

8.8 The UK as a Role Model of Islamic Finance for other European Countries

As discussed in section 8.7, when interviewees were asked whether the United Kingdom offers an Islamic banking model for other European countries to follow, ten interviewees out of 13 participants stated their opinions. From this, three clearly differing views emerged, which were grouped in three clusters.

Five of the ten interviewees who offered opinions on the appropriateness of the model are grouped in Cluster 2. The five indicated that the United Kingdom does not offer an Islamic banking model for other European countries to follow. For example, Prof Dr. Abdul Ghafar Ismail and Nafisa Chaudhry argued that each country has a different demand pattern and financial environment. However, they also agreed that the United Kingdom's model is an interesting case study from which to learn about the approach of the government and regulators toward Islamic banking and finance. Prof. Dr. Humayon Dar stated that currently five investment banks are operating in the United Kingdom but they "are not very successful in stimulating the general public."

Only two interviewees stated that the United Kingdom's Islamic banking model could be suitable for implementation in other European countries. However, Waheed Qasir stressed that, "[The] Islamic banking window model has not proved to be successful." Therefore, a full-fledge bank would be the better option. It should be noted that Mr. Waheed Qasir is from the United Kingdom and is well informed about the development of Islamic finance in the United Kingdom over the years. The second interviewee, Dr. Muhammad Umer Chapra (of Saudi Arabia) has, through is scholarly contributions, earned a prominent and respectable position in the Islamic finance industry.

Three interviewees were unable to provide thorough analysis due to their lack of information about the market in the United Kingdom, as can be seen in Cluster 3. However, Dr. Nikolaus Siegfried argued that the United Kingdom provides a special case because the Muslim community has a particular interest in Islamic banking products.

Part 2: Research Question 2
What challenges are to be expected for Islamic banking in Germany and in the European Union?

The findings of this study showed that the Islamic banking and finance in Germany and in the European Union faces a number of challenges such as: lack of awareness about Islamic banking and finance, weak demand, strong competition from conventional counterparts, lack of standardized Islamic financial institution at European level, misconceptions and growing prejudices against Muslims (Islam), a lack of legal and regulatory solutions specific to different Islamic products, and a lack of enabling institutions.

The following sections provide an overview of the data analyzed to draw the conclusion stated above. In total, nine questions were asked to the interviewees in order to answer Research Question 2. Some of the interview questions are specific in nature and were only asked to the most relevant person.

8.9 Challenges for Islamic Banking in Europe

In response to the challenges of Islamic banking in Europe, a total of 11 interviewees expressed their views from 13 participants. In Cluster 1, an overwhelming majority (10 out of 11) of the interviewees mentioned a number of challenges that were summarized into four main challenges: capacity of Islamic financial institutions, negative image of Islam in general, regulatory framework, and low market demand of Islamic banking products. Therefore, three broad themes were generated and can be seen in Cluster 1.

Contrary to the opinions grouped in Cluster 1, only one interviewee (Andreas Ernst, Legal Counsel) stated that, from a legal perspective, there are no challenges to offering Islamic banking and services in Germany. He accentuated that under German law it is possible to draft contracts based on Islamic finance principles. However, dispute resolution may be a challenge. Dr. Nikolaus Siegfried, who is grouped in Cluster 1, stated that there is a "lack of interest from the client side," which might be considered as a challenge for Islamic finance. Dr. Siegfried further stated that there are no regulatory and supervisory challenges, and pointed out the examples of Landesbank Berlin AG and KT Bank AG.

8.10 Legal and Product Development Challenges

In order to determine the specific regulatory challenges that KT Bank AG in Germany faces, Mr. Uğurlu Soylu (Managing Director of KT Bank AG) was asked a question about the tax treatment arising from Islamic mortgage contracts.

Double stamp tax duty (when a bank buys a real estate and then resells it to a consumer and taxes must be paid to the government on both transactions) is the major challenge in Islamic mortgage contacts. This problem was solved in the United Kingdom by amending the law. However, in Germany it is not possible to propose legal changes at present. The bank has managed to overcome this issue by incorporating a special company known as a Special Purpose Vehicle (SPV). With the SPV in place, property will be bought in the name of the SPV and later the bank will sell shares of the property to consumers. As soon as a consumer pays all instalments to the bank, ownership of the property will be transferred to the consumer.

8.11 European Regulatory Frameworks and Space for Islamic Law

A suitable regulatory framework may play an important role for the development of Islamic banking in Germany. Therefore, Mr. Andreas Ernst, Legal Counsel at Enercon GmbH, argued that it is not possible to change European legal systems for the purpose of Islamic banking. However, it is possible to include some Islamic commercial provisions.

8.12 Regulators Approach toward Islamic Banking in Germany

The aim of Part 2 is to ascertain the different challenges of Islamic banking in Germany and the European Union. Therefore, a discussion follows addressing the approach of regulators like BaFin toward the introduction of Islamic banking in Germany.

Uğurlu Soylu, Managing Director at Kuveyt Türk Katılım Bankası A.Ş. (KT Bank AG) agreed with other interviewees who highlighted the fact that financial market regulators in Germany have not played a proactive role. However, it should be noted that BaFin has not posed hurdles, but the application for a bank license took longer than anticipated.

8.13 Legal and Regulatory Requirements

To further address the regulatory approach toward Islamic banking in Germany, Mr. Uğurlu Soylu (Managing Director of KT Bank AG) was asked a question about whether the regulatory requirements to obtain a license were the same for both conventional banks and Islamic banks. As KT Bank AG has recently obtained a full-fledge Islamic banking license Mr. Uğurlu Soylu was the most suitable person to ask for this question. Based on the response, this study found that the licensing procedure is no different for an Islamic Bank than for a conventional bank.

8.14 Political Support to Islamic Banking in Germany

As was discussed in Part 1 of this chapter, one of the main reasons for the success of Islamic banking in the United Kingdom was the political support provided. In order to verify whether the German government provided proactive support to Islamic banking or to the licensing of KT Bank AG. Mr. Uğurlu Soylu (Managing Director of Kuveyt Türk Katılım Bankası A.Ş.) pointed out that the bank did not establish close contacts with the ruling political parties, as management believed that the issuance of a banking license was primarily a legal matter. This argument proved to be correct and BaFin issued a full-banking license to KT Bank AG in March 2015.

As was discussed in Chapter 4, and in the literature review provided in Chapter 6, there is difference in the regulatory approaches to Islamic banking and finance in the United Kingdom and Germany. Therefore, the following three questions were designed to provide an in-depth discussion of the role of BaFin in regulating Islamic banking in Germany. The aim of these questions was to determine whether regulators perspectives toward Islamic banking were a challenge.

8.15 BaFin Policy regarding Issuing Banking License in Germany

According to Dr. Johannes Engels, Senior Policy Officer at BaFin, all financial institutions aiming to start banking business in Germany have to fulfil certain requirements. Therefore, any institution can obtain permission to start operations in Germany by adhering to established rules and procedures.

8.16 BaFin Policy toward Islamic Banking in Germany

According to Dr. Johannes Engels, Senior Policy Officer at BaFin, BaFin treats Islamic banking as a form of business similar to other types of banking institutions operating in the market. Therefore, BaFin has no special requirements for Islamic banking.

8.17 Islamic Banking via European Union Passport in Germany

It should be noted that so far no financial institution has applied to open an Islamic bank in Germany through the European Union passport option. Theoretically, if any bank from the United Kingdom is willing to start a branch in Germany that bank should first contact the local supervisor (for example the Bank of England in the UK) and apply for notification. The notification the Bank of England requests that BaFin allow that bank to commence operations in Germany.

Part 3: Research Question 3
What will be the future of Islamic banking look like in Germany and in the European Union?

The findings of this study showed that the future of Islamic banking in Germany and the European Union is favorable as the message of Islamic finance is spreading beyond Muslim countries. The success of the first *Shari'ah*-compliant Islamic bank, KT Bank AG, will depend on its operating model. However, the growth of Islamic banking and finance in Germany will be slow and gradual. On the other hand, Islamic finance has limited growth potential in the United Kingdom.

The following sections provide an overview of the data analyzed to draw the above conclusion. In total, interviewees were asked five questions designed to answer Research Question 3. Some of the questions have a broader perspective regarding the future of Islamic banking in Europe, but a few questions were specifically designed to analyze the viability of the KT Bank AG in Germany.

8.18 Future of Islamic Banking in Europe

As far as the future of Islamic banking in Europe is concerned, ten interviewees out of 13 participants expressed their views and were grouped into three clusters on the basis of their assessment. Seven interviewees, a vast majority, cited that the future of Islamic banking is bright and are grouped in Cluster 1. However, an important point brought to attention by Mr. Waheed Qasir is that Islamic financial institutions should strive to offer competitive products and services. Moreover, Dr.Muhammad Umer Chapra argued that Islamic banking and finance is gaining attention and refers to the main causes of financial crises, which he said basically stem from the inherent weakness of the conventional financial system.

However, Dr. Nikolaus Siegfried maintains that the future of Islamic banking is not favorable, mainly due to low demand as shown in Cluster 2. Among ten interviewees, Dr. Siegfried held consistent views about the low demand of Islamic banking and finance in Europe.

It should be noted that Prof. Dr. Humayon Dar was the only interviewee out of ten who emphasizes a different perspective about the future of Islamic banking and finance in Europe, as is shown in Cluster 3. In his opinion, the future of Islamic banking and finance lies in the Muslim countries because many of these Muslim countries have less than 1% market share of Islamic banking.

Prof. Dr. Volker Nienhaus stated that different scenarios are possible concerning the future of Islamic banking. However, he did not explain each possibility in detail.

8.19 Success Prospects of KT Bank AG in Germany

As was discussed in Chapter 5, the hallmark of Islamic banking in Germany was the establishment of KT Bank AG in July 2015. On the question of the success prospects of KT Bank AG, seven of the 13 participants surveyed for this study responded to this question. The responses are grouped into two clusters.

Five of the interviewees stated that KT Bank AG will be successful in Germany provided it is well managed and it adopts a suitable operating model. Furthermore, financial viability of the bank and winning consumer trust will also be important factors. It should be taken into account that most of the interviewees in Cluster 1 agreed that competitive products and services will be key differentiating factors.

On the other hand, two interviewees in Cluster 2 stated that KT Bank AG faces different challenges such as gaining market share from conventional banks, because retail clients are considered to be loyal to their current financial institutions. Moreover, meeting expectations of those consumers who are looking for higher returns on their investments would be difficult because currently interest rates are low. Both interviewees have many years of experience dealing with Islamic banking and finance in Germany, the United Kingdom, and internationally.

8.20 Concluding Remarks

The purpose of Chapter 8 was to answer the three qualitative research questions by collecting data in 13 interviewees. Research Question 1 was related to the success factors of Islamic banking in the United Kingdom and Germany. Three factors were identified as determinants of success for Islamic banking and finance in the United Kingdom: 1) the proactive approach on the part of the government, a strategic location in the city of London, and the existence of a religious consumer base, 2) success factors for Islamic banking in Germany included pricing and quality of Islamic financial products, availability of a large Muslim population (the presence of the Turkish community and their potential to use *Shari'ah*-compliant products and services), and 3) a value proposition present in the availability of Islamic banking and finance, and its unique Islamic specific features, for the German consumers.

Regarding Research Question 2, this study found that Islamic banking faces challenges including:

a) A lack of awareness about Islamic banking and finance
b) Weak demand
c) Strong competition from conventional counterparts
d) A lack of standardized Islamic financial institution at European level
e) Misconceptions and growing prejudices against Muslims (Islam)
f) A lack of legal and regulatory solutions specific to different Islamic products
g) A lack of an enabling environment for institutions is a major challenge that Islamic banking and finance will face in Germany and European Union.

From a legal point of view it is possible to incorporate Islamic commercial provisions in the absence of a regulatory framework in financial contracts in Germany. In Germany neither the government nor the BaFin has played a proactive role, unlike government officials and regulators in the United Kingdom. However, there were no obstacles for Islamic banking. Some of the interviewees also pointed out that in Germany and the European Union it is not currently possible to amend laws but it is quite possible to add Islamic commercial provisions to offer Islamic banking and finance products.

Regarding Research Question 3, the findings of this study showed that the future of Islamic banking in Germany and the European Union looks promising. However, the growth of Islamic banking and finance in Germany will be slow and gradual. On the other hand, Islamic finance has also limited growth potential in the United Kingdom. Furthermore, the success of the first *Shari'ah*-compliant Islamic bank, KT Bank AG, will depend on its operating model.

Chapter 9: Empirical Analysis of the Quantitative Data

9.1 Introduction[11]

The main objective of Chapter 9 is to analyze the knowledge, attitudes, and practices of Muslims living in Germany toward retail Islamic banking and finance products using the statistical approaches proposed in Chapter 7. This study provides important insights into current behaviors of German retail banking consumers and Muslim umbrella organizations, and measures consumer openness, understanding, and expectations toward Islamic banking and finance. In Chapter 9, an analysis based on the retail banking questionnaire and Muslim umbrella organization's questionnaire will be described. The aim of this study was to explore the awareness levels of Muslims about the existence of Islamic financial system and identify the factors that affect the respondents' attitudes toward choosing different banking products and services based on the respondents' religious orientations. This study also investigated Muslim consumer willingness to switch to Islamic banking.

This chapter is divided into three main sections. The three sections are further divided into different parts based on various themes. In Section 1, results of the analysis of the retail banking survey are presented. Section 2 provides the results of the Muslim Umbrella Organization's survey. Finally, Section 3 discusses the various hypotheses proposed by this study and describes the quantitative and qualitative empirical findings associated with each. The results of these hypotheses will be critically evaluated in the framework of different studies discussed in the literature review (Chapter 6).

9.2 Section 1: Analysis of the Retail Banking Survey

The survey was conducted in nine cities of Germany including Berlin, Hamburg, Cologne, Frankfurt am Main, Munich, Duesseldorf, Essen, Duisburg, and Bochum. The retail banking questionnaire was comprised of five parts.

Demographic and personal information of the respondents is discussed in Part 1 (9.2.1). General banking and finance information provided by the respondents is described in Part 2 (9.2.2), and Part 3 provides an overview of consumer perceptions about Islamic banking. Part 4 is about consumer willingness to switch to Islamic banking, and Part 5 reviews the relevance of Islamic products and services to the needs of consumers.

---

11 All tables in Chapter 9 are based on primary data collected by the researcher of this study through surveys.

9.2.1 Part 1: The Main Characteristics of the Respondents

The main characteristics of the retail banking sample are shown in Table 6. Of the respondents, 71.90% were male and 28.10% were female. The sample consisted of 402 respondents and all respondents were followers of the Muslims religion. The purposeful sample consisted of Muslims because the focus of this research was to gain insights into the perceptions, attitudes, and practices of the Muslim population living in Germany toward Islamic banking and finance. Almost half of the respondents (47.51%) were aged 18–30 years, and 35% of the respondents were aged 31–45 years. Therefore, we can conclude that the majority of the respondents in this study are from 18 to 45 years. As far as the educational level of the respondents is concerned, 32.91% had earned a university Master's or Ph.D., 20.76% had earned a university bachelor's degree, and 20.00% had a higher secondary school education. In addition to this, 12.15% of the respondents had vocational education. Regarding the professions of the respondents, 40.55% were salaried employees, 22.92% were students, 11.59% were businessmen or businesswomen, and 9.57% housewives. Regarding nationality, 32.92% of the respondents were German, 24.18% were Turkish, and 21.45% were South East Asian. As far as the monthly gross income was concerned, 35.05% of the respondents reported incomes of less than 1,000€ per month, 20.62% reported income between 1,000–2,000€ per month, and 23.20% reported income in the rage of 2,000–3,000€ per month.

Overall, the profile analysis of the respondents showed that the majority of them were males and were young people (47.50% of the respondents were 18 to 30 years of age). Moreover, the data also indicated that respondents were educated. It is worth mentioning that respondents were not asked to indicate their country of origin in the demographic survey. Therefore, it is supposed that the majority of the respondents who disclosed their nationality as German had a Turkish and migratory background. The data also revealed a relatively low income level for the respondents even though most earned a salaried income.

It should be mentioned that the data collection process was not very easy and many people declined to participate in the survey. Therefore, the survey drew 22% of its sample from students. It is also worth mentioning that the conversations with students indicated that most of them were also working part time. This could be the key reason that 35.05% of the respondents reported income levels below €1,000 per month.

Table 6: Profile Analysis of the Respondents

Variables	Frequency	Percentage	Variables	Frequency	Percentage
Gender			**Nationality**		
Male	289	71.90	German	132	32.84
Female	113	28.10	Turkish	97	24.13
Total	***402***	***100.00***	Arabic (Middle East & Far East)	20	4.96
Religion			African	4	1.00
Muslims	402	100.00	South East Asian (Pakistani, Indian & Bangladeshi)	86	21.39
Monthly Gross Income in €			Other	63	15.67
Less than 1,000	136	35.05	***Total***	***402***	***100.00***
1,001–2,000	80	20.62	**Age group in Years**		
2,001–3,000	90	23.20	18–30	191	47.51
3,001–4,000	39	10.05	31–45	141	35.00
4,001–5,000	23	5.92	46–60	60	14.93
5,001–6,000	5	1.29	61–75	7	1.74
More than 6,000	15	3.87	Above 76	0	0
Total	***388***	***100.00***	***Total***	***402***	***99.18***
Education Level			**Profession**		
Higher secondary school	79	20.00	Salaried employees	161	40.55
Vocational education	48	12.15	Business person	46	11.59
University bachelor	82	20.76	Wage earner	12	3.02
University master/ Ph.D.	130	32.91	Retired	10	2.52
Shari'ah education	2	0.50	Unemployed	9	2.27
Other	54	13.67	Housewives	38	9.57
Total	***395***	***99.99***	Student	91	22.92
			Other	30	7.56
			Total	***397***	***100.00***

9.2.2 Part 2: General Banking and Finance Information

The main purpose of Part 2 is to ascertain information provided by the respondents about their banking relationship with existing financial institutions. This section will also to capture the important bank selection criteria that are considered by the respondents when selecting a financial institution. The overwhelming majority, 71.64% (n=288 from 402 respondents) selected "Yes" when asked, "Do you or have you previously used products/services such as bank loan and saving account etc. offered by a bank?" These individuals indicated that they had an existing relationship with banks and had used products and services such as loans and saving accounts. However, 28.36% (n=114) of the respondents had not yet used banking products. This finding shows that there is significant under-penetration of banking and finance products and services among surveyed Muslim retail consumers in Germany.

Availability of Automated Teller Machine (ATM) services was understandably the most important service sought by 66.42% (n=267) of the respondents when selecting a bank, as shown in Table 7. Low fees were the second most important bank selection criteria, and 60.45% (n=243) of the respondents considered it very important. Free online bank transfer facility/phone banking services was the third most important bank selection criteria as stated by 51.00% (n=205) of the respondents.

However, 37.06% (n=149) of the respondents said that they would consider Islamic banking while selecting a bank, as can be seen Table 7. Two possible findings can be extracted from the information provided in Table 7. First, there could be a correlation between those respondents who stated that they had not yet taken out any loans or opened any savings bank accounts (28.36%) and those who indicated that Islamic banking was an important screening criterion for selecting a bank (37.06%). Second, data showed that most of the respondents tended to establish a relationship with those banks that offered essential banking features and facilities such as ATM cards, online payment processing, low fees, and convenient location.

Table 7: Most Important Banking Products and Services for Bank Selection

Q9: Which of the below is most important to you when you are selecting a bank (multiple options possible)?		
Variables	**Frequency**	**Percentage**
Availability of ATM	267	66.42
Low Fee	243	60.45
High consumer services	142	35.32
Free online bank transfer facility/Phone banking services	205	51.00
Higher profit on saving accounts	69	17.16

Q9: Which of the below is most important to you when you are selecting a bank (multiple options possible)?		
Variables	**Frequency**	**Percentage**
Nearest location of Branch/ Flexibility in meetings	155	38.56
Islamic banking (interest-free banks)	149	37.06
Other	12	2.99
Total	***402***	

9.2.3 Part 3: Perceptions of Consumers About Islamic Banking

Part 3 consists of a number of questions that deal with consumer perceptions about Islamic banking. This section draws significance because it generalizes some of the answers of Quantitative Research Question 1, as discussed below.

Quantitative Research Question 1
What are the perceptions of Muslim consumers about Islamic banking and finance?

The findings of this study showed that the majority (more than two-thirds) of the Muslim consumers had knowledge about the key principles and tenets of Islamic banking and finance, including prohibition of *Riba*. Moreover, two-thirds of the respondents considered that charging and paying interest to be prohibited in Islam. An overwhelming majority of the respondents identified as religious. And more than two-thirds of the respondents highlighted a perceived lack of Islamic banking services in their neighbourhood. The findings of this study also revealed that almost two-third of the respondents showed strong interest in buying *Shari'ah*-compliant products and services even if they had to pay higher prices. It should be noted that one-third of respondents were using mortgage services from conventional banks.

The following sections (from 9.2.4 to 9.2.11) provide an overview of the data analyzed to draw this conclusion. In total, nine questions were asked to address Research Question 1.

9.2.4 Knowledge About Islamic Banking and Finance

In this section of the survey, Muslims were asked about their knowledge concerning Islamic banking and finance. The results show that over 50.25% (n=200) said that they were aware of the fact that Islamic banks provide interest-free (*Riba*) banking products (Please See Table 8 Below). This implies that most of respondents know the basic tenets of Islamic banks. Furthermore, 30.15% (n=120) stated that Islamic banks follow *Shari'ah* rules and over 23.00% (n=94) selected all of the options when given the opportunity to do so (Islamic banks follow *Shari'ah* rules, Islamic banks avoid interest (*Riba*), and *Musharakah*, *Mudarabah*, *Sukuk* and *Qard Hasan* are the key products offered by Islamic banks). However, almost 25.00% (n=99) of the respondents said that they did not know about Islamic banking as can be seen in Table 8. The results also suggest that a wide majority of the respondents have no knowledge about different Islamic banking instruments and products such as *Musharakah, Mudarabah* and *Sukuk*. Another conclusion, which may be derived from Table 8, is that the lack of interest in Islamic financial products by one-fourth of the respondents is an important factor of poor knowledge.

Table 8: Perception of Consumers About Islamic Banking

Q10: What is your knowledge about Islamic banking and finance (multiple options possible)?		
Variables	**Frequency**	**Percentage**
Islamic banks follow *Shari'ah* rules	120	30.15
Islamic banks avoid interest (*Riba*)	200	50.25
Musharakah, Mudarabah, Sukuk and *Qard Hasan* are the key products offered by Islamic banks	37	9.30
All of above	94	23.62
Do not know	99	24.87
Total	***398***	

9.2.5 Religious Characteristics of the Muslims

Islamic banking draws its origin from *Shari'ah* and a number of teachings are mentioned in the *Quran* about the prohibition of *Riba,* as discussed in detail in Chapter 2. Therefore, it was important to ask the respondents about their level of religiosity. The results showed that 43.86% (n=175) of the respondents (please see Table 9 below) said that they were religious (i.e., in the context of fulfilling the basic rituals of *Shari'ah* like prayers, avoiding interest, paying *zakat, and so forth.*). It is worth mention that, the notion *religious* is sometimes also taken as simply being Muslim and observing certain basic obligations such as prayers.

In addition to this, 19.55% (n=78) of the respondents said they were very religious, as can be seen in Table 9. It seems that the data in Table 9 (religious characteristics of the Muslims) and 8 (perceptions of consumers about Islamic banking) shows strong connection between level of religiosity and knowledge about Islamic banking and finance. Those who are religious or very religious tended to show higher knowledge about the existence of basic rules and features of Islamic banking. In total an overwhelming majority (73.43%) of the respondents identified as religious (degree of religiousness varies from religious to very strongly religious).

Table 9: Religious Characteristics of the Muslims

Q11: How will you characterize your religious approach (fulfilling the basic rituals of *Shari'ah* i.e., prays, avoiding interest, paying *zakat* etc.)?		
Variables	**Frequency**	**Percentage**
Not very strongly religious	14	3.51
Not very religious	18	4.51
Not religious	22	5.51
Neutral	52	13.03
Religious	175	43.86
Very religious	78	19.55
very strongly religious	40	10.02
Total	***399***	***99.99***

9.2.6 Awareness Level About Islamic Banking and Finance

When respondents were asked whether they had heard about Islamic banking and finance before this study, only 28.21% (n=112) of the respondents were confident that they were familiar with Islamic banking and 26.95% (n=107) said that they had some information as shown in Table 10. These results revealed that 55.16% (very much awareness and somewhat awareness) of the respondents who had good awareness about Islamic banking and finance. But 15.87% (n=63) stated that they had less awareness about Islamic banking and finance. Therefore, in total 71% of the respondents indicated they had awareness but a lower degree of awareness.

On the other hand, 11.84% (n=47) said they had no information about Islamic banking and finance. Moreover, 15.87% (n=63) of the respondents said that they knew little, as Table 10 depicts. These results demonstrate critical trends and future implications for KT Bank AG and other Islamic financial institutions in Germany. The results also show that poor awareness cannot generate enough business for these institutions. Therefore, it is very important for these institutes to engage with potential consumers through effective marketing campaigns. Once some consumers enjoy good *Shari'ah*-compliant banking experience they can recommend them to other family members and friends.

Table 10: Awareness About Islamic Banking and Finance

Q12: Have you heard about Islamic banking and finance before this?		
Variables	**Frequency**	**Percentage**
Not at all	47	11.84
Not as such	19	4.79
Little	63	15.87
Neutral	11	2.77
May be	38	9.57
Somewhat	107	26.95
Very much	112	28.21
Total	***397***	***100.00***

9.2.7 Awareness and Prohibition of *Riba*

As it can be seen in Table 11, 38.94% (n=155) of the respondents said they were very familiar with the word *Riba* and 23.37% (n=93) said they had some information about it. Moreover, 8.54% (n=34) of the respondents stated they had less awareness about *Riba*. In total, it was concluded from the data that 70.85% of the respondents had awareness about the prohibition of *Riba*. Only around 20% (n=79) of the respondents were unaware of the term *Riba*, as can be seen in Table 11. The possible reason for high levels of familiarity with *Riba* could be the fact that it is mentioned several times in the *Quran* and religious scholars advocate the prohibition of *Riba* in religious gatherings. The findings in respect to the prohibition of *Riba* were also similar to the findings discussed in Chapter 6, Section 6.3.1. The majority of the respondents stated that Islamic banks avoid *Riba*. Those who claimed the higher degree of familiarity with *Riba* did so primarily because they are familiar with the *Quran*, which frequently mentions *Riba*. Another reason for understanding *Riba* might be the fact that Islam prohibits *Riba* and religious Imams often discuss this matter during religious gatherings.

Table 11: Awareness About Riba *(Interest)*

Q13: Are you familiar with the word *Riba* (Interest)?		
Variables	**Frequency**	**Percentage**
Not at all	57	14.32
Not as such	22	5.53
Little	26	6.53
Neutral	11	2.76

Q13: Are you familiar with the word *Riba* (Interest)?		
Variables	**Frequency**	**Percentage**
May be	34	8.54
Somewhat	93	23.37
very much	155	38.94
Total	***398***	***99.99***

As table 12 shows 47.10% (n=187) of the respondents had a clear understanding that charging and paying interest is prohibited in Islam. Furthermore, 18.14% (n=72) had sufficient awareness that charging and paying interest is prohibited. However, almost 13.00% (n=41) of the respondents believed that charging and paying interest is not prohibited. From these results we can draw the conclusion that about half of the respondents believed that interest is not allowed. (The findings of this question reiterate the results of their familiarity with *Riba,* as shown in Table 11, Awareness about *Riba*). Two factors could explain the small number of respondents who believed that charging and paying interest (*Riba*) in financial transactions is not prohibited in Islam. First, lack of information about interest and, second, a difference of opinions in true interpretation of *interest.*

Table 12: Prohibition of Charging and Paying Interest

Q14: Do you consider charging and paying interest is prohibited in Islam?		
Variables	**Frequency**	**Percentage**
Not at all	30	7.56
Not as such	21	5.29
Little	13	3.02
Neutral	38	9.57
May be	36	9.07
Somewhat	72	18.14
Very much	187	47.10
Total	***397***	***99.75***

9.2.8 Availability of Islamic Banks in Neighborhood

Over 70% (n=277) of the respondents were aware of the fact that there were no Islamic banks or no availability of Islamic financial services in the city or region in which they lived (please see Table 13). However, 11.23% (n=44) of the respondents did not express an opinion. The lack of response could be the result of a lack of information about the existence of Islamic banks. Nevertheless, only a small number of the respondents (2.04%, n=8) said that they were familiar with the existence of such services, as can be seen in Table 13.

The results obtained are compatible with the findings of the following section (9.3.3), which shows that the vast majority of the respondents were not aware of the availability of Islamic financial services in the neighborhoods in which they lived. These findings were expected, and the respondents have highlighted three main reasons. First, 49.21% cited that there was no presence of Islamic banks or financial institutions. Second, 43.65% stated that no Islamic bank had approached them. This means that there were no adequate marketing efforts promoting Islamic financial products and services. Finally, a lack of awareness on the part of the respondents is also an important factor in this regard.

Table 13: Availability of Islamic Banks

Q15: Are there any Islamic banks/ Islamic banking and finance services available in your city/region?		
Variables	**Frequency**	**Percentage**
Not at all	240	61.23
Not as such	37	9.44
Little	14	3.57
Neutral	44	11.23
May be	38	9.69
Somewhat	11	2.81
very much	8	2.04
Total	***392***	***99.93***

9.2.9 Investment in *Shari'ah-compliant Products*

The results of the question about investment in *Shari'ah*-compliant products can be broadly categorized in three groups. About 37.66% (n=148) of the respondents stated that they had not thought about making an investment in *Shari'ah*-compliant products and services, as shown in Table 14. As discussed earlier in the literature review, consumers from Turkish origin (in general) and first generation German-Turks (particularly) were very thoughtful while engaging in such investments. Moreover, investments in a particular area require meticulous analysis of available information and thus also demand reasonable time and specific expertise.

On the other hand, a significant number of the respondents (39.69%, n=156) said that they had thought to invest in Islamic products. It is assumed that these are *Shari'ah* sensitive Muslims who are genuinely looking for *Shari'ah*-compliant investment opportunities in which to invest their savings for higher returns and thus subsequent wealth creation. As can be seen in Table 14, 22.65% (n=89) of the respondents did not disclose their intention and remained neutral. One possible reason could be a lack of awareness for various investment avenues available within *Shari'ah*-compliant banking.

Table 14: Investment in Shari'ah*-compliant Products*

Q16: Have you ever thought to invest in *Shari'ah*-compliant products of an Islamic bank?		
Variables	**Frequency**	**Percentage**
Very strongly disagree	54	13.74
Strongly disagree	35	8.91
Disagree	59	15.01
Neutral	89	22.65
Agree	74	18.83
Strongly agree	34	8.65
Very strongly agree	48	12.21
Total	***393***	***100.00***

9.2.10 Mortgage from non-Islamic Western Banks

The analysis shows mixed results when respondents were asked whether they avoid taking mortgage loans from non-Islamic Western banks because these services include interest. As can be seen in Table 15, 41.67% (n=165) of the respondents stated that they do not avoid mortgage loans from conventional banks. It is supposed that the lack of *Shari'ah*-compliant mortgage products in Germany is the main reason behind this trend.

The analysis further shows that 38.38% (n=152) of the respondents said they avoid services of non-Islamic banks because of the element of interest. Two factors may contribute in this regard. First, as 37.06% of the respondents cited in Part 2 (Section 9.2.2) of Chapter 9, they filter products and services of financial institutions on the basis of *Shari'ah*-compliant banking. Second, prohibition of *Riba* is one of the important considerations, as has been discussed in detail in the preceding sections of this chapter. As table 15 shows, 19.95% (n=79) of the respondents remained neutral.

Table 15: Mortgage Loans from Non-Islamic Banks

Q17: Do you avoid taking mortgage loans from non-Islamic Western banks because the products and services involve interest?		
Variables	**Frequency**	**Percentage**
Very strongly disagree	68	17.17
strongly disagree	31	7.83
Disagree	66	16.67
Neutral	79	19.95
Agree	41	10.35
Strongly agree	45	11.36
Very strongly agree	66	16.67
Total	***396***	***100.00***

9.2.11 Willingness to Use Products and Services of Islamic Banks Despite Higher Costs

In order to comprehend the relationship between religiosity and motivation of the Muslim respondents to buy *Shari'ah*-compliant products, a question was asked exploring whether they would use these products even if they (the respondents) had to pay higher price. From this analysis two main outcomes can be summarized. Over 52.77% (n=210) of the respondents showed willingness to buy products and services despite higher price, as can be seen in Table 16. This is a critical trend because it shows strong commitment and dedication of the Muslim consumers toward Islamic banking irrespective of financial disadvantage to purchasing similar but less-expensive conventional products and services.

On the contrary, some 28.64% (n=114) of the respondents indicated that they would not pay higher price if Islamic banks offered more expensive products and services (please see Table 16). This behavior indicates that the Islamic banks should carefully structure and price products and services to gain a wider market share of less *Shari'ah*-sensitive consumers. This result further accentuates the findings of the literature review, which showed that a number of Muslims living in Germany have low incomes and, therefore, affordable products and services should be marketed. Alternatively, this situation also signals Islamic financial institutions to present themselves as a viable option to consumers despite growing competition among industry players. Generally, retail consumers presume that Islamic banking and finance products are relatively cheaper than their conventional counterparts.

Table 16: Willingness to Get Services of Islamic Banks Despite Higher Costs

Q18: Are you willing to get services of Islamic banks even if you have to even pay higher price for them?		
Variables	**Frequency**	**Percentage**
Very strongly disagree	51	12.81
strongly disagree	19	4.77
Disagree	44	11.06
Neutral	74	18.59
Agree	88	22.11
Strongly agree	44	11.06
Very strongly agree	78	19.60
Total	***398***	***100.00***

In summary, Table 17 (Summary Statistics of Main Variables) provides the key statistics describing the main variables of this study. The respondents had higher degree of familiarity with *Riba* and most of them believed that interest is prohibited in Islam. On the contrary, a vast majority of the respondents stated that they do not have access to Islamic banking and finance products due mainly to the non-existence of Islamic financial institutions in Germany. However, the respondents were also willing to receive services of Islamic banks despite higher price.

Table 17: Summary Statistics of Main Variables of Part Three

Summary Statistics of Main Variables				
Variables	**N**	**Mean**	**Standard Deviation**	**Variance**
Religious characteristics of the respondents	399	4.880	1.3802	1.905
Awareness about Islamic banking and finance	397	4.872	2.0928	4.380
Familiar with the word *Riba*	398	5.116	2.2064	4.868
Prohibition of charging and paying interest in Islam	397	5.501	1.9327	3.735
Availability of Islamic banks/ Islamic banking and finance services in city/region	392	2.153	1.7066	2.913

Summary Statistics of Main Variables				
Variables	**N**	**Mean**	**Standard Deviation**	**Variance**
Intention to invest in *Shari'ah*-compliant products of an Islamic bank	393	3.987	1.8398	3.385
Avoidance of taking mortgage loans from non-Islamic Western banks due to interest	396	3.992	2.0233	4.094
Willingness to get services of Islamic banks despite higher price	398	4.440	1.9230	3.698

9.3 Part 4: Consumer Willingness to Switch to Islamic Banking

In the preceding sections of this chapter, a detailed discussion of the knowledge and awareness of the Muslim consumers toward Islamic banking and finance in Germany was discussed. The primary objective of this section (9.3) is to critically evaluate the Muslim consumer's actual willingness to switch from conventional banking to Islamic banking. Moreover, this section will discuss prominent reasons some of the respondents indicated there were not willing to switch to Islamic banking. Part 4 will provide insights into the findings related to Quantitative Research Question 2.

Quantitative Research Question 2

What are the perceptions and willingness of Muslim consumers to switch Islamic banking?

The findings of this study revealed that two-thirds of the Muslim consumers were willing to embrace Islamic banking and finance, and an additional one-fourth of the respondents were indecisive about switching to Islamic banking. Almost two-third of the respondents cited the fact that Islamic banks do not charge interest as a key reason to switch to Islamic banking.

Half of the respondents expressed that the lack of *Shari'ah*-compliant banking products and services in their neighbourhoods was a primary reason of not engaging in Islamic banking. More than one-third of respondents identified the fact that no Islamic banks had approached them as the second most influential reason for not doing Islamic banking.

The following sections (from 9.3.1 to 9.3.3) provide an overview of the data analyzed to draw the above conclusion. In total, three questions were asked to address Research Question 2.

9.3.1 Willingness to Switch Toward Islamic Banking

Apart from knowledge and awareness about Islamic banking and finance, it is important to analyze the willingness to use retail Islamic banking and finance because this is seen as a clear measure of actual demand. As seen in Table 18, two significant trends can be identified.

First, the results showed that a vast majority (65.42%) of the respondents were willing to embrace Islamic banking. This finding reiterates the already discussed point that over 52.77% of retail consumers are prepared to pay higher price for Islamic banking and finance products and services. Second, approximately 26.62% of the retail Islamic banking consumers who responded to the survey were indecisive about switching to Islamic banking. It is worth mentioning that these consumers are not sure at the moment whether they want to engage in Islamic banking or not. Therefore, providing them with information capable of building an adequate awareness, which could dispel their concerns and misconceptions about Islamic banking products, might also motivate them to engage in Islamic banking.

Table 18: Consumer's Willingness to Switch Islamic Banking

Q19: Are you willing to do Islamic banking?		
Variables	**Frequency**	**Percentage**
Yes	263	65.42
No	32	7.96
Not sure	107	26.62
Total	***402***	***100.00***

9.3.2 Motivations to Do Islamic Banking

Those respondents who showed a willingness to engage with Islamic Banking products and services were further asked to give reasons for which they would engage in Islamic banking. As can be seen in Table 19, three main arguments emerged in favor of using Islamic banking. First, the overwhelming majority of the respondents (61.72%, n=187) stated that they wanted to switch to Islamic banking because Islamic banks do not charge interest. This finding gives an indication of general awareness among retail Islamic banking consumers about Islamic and conventional banking systems.

Second, about 30% (n=92) of the respondents stated that Islam prohibits *Riba* and that is why they are religiously obligated to use *Riba*-free banking services (please see Table 19). This shows recognition of the prohibition of *Riba* among retail consumers. Finally, some 27% (n=82) of the respondents stated that they wanted to switch to Islamic banking because Islamic banking and finance products and services offer them religious satisfaction and comfort. These arguments indicate that the majority of the consumers have shown their sensitivity to the permissibility of *Shari'ah*-compliant products and services over other perceived benefits such as higher rate of return on investments.

Table 19: Reasons that Motivate Consumers to Do Islamic Banking

Q20: If your answer is Yes then, what might be reason/s that motivates you to do Islamic banking (multiple options possible)?		
Variables	**Frequency**	**Percentage**
Islamic banks do not charge interest (*Riba*)	187	61.72
Islamic banks fully apply *Shari'ah* principles	35	11.55
Islam prohibits *Riba*, that is why I am religiously obligated to use *Riba* free services	92	30.36
Islamic products/services offer me religious satisfaction and comfort	82	27.06
Islamic banks offer higher rate of return on deposits on investments	33	10.89
Islamic banks apply Profit and Loss sharing (PLS) methods i.e., *Musharaka*	52	17.16
Islam financial institutions (banks, insurance companies etc.) aims to serve Muslim communities	50	16.50
Islamic banks gives interest-free loans i.e., *Qard Hasan* to poor people and students	65	21.45
Islamic banks provide reliable services because they have *Shari'ah* scholars to certify their products	29	9.57
All of above	54	17.82
Do not know	35	11.55
Other	09	2.97
Total	***303***	

9.3.3 Reasons for Not Doing Islamic Banking

It is important to further investigate the rationale of those consumers who are not willing to do Islamic banking because the findings may have serious implications for the relevant stakeholders. As can be seen in Table 20, 49.21% (n=62) of the respondents said that no bank in their locality was offering Islamic banking products. This finding is quite expected because until July 2015 there was no fully *Shari'ah*-compliant bank in Germany. Likewise, 42.06% (n=53) of the respondents cited that they were not aware of the presence of Islamic banks.

On the other hand, 43.65% (n=55) of the respondents said that no Islamic bank had approached them as it can be seen in Table 20. Obviously, in the absence of any Islamic financial institution it was not logical to market products and services. Overall, these factors show that a lack of availability of Islamic products and services is one of the major reasons for not engaging in Islamic banking.

Table 20: Reasons for Not Doing Islamic Banking

Q21: If your answer is No then, what might be the reason/s for not doing Islamic banking (multiple options possible)?		
Variables	**Frequency**	**Percentage**
Because no banks in my locality offer Islamic banking services	62	49.21
No Islamic banks have approached me	55	43.65
I do not know about Islamic banks presence	53	42.06
Other	21	16.67
Total	***126***	

9.4 Part 5: Relevance of Islamic Products

After having discussed the knowledge, attitudes, and willingness of Muslim consumers regarding Islamic banking and finance, this section aims to shed light on the preferences of retail consumers for different products and services and provides insight into the results related to Quantitative Research Question 3.

Quantitative Research Question 3
What are the relevant Islamic products/services of Muslim consumers?

The findings of this study revealed that more than half of the Muslim retail consumers surveyed selected a Giro accounts facility as the most desired service. Savings account services were cited as a second priority by more than one-third of the respondents. Moreover, mortgage financing was cited as the third most attractive product by one-third of the respondents. Table 21 provides an overview of the data analyzed to draw this conclusion.

As can be seen in Table 21, more than half of the respondents (55.22%, n=217) selected a Giro account facility. The selection of a Giro account as the top most desired service indicates that most of the consumers who responded to the survey are interested mainly in routine banking functions such as payment of expenses and receipt of income through banking channels.

Savings accounts are the second most attractive service cited by the consumers (44.27%, n=174) (please see Table 21). The main motive for obtaining savings accounts could be to seek some profit on the deposited money. Surprisingly, mortgage financing is ranked third by 36.64% (n=144) of the respondents. This outcome is quite a significant development because, as discussed in the literature review in Chapter 6, the most previous studies indicated huge demand for mortgage financing in Germany.

It is also worth mentioning that this study surveyed some retail businesses in order to assess their financial needs and most of them cited business loans (28.50%, n=112). Car financing, educational loans, and investment accounts are among the notably desired products and services.

Table 21: Top Three Products Desired by the Respondents

Q22: If you have money and also the opportunity to benefit from the products and services of an Islamic bank. Which Top three products will you select?		
Variables	**Frequency**	**Percentage**
Giro account (for bank transfers)	217	55.22
Saving accounts (to obtain higher return/profit)	174	44.27
Mortgage services/Home financing (getting loan to buy home)	144	36.64
Car financing	95	24.17
Remittances	37	9.61
Investment accounts	81	20.61
Business loans	112	28.50
Educational loans	85	21.63
Other	40	10.18
Total	***393***	

In the preceding sections the knowledge, awareness, and perceptions of the Muslim consumers surveyed in this study toward Islamic banking and finance were discussed using descriptive statistics. In the following section, Part 6, inferential statistical analysis of the retail banking survey is made.

9.5 Part 6: Inferential Statistical Analysis of the Retail Banking Survey

Further analysis was conducted to examine the relationships between different variables. This section will explain the in-depth results obtained through inferential statistical techniques, which promote clarity about the relations between different variables.

9.5.1 Determination of Correlation Among Different Variables

Correlation analysis was conducted to statistically test the relationships among the variables used in the current study and to further reinforce the results. From a theoretical standpoint, two variables can be related in three ways: (1) positively related, (2) not related, or (3) negatively related (Field, 2014). A positively related or correlated relationship means that if one variable increases the other one also increases and vice versa. However, on the other hand a negatively related or correlated relationship means that if one variable increase the other also decreases, which indicates no relationship between the variables tested.

The results revealed that variables such as religious characteristics, including: a) awareness about Islamic banking, b) familiarity with *Riba*, c) perceptions of prohibition of charging and paying interest, d) intention to make investments in *Shari'ah*-compliant Islamic products, e) avoidance of non-Islamic products and the willingness to pay even higher prices for Islamic products, correlate positively with each other, $p<.05$.

For example, the results reveal that respondents who characterized their religious approach as stronger than others also tended to have heard about Islamic banking more often, considered investing in *Shari'ah*-compliant Islamic products, or avoided non-Islamic products more often. At the same time, knowledge about Islamic banking and finance is positively associated with the intention to make investments in *Shari'ah*-compliant Islamic products, the avoidance of non-Islamic products, and the willingness to pay even higher prices for Islamic products.

One-Way ANOVA
ANOVA is also commonly known as analysis of variance, a statistical technique to test the equality of more than two means simultaneously by using variance.

Purpose:
The purpose for using ANOVA was to ascertain if there was a difference between groups of participants based on the testing of certain variables. A t-test is also commonly used to measure differences between two means when two sets of data are compared. In the current study more than two groups of data were used, and for that reason ANOVA was employed. ANAOVA is frequently used to test hypotheses in quantitative research. If the p-value in ANOVA is less than 0.05 then the null hypothesis is rejected (Almutairi, 2010). There are two types of ANOVA. In a one-way ANOVA more than two levels of a single independent variable are used.

However, in case of a two-way ANOVA more than two levels of multiple variables are used (Field, 2014).

9.5.2 Willingness to do Islamic Banking and Religious Characteristics of the Respondents

The purpose of this analysis was to examine the relationship between the respondents' willingness to engage in Islamic banking and respondents' religious characteristics. There is a dependent variable (religious characteristics) and an independent variable (willingness to do Islamic banking). Results of the descriptive statistical analysis are shown in the form of Mean (*M*), standard deviation (*SD*), and the sample population in each group (N). Mean is a statistical measure that shows an average of particular data, and standard deviation is a statistical measure that shows how widely individual observations are dispersed in a particular data set. Standard deviation would be higher if individual observations vary substantially from the group mean, and vice versa.

The responses related to willingness to engage in Islamic banking are grouped in three categories namely *No*, *Not Sure*, and *Yes*, and *N* shows the number of individuals who selected these three options from a total sample size of 399. Participants who are willing to engage in Islamic banking characterize their religious approach to be significantly stronger (M=5.307, SD=1.1359) than participants who do not engage in Islamic Banking (M=3.094, SD=1.4670), $F(2, 396) = 60.464$, $p < 0.001$. This analysis shows that a willingness to engage in Islamic banking is related to the strength of one's religious characteristics. If someone is more inclined toward religion it is expected that the person will also be more willing to use Islamic banking products.

9.5.3 Gender and Level of Awareness of the Respondents

The purpose of this analysis was to examine the relationship between gender and the level of awareness about Islamic banking using an ANOVA.

A one-way ANOVA revealed a significant effect of gender on the level of the awareness of the respondents, $F(1,395)=16.886$, $p< 0.001$. This study concluded that male (M=5.137, SD=2.0259) respondents seem to be more familiar with Islamic banking and females (M=4.196, SD=2.1174) are less aware. This analysis revealed that male and female Muslim respondents are not equally familiar with Islamic banking and finance in Germany.

9.5.4 Gender and Perceptions of Making Investments in *Shari'ah*-compliant Products

The purpose of this analysis was to examine the relationship between gender and respondents behavior in making decisions about investments in *Shari'ah*-compliant products using an ANOVA.

A one-way ANOVA revealed no significant effect of gender on respondents behavior in making decisions about investments in *Shari'ah*-compliant products, $F(1, 391) = 1.922$, $p > 0.05$. Therefore, this study concluded that there was no significant difference between female and male respondents' behavior in making investments in *Shahri'ah*-compliant products. However, male (M=4.067, SD=1.8047) respondents considered making investments in Islamic products to a slightly higher extent than did female respondents (M=3.780, SD=1.9214). The overall analysis shows that in general, Muslim respondents decided to remain neutral and this can be interpreted, as they were not fully sure about making *Shari'ah*-compliant investments. One reason could be a lack of availability of such products and services.

9.5.5 Gender and Perceptions of Avoiding Mortgage Loans from Non-Islamic Banks

The purpose of this analysis was to employ ANOVA to examine the relationship between gender and the respondents' behavior in avoiding mortgage loans from non-Islamic banks.

A one-way ANOVA revealed a significant relationship between gender and respondents' behavior in avoiding mortgage loans from non-Islamic Western banks, $F(1, 394) = 10.594$, $p < 0.00$.

Furthermore, male (M=4.196, SD=2.0633) respondents showed a higher tendency to avoid mortgage loans when compared to females (M=3.468, SD=1.8232). This finding indicates that Muslim respondents use products and services of non-Islamic Western banks despite knowing that these products and services are not *Shari'ah*-compliant.

9.5.6 Gender and Perceptions of the Respondents to Pay Higher Prices to Obtain Services of Islamic banks

The purpose of this analysis was to employ ANOVA to examine the relationship between gender and the respondents' willingness to acquire services of Islamic banks even if the products and services are only available at higher prices.

A one-way ANOVA revealed a significant relationship between gender and participant willingness to acquire services of Islamic banks even if they have to pay higher prices, $F(1, 396) = 4.964$, $p < 0.05$. Furthermore, male (M=4.573, SD=1.9466) respondents tend to use services of Islamic banks to a higher extent than did females (M=4.098, SD=1.8255). It is worth mentioning that Muslim respondents were, in general, hesitant to pay higher prices for the products offered by Islamic banks, because the mean values of both male and female were in a neutral range. As we discussed in the descriptive analysis section earlier, almost 20% of the Muslim respondents had not disclosed their willingness to pay higher price for Islamic financial products. This can be interpreted to mean that pricing of products is an important consideration even if the products are *Shari'ah*-compliant.

9.5.7 Awareness of Islamic Banking and Educational Backgrounds

The purpose of this analysis was to use ANOVA to test for a relationship between groups of respondents with different educational backgrounds and their level of awareness about Islamic banking. For this purpose, respondents were divided into one group with higher education (those respondents who have university education) and one group with lower education (those respondents who have a higher secondary schooling, vocational training, *Shari'ah* education, and others).

A one-way ANOVA revealed a significant relationship between different education backgrounds and level of awareness of Islamic banking, $F(1, 395) = 57.346$, $p < 0.001$. Respondents with higher education levels (M=5.585, SD=1.7324) tended to have greater knowledge about Islamic banking than did respondents with lower educational levels (M=4.095, SD=2.1774). This result indicates that the higher the educational level, the more aware the respondent was about Islamic banking and finance.

9.5.8 Nationality and Level of Awareness of Islamic Banking

The purpose of this analysis was to use ANOVA to examine the relationship between different nationalities and their level of awareness about Islamic banking.

A one-way ANOVA revealed a significant relationship between different nationalities and level of awareness about Islamic banking, $F(5, 391) = 12.844$, $p < 0.001$.

Therefore, results revealed that Turkish respondents (M=3.979, SD=2.2756) were least aware about Islamic banking, and South East Asian respondents (M=6.098, SD=1.2825) were well aware of Islamic banking. These results also validated the views of several scholars (discussed in Chapter 8) who claimed that Muslims from South East Asian countries have higher aspirations for Islamic banking than do Muslims from Turkey and the Balkan states. Results also indicated that German respondents (M=4.455, SD=2.0726) had sufficient knowledge about Islamic banking.

9.5.9 Nationality of Respondents and Demand for Islamic Products and Services

It was important for this study to analyze whether consumer nationality expressed similar or different levels of demand for specific products and services. Therefore, for each product and service calculations were done to determine the cross nationality of the most demanded products and services, as shown in Table 22. The findings indicate that Germans find Giro accounts (55.30%), savings accounts, and mortgage financing (40.15%) very attractive. Similarly, Turkish consumers expressed more interest in Giro accounts (62.89%) and savings accounts (46.39%). Unlike the studies cited in the literature review for this study, the findings of the current study indicate that mortgage financing is not a highly desired product

(29.90%) by the Turkish community. Furthermore, only 11.34% of the respondents indicated an interest in remittances services. Again, referring to the literature, a significant number of Turkish people tend to do investments in real estate in Turkey, but the aforementioned findings indicate a changing trend. On the other hand, this study also found that the Turkish community is interested in business and educational loans. From the demand for educational loans it can be interpreted that a younger generation of Turks are eager to educate themselves than were their ancestors.

It has been found that a small number of the respondents from Arabic origin participated in the survey. However, most of the Arabic respondents (65%) expressed interest in Giro accounts (shown in Table 22). Regarding South East Asian respondents, the findings suggest that the majority of them are interested in Giro (43.02%) and savings account (36.05%). However, about 32.56% of the respondents also expressed interest in business loans. In addition to this, almost 26% of the responders were interested in investment accounts. Respondents from other nationalities also expressed keen interest in Giro and saving accounts. The overall analysis reveals that only a small number of people are interested in remitting money to their countries of origin. Although it was unanticipated, this study also found a moderate demand for mortgage and car financing.

Table 22: Cross Nationality Analysis of Most Demanded Products and Services

Country	Nationality Frequency	Giro Account		Savings Account		Mortgage Financing		Car Financing		Remittances		Investment Accounts		Business Loans		Educational Loans		Other	
		F	%	F	%	F	%	F	%	F	%	F	%	F	%	F	%	F	%
German	132	73	55.30	53	40.15	53	40.15	31	23.48	9	6.82	20	15.15	40	30.30	22	16.67	8	6.06
Turkish	97	61	62.89	45	46.39	29	29.90	27	27.84	11	11.34	12	12.37	21	21.65	21	21.65	16	16.49
Arabic	20	13	65.00	8	40.00	6	30.00	5	25.00	3	15.00	5	25.00	3	15.00	5	25.00	7	35.00
African	4	3	75.00	3	75.00	1	25.00	0	0.00	0	0.00	1	25.00	1	25.00	1	25.00	0	0.00
South East Asian	86	37	43.02	31	36.05	25	29.07	19	22.10	10	11.63	22	25.58	28	32.56	17	19.77	7	8.14
Other	63	27	42.86	26	41.27	23	36.51	9	14.29	4	6.35	11	17.46	12	19.05	18	28.57	2	3.17

In order to further differentiate demand patterns of Islamic financial products and services on the basis of nationality, a *t*-test was conducted. A *t*-test is a statistical technique used to determine if two sets of data are similar. As we know, Islamic banking originated from the Middle East and it is assumed that Arabic people would demonstrate a higher demand for *Shari'ah*-compliant products and services than Turkish people because Islamic banking has recently gained recognition and momentum in Turkey.

Descriptive statistics revealed that (in general) people from the Arabic origins express a slightly higher level of demand (M=4.125, SD=1.7078: investment in *Shari'ah*-compliant products and M= 4.294, SD=1.8630: willingness to get services despite higher price) of Islamic products and services than the Turkish people (*M*=3.771, *SD*=1.7680: investment in *Shari'ah*-compliant products and *M*= 3.938, *SD*=1.9019: willingness to get services despite higher price).

Statistically there is no significant difference between the demand of people from Arabic and Turkish origins ($p > 0.05$), of independent samples tested. Instead, people from both countries indicated considerably high demand. It should be noted that the sample size of Arabic people (N=16) is too small to make general conclusions, but we can infer that the rest of Arabic population in Germany will also exhibit similar demand patterns.

9.6 Section 2: Descriptive Statistical Analysis of the Survey of Muslim Umbrella Organizations

In Germany, most Muslims from different countries of origin have established their representative umbrella organizations. These organizations provide a platform for social and religious gatherings, thus an empirical study was also conducted to take into consideration their level of knowledge, awareness, and practices toward Islamic banking and finance. In total eight Muslim umbrella organizations participated in the survey. Therefore, the primary objective in this section (9.6) is to compare the results with the retail Islamic banking survey (Section 1: Analysis of the Retail Banking Survey) for a better understanding of overall trends and perceptions of Muslims in Germany. Section 2 also provides insights to the findings of this study as they relate to Quantitative Research Question 4.

Quantitative Research Question 4
What are the perceptions of Muslims in Germany concerning Muslim umbrella organizations (*Muslimische Dachverbände*) toward Islamic banking and finance in Germany?

This study found that an overwhelming majority of the Muslim umbrella organizations that participated in this study were well aware of the Islamic financial system. Almost two-thirds of the Muslim umbrella organizations expressed a willingness to use interest-free products and services provided by an Islamic bank and to recommend them to their members. Regarding relevant products and services, an overwhelming majority intended to use giro and savings accounts. More than two-thirds of the Muslim umbrella organizations indicated that Muslims living in Germany desired Islamic banking and finance products. Finally, a majority of the Muslim umbrella organizations also believed that these products and services would bring benefits for the Muslim community living in Germany.

The following sections (from 9.6.1 to 9.6.7) provide an overview of the data analyzed to draw this conclusion. In total, seven questions were asked to address Research Question 4.

9.6.1 Awareness About the Existence of the Islamic Financial System

Before analyzing the perceptions of Muslim umbrella organizations and asking difficult questions concerning products and services of Islamic banking and finance, a very basic question was asked about the existence of the Islamic financial system. Almost all the Muslim organizations (87.50%, n=7) knew about the existence of such systems. This finding shows that there is wide spread awareness about Islamic banking and finance.

9.6.2 Usage and Recommendation of Interest-free Products to the Members

In Islamic community circles, the use and recommendation of particular products or services, especially by religious organizations, generally has a considerable significance for Muslim consumers because of the recommendation provided by religious organizations. This might give Muslim consumers satisfaction and peace of mind, thus increasing the marketing impact. When the organizations were asked whether they would use interest-free products and services of Islamic banks and also recommend them to their members, the majority of (62.50% ,n=5) of the respondents indicated a willingness to do so. However, 37.50% (n=3) of the respondents were not sure about using interest-free products and services of an Islamic bank or about recommending them to their members. These organizations may not be familiar with the actual practice of Islamic banking and finance in Germany.

9.6.3 Desired Products and Services by the Muslim Organizations

Giro and savings accounts are the most desired products i.e., 80.00% (n=4) by the Muslim umbrella organizations. Interestingly, the findings of the retail Islamic banking survey also found that the majority of the respondents viewed Giro and savings accounts as the most important products and services. However, Muslim umbrella organizations also cited educational loans as the third most desired product.

It is worth mentioning that these organizations have not shown strong interest in loans from Islamic banks for the construction of mosques. Similarly, they have not exhibited enough demand for mortgage financing, investment accounts, or car financing.

9.6.4 Reasons for Not Doing Islamic Banking

The preceding section (9.6.3) explained that some organizations (37.50%) are not sure about or do not know about the use of interest-free products and services provided by Islamic banks. Most of the respondents (66.77%, n=2) indicated two reasons for not engaging in Islamic banking. First, no banks in their locality offered Islamic banking services. Second, no Islamic bank had approached them. These findings were expected as they are similar to the findings from the retail Islamic banking survey and because Islamic banking started only recently in Germany.

9.6.5 Demand of Islamic Banking Products Among Muslims

After having analyzed the knowledge and identified the most desired products and services, it is also important to assess the demand of such products and services. Results showed that 75% (n=6) of the organizations believe that Muslims living in Germany desired Islamic banking products. This finding is quite similar to the finding of the retail Islamic banking survey, which found that over 65% of the respondents stated a willingness to switch to Islamic banking.

However, 25% (n=2) of the respondents were not sure about the level of demand. From the given information, it is not possible to precisely predict the reasons for inadequate demand.

9.6.6 Benefits of Islamic Banking Products for the Muslim Community

The literature review revealed that, until 2015 when KT Bank AG opened in Germany, Muslims in Germany remained financially exclusive. Therefore, this study attempted to assess some perceived benefits of Islamic banking and finance for the Muslim community. Most of the respondents (87.50%, n=71) agreed that offering Islamic banking products and services would bring benefits for the Muslims living in Germany. One of the most obvious benefits is financial inclusion and religious satisfaction available with the availability of *Shari'ah*-compliant products and services.

9.6.7 Religious Characteristics of Members of Muslim Organizations

Finally, through this study an attempt was made to determine the level of religiosity among the members of Muslim umbrella organizations. As we know from the findings of the retail Islamic banking survey, consumers who exhibit higher levels of religiosity generally exhibit a higher tendency toward using *Shari'ah*-compliant products and services.

This study found that half of the Muslim organizations (50%, n=4) said that their members were religious, and over 37% (n=3) declared their members very religious. Therefore, findings pertaining to this question were similar to those for the question asked in the retail banking survey. For example, over 40% (n=175) of the respondents said they were religious and about 20% (n=78) said that they were very religious.

9.7 Section Three: Hypothesis Testing

This section describes how hypotheses were tested against the available qualitative[12] and quantitative evidence. Hypothesis 5 was tested using descriptive statistical findings due to nature of data. Hypotheses 1 to 4 are tested through both descriptive and inferential statistical tools (analysis of variance and t-test), and Hypotheses 6 and 7 were tested using qualitative analysis. A summary of findings of each hypothesis is presented in Table 23.

Hypothesis 1:
H1: Muslims living in Germany are familiar with the concept of Islamic finance.
Ho: Muslims living in Germany are not familiar with the concept of Islamic finance.

The results show that 55.16% Muslim respondents (n=219) have already heard about Islamic banking and finance before this study and they were familiar with Islamic banking and finance. Of the respondents, 55.16% were aware of Islamic banking and finance, but 15.84% (n=63) were aware but had less information. Thus, we can say that 71% of the respondents had heard about Islamic banking but that their level of awareness varies. This can be interpreted to indicate that Muslims generally know that Islam is a complete code of life and that Islam proposes an economic and financial system that is different from the conventional system. Contrary to this, only 9.30% of Muslims (n=37) were familiar with the key products of Islamic finance, such as *Musharakah*, *Mudarabah*, *Sukuk* and *Qard Hasan*.

As far as Muslim umbrella organizations (n=8) were concerned, more than 87% reported that they had awareness about the existence of the Islamic financial system. This finding indicates that there is widespread awareness about Islamic banking and finance.

A one-sample statistical test was conducted to test Hypothesis 1. A test value of four was applied, which would mean that a resulting value above four (neutral value) would indicate that Muslims living in Germany are familiar with the concept of Islamic finance. There was a significant effect to be found, $t\ (396) = 8.30$, $p < 0.001$. This finding can also be verified with the descriptive results (N=397, M=4.88, SD=2.0928) obtained from the one-sample test because the mean value was 4.88 (M=4.88), which was greater than the test value of four (4) and reveals that Muslims in Germany are familiar with the concept of Islamic finance.

These findings support Hypothesis 1: *Muslims living in Germany are familiar with the concept of Islamic finance.* This result shows that Muslims living in Germany can theoretically differentiate between conventional financial systems and Islamic financial systems. This awareness about basic tenants of the Islamic financial system

12 Generally hypotheses are tested using statistical tools (both descriptive and inferential. Please see Faisal *et al.*, n.a, pp. 9–10, available at: https://www.academia.edu/5218913/AWARENESS_OF_ISLAMIC_BANKING_IN_INDIA-An_Empirical_Study). However, some researchers have also tested hypothesis through qualitative studies (please see Hassan, 2011). Therefore, mixed tools are used due to nature of data.

could help Islamic banking and finance institutions in Germany (like KT Bank AG) to explore market potential.

Critical Evaluation and Discussion:

The majority (55.16%) of the respondents cited that they have heard about Islamic banking and finance. However, less than one-third were aware that *Musharakah*, *Mudarabah*, *Sukuk* and *Qard Hasan* are the key products offered by Islamic banks.

On the other hand, the survey findings indicated that Muslim umbrella organizations have a higher level of awareness about the existence of the Islamic financial system. The results are not consistent with the views presented in the literature review that claimed that the German market has potential but lacks awareness among the business community and other market participants (Guski, 2009). Current research showed a relatively good understanding on the part of Muslims living in Germany, but also indicated that they had limited information about the specific products of Islamic banking and finance.

As far as the awareness about Islamic banking and finance is concerned, the Institute of Islamic Banking and Finance (IFIBAF) study from 2010 showed that 63.5% of the respondents knew about Islamic banking and finance, but this study found that 55.16% of the respondents have heard about it. This gap might be due to the fact that the Institute of Islamic Banking and Finance (2010) study is based on 1000 respondents whereas the current study employed sample of 402. However, findings of this study about the lack of awareness of different instruments and products confirm the results of Alexander *et al.*'s (2010) study, which revealed that 23% of the respondents showed familiarity with *Qard Hasan* and 18% with *Mudarabah*.

Hypothesis 2:

H2: Muslims living in Germany are familiar with the *Riba* and consider charging and paying interest is prohibited in Islam.

Ho: Muslims living in Germany are not familiar with the *Riba* and do not consider charging and paying interest is prohibited in Islam.

The descriptive statistical results show that more than two-thirds of the Muslim respondents are familiar with *Riba* (70.85%, n=282). In addition to this, more than two-thirds also believe that charging and paying interest is prohibited in Islam.

It should be noted that Hypothesis 2 is composed of two elements: a) familiarity of Muslim respondents with *Riba*; b) perceptions of Muslim respondents toward prohibition of charging and payment interest in Islam. Therefore, two separate ANOVA tests were conducted.

A one-way between subjects ANOVA was conducted to relate gender to the respondents' level of the awareness of *Riba*. There was no significant effect to be found, $F<1$ [$F(1, 396) = 0.157$, $p > 0.05$]. Therefore, we can conclude that both male (M=5.143, SD=2.2197) and female (M=5.045, SD=2.1800) respondents seem to be equally familiar with *Riba*. This means that both male and female Muslim respondents have familiarity with *Riba*.

The second ANOVA test was performed to examine the relationship between gender and the perceptions of Muslims regarding charging and paying interest. A one-way between subjects ANOVA revealed a significant effect of gender on the level of prohibition of charging and paying interest, $F\,(1,\,395) = 9.475$, $p < 0.002$. Furthermore, we can conclude that male (M=5.685, SD=1.8822) respondents consider charging and paying interest as more prohibited in Islam than females do (M=5.027, SD=1.9884).

The results of these statistical analyses support Hypothesis 2: *Muslims living in Germany are familiar with the Riba and consider charging and paying interest as prohibited in Islam.* Moreover, both male and female Muslim respondents have almost equal familiarity with *Riba*. This result may have far reaching positive implications on Islamic banking and finance in Germany because evidence suggests that the Muslim respondents are not only aware of the concept of *Riba* but also believe that charging and paying interest are not permitted in Islam. This means that they would tend to buy *Shari'ah*-compliant products and services in Germany.

Critical Evaluation and Discussion:

As far as familiarity of Muslims with *Riba* is concerned, this study found that 70.85% of respondents had awareness about *Riba*. The findings of this study about *Riba* replicate the findings of the study conducted by Alexander *et al.* (2010) and Farhoush and Schmidt (2011). Alexander *et al.* found that 61% of the respondents stated that *Riba* is prohibited in Islam and Farhoush and Schmidt stated that 70% of the Muslims living in Germany argued that conformity with the prohibition of *Riba* were important to them as was discussed in the literature review for the current study.

However, *Riba* findings of this study contradict the claims of Gassner (2003a), who argued that 23.2% of the Turkish people living in Germany find *Riba* unacceptable because it is prohibited in Islam. The main difference in Gassner's results and this study might be that this study had a wider focus, and Gassner's study was mainly concerned with people with Turkish backgrounds.

Hypothesis 3:
H3: Muslims living in Germany consider themselves religious.
Ho: Muslims living in Germany do not consider themselves religious.

This study found that an overwhelming majority (73.43%, n=293) of the retail banking consumers stated that they were religious (from religious to very strongly religious).

As far as the findings of the Muslim umbrella organizations survey are concerned, an overwhelming majority (87.50%, n=7) stated that they believed their members were religious (it was observed while collecting the data from field survey that the respondents often faced difficulty in choosing between religious, very religious, and very strongly religious when selecting a descriptive word with which to label themselves). Thus, it can be interpreted that the degree of religiousness is a subjective matter that depends on the self-awareness of the individual.

Hypothesis 3 was tested statistically through analysis of variance (ANOVA). Gender was a determining factor in the level of the religious characteristics reported by the respondents, with (M=5.014, SD=1.3142) male respondents reporting they were more religious (not enough difference but still significant) and females (M=4.536, SD=1.4883) are less religious, $F(1, 397) = 9.887$, $p < 0.002$. This analysis shows that religious characteristics vary between males and females.

The results of this statistical analysis, and the findings of retail Islamic banking and Muslim umbrella organizations surveys, support Hypothesis 3: *Muslims living in Germany consider themselves religious.* From these results it can be inferred that the existence of a religious consumer base is one of the vital factors for the success of Islamic banking and finance in Germany.

Critical Evaluation and Discussion:

The current research found that 73.43% retail banking consumers self-identified as religious. This finding is in agreement with Farhoush and Schmidt's (2011) finding that 70% of the respondents were very religious. The study of Deutsch-Emiratische Industrie und Handelskammer (2010) also revealed that 74% of people surveyed considered themselves religious.

It is worth mentioning that the survey for the Muslim umbrella organizations showed that the religious characteristics of 87.50% of their members ranged from *religious* to *very religious.* It should also be noted that the sample size was small and therefore these results may not be generalized for the rest of the Muslim organizations, but overall findings of this study are in agreement with the studies of Farhoush and Schmidt (2011) and Deutsch-Emiratische Industrie und Handelskammer (2010).

Hypothesis 4:
H4: Muslims living in Germany will use *Shari'ah*-compliant Islamic finance products and services if provided with these.
Ho: Muslims living in Germany will not use *Shari'ah*-compliant Islamic finance products and services if provided with these.

The researcher hypothesized a positive relationship between Muslims living in Germany and the use of *Shari'ah*-compliant Islamic finance products and services if such products and services are provided. According to the retail banking survey the majority of respondents (52.77%, n=210) expressed an interest in using such products even if they had to pay higher prices for them. It is worth mentioning that two-thirds (65.42%, n=263) of retail banking consumers also stated that they are willing to use Islamic financial products and switch to Islamic banking. This hypothesis had two parts: interest in *Shari'ah*-compliant products; and willingness to switch and use Islamic products. Therefore, interest in products and services, willingness to switch, and willingness to pay higher prices are different factors that determine whether the Muslim consumers will use *Shari'ah*-compliant products and services if provided with the opportunity to do so. The majority (over 62%) of Muslim umbrella organizations have cited that they would like to use *Shari'ah*-compliant Islamic finance products and services.

Hypothesis 4 was also tested statistically through analysis of variance (ANOVA). The purpose of this analysis was to examine the willingness of the respondents to do Islamic banking.

A one-way between subjects ANOVA was conducted to relate the respondents' willingness to do Islamic banking to the level of the respondents' awareness of Islamic banking. Willingness to do Islamic banking (three options: Yes, No, Not Sure) had a significant effect on awareness level, showing that respondents who are willing to do Islamic banking have heard more about Islamic banking before, $F(2, 394) = 21.022$, $p < 0.001$.

Furthermore, there is a significant difference between willing to do Islamic banking (Yes) (M=5.340, SD=1.8449) and not willing (No) (M=3.687, SD=2.2352) to do Islamic banking. As such, there is no significant difference between those who are not willing (M=3.687, SD=2.2352) and those who are not sure (M=4.085, SD=2.2557). This indicates that those respondents who stated that they were willing to do Islamic banking and finance had heard more about it than those respondents who said that they were not sure or not willing.

This could be looked at from another perspective. As was discussed while explaining the profile analysis of the respondents, the number of males in the sample for this study was higher than the number of females (72% vs. 28%). It appears, based on this, that the findings are over-emphasized because of the higher male representation.

Moreover, the results of the ANOVA also revealed that the male respondents had higher degrees of familiarity than female respondents with Islamic banking and finance. The reason why males were more familiar with Islamic banking could have been their exposure to, and interaction with, such topics. As we know, most of the Muslim women who responded to this study were housewives and were less concerned with financial matters.

The findings stated above are related to the analysis of data gathered in the retail Islamic banking and Muslim umbrella organizations surveys and support Hypothesis 4: *Muslims living in Germany will use Shari'ah-compliant Islamic finance products and services if provided with these.* The results revealed that it is important to inform people about Islamic banking, and that the level of awareness about Islamic banking is connected to the willingness to do Islamic banking.

Critical Evaluation and Discussion:

The findings of the retail banking survey indicated that 65.42% of the respondents were willing to switch to Islamic banking. This finding is in line with previous studies discussed in the literature review with reference to Nawas (2013), Deutsch-Emiratische Industrie und Handelskammer study (2010), Evens (2014), and the IFIBAF (2010).

Nawas (2013) found that 74% of German Muslims have shown strong interest in Islamic financial products. As was mentioned earlier, this study found that 65.42% of the Muslim retail banking consumers living in Germany are willing to switch to Islamic banking. The IFIBAF study from 2010 found that 72% of the respondents showed interest in Islamic financial products. Again, this high degree of interest might be due to the fact that the sample contained 1000 respondents whereas our study employed a sample of 402. Alexander *et al.*'s (2010) study found that 84% of the respondents showed interest in Islamic banking and finance. But it should be noted that the current study is based on a smaller sample size of 111. On the other hand, the Deutsch-Emiratische Industrie und Handelskammer study (2010) found that 60% of the respondents were willing to leverage Islamic banking and *Shari'ah*-compliant investment products. Evens (2014) also found that 62% of the respondents showed a willingness to buy Islamic insurance products.

Hypothesis 5:

H5: Muslims living in Germany report a desire for mortgage finance.
Ho: Muslims living in Germany do not report a desire for mortgage finance.

The retail banking consumers were asked to prioritize the most important Islamic banking products. The finding showed that Giro accounts ranked first (55.22%), saving accounts ranked second (44.27%), and mortgage services or home financing ranked third (36.64%). The question was structured in a way that the Giro account and saving accounts were the first two products listed followed by mortgage financing, therefore it is believed that the respondents selected the top two products from the list. Selection of mortgage financing indicates that it is still a highly desired product. This may be indicative of the fact that, in Germany, Giro accounts are a basic necessity when starting a relationship with a bank, and savings account are a German tradition. Therefore, in the light of these arguments, it can be concluded that Muslims in Germany have a strong desire for mortgage financing.

On the other hand, findings of the Muslim Umbrella Organizations survey revealed that mortgage services or home financing was not included in the top three products. Giro and savings accounts (80%) were first, followed by educational loans (60%).

The findings of the retail Islamic banking and Muslim Umbrella Organizations surveys partially support Hypothesis 4: *Muslims living in Germany report a desire for mortgage finance.* This finding suggests that financial institutions providing *Shari'ah*-compliant products and services should also offer other products and services to address the needs of the consumers. No doubt that mortgage financing is one of the important products required by the Muslims, but other products such as savings accounts and educational loans are also important.

Critical Evaluation and Discussion:

The findings of the retail Islamic banking survey revealed that Giro account (55.22%) facility, savings accounts (44.27%), and mortgage services or home financing (36.64%) were highly desired products by the Muslims. These findings about product and service preferences, especially about mortgage financing, were unexpected compared to the other studies, including the Deutsch-Emiratische Industrie und Handelskammer (2010) and Farhoush and Schmidt (2011). The Deutsch-Emiratische Industrie und Handelskammer (2010) study found that 62% of the respondents desired mortgage finance, 43% insurance products, and 42% investment funds. Similarly, Farhoush and Schmidt (2011) found that 75% of the respondents indicated a willingness to use *Shari'ah*-compliant savings account, 73.4% were willing to use loans for mortgage, and 52% were willing to use mutual funds. It is worth noting that the findings of this study show that loans for mortgage financing are ranked third in order of importance for the products listed.

There might be two reasons behind this trend. First, there is a sufficient gap in the findings of this study and the findings of previous studies. Meanwhile, there might have been a shift in the preferences of Muslim consumers during the period between the earlier studies and the current studies. Second, and more importantly, 12% of the sample population for this study is composed of retail businessmen and their main preferences are Giro accounts and savings accounts rather than mortgage financing.

Hypothesis 6

H6: There are market entry barriers for the *Shari'ah*-compliant products in Germany.

Ho: There are no market entry barriers for the *Shari'ah*-compliant products in Germany.

As was discussed in the literature review, researchers such as Schönenbach (2012) believe that there are market entry barriers for the *Shari'ah*-compliant products in Germany. However, this study found contrary results and concluded that there are no market entry barriers. This argument can be supported through two main findings. First, the issuance of full-fledge banking license to the KT Bank AG in March 2015 proves that there were no restrictions imposed by regulatory authorities. Second, the findings of the qualitative study confirmed this outcome. In this regard, the two most relevant stakeholders are the KT Bank AG and the BaFin. Mr. Uğurlu Soylu, Managing Director of the KT Bank AG stated:

> "BaFin gave a clear signal that there is no legal barrier in Germany to obtain a license for an ethical based products."

However, he also admits that there were no proactive measures to create an enabling environment.

Similarly, Mr. Johannes Engels, Senior Policy Officer at the BaFin also confirmed that there is no market entry barrier for Islamic banking in Germany and stated that:

> "There is absolutely no restriction on the base of religion or region. All institutions and individuals can apply for a license and we examine their application carefully. Anyone can open a bank by fulfilling the legal requirements."

These findings do not support Hypothesis 6: *There are market entry barriers for the Shari'ah-compliant products in Germany.* In light of above results this study concluded that there are no barriers to entry. However, the lack of proactive attitude is self-evident in the promotion and facilitation of Islamic finance in the country, as was previously discussed. These results indicate that financial institutions that are willing to explore the German banking and finance market by offering *Shari'ah*-compliant products and services will not face market entry barriers.

Critical Evaluation and Discussion:

Regarding the regulatory framework of Islamic banking in Germany, the findings of this study are not consistent with the studies discussed in the literature review. This study found that there were no regulatory barriers for Islamic banking in Germany, but Ernst (2011) identified the Islamic law and lack of support as barriers in the development and growth for Islamic banking because Islamic law is not compatible with existing German and European legal framework. However, the establishment of KT Bank AG reinforces to the findings of this study, which indicate that there are no restrictions from regulatory authorities. Furthermore, from a legal point of view, it is possible to include some Islamic commercial provisions to provide a mechanism to do Islamic banking. This is especially true in the case of wholesale banking and finance. But, in the case of retail banking, it would be difficult to offer Islamic banking products without the underlying legal provisions covering such matters as consumer protection.

The argument made by Colditz (2009) seems partially supportive of Ernst's (2011) argument that German financial institutions have not demonstrated a strong interest in Islamic banking and finance except for in the instance of the *Sukuk* bond issued in 2004. However, the recent entry of KT Bank AG in the German marketplace suggests that there is interest from financial authorities to facilitate or support Muslims in financial inclusion.

Hypothesis 7

H7: The United Kingdom's experience with *Shari'ah*-compliant financial products provides an Islamic banking model for European countries like Germany.
Ho: The United Kingdom's experience with *Shari'ah*-compliant financial products does not provide an Islamic banking model for European countries like Germany.

The analysis of interviews in the qualitative study revealed that the majority of the interviewees believed that the United Kingdom's model of Islamic banking is not totally applicable to the German market. Of the 13 participants, 10 responded to this question, and only two said that the United Kingdom's model is relevant for Germany. However, five interviewees argued that the United Kingdom's model of Islamic banking is not applicable to Germany because every country has its own history, culture, financial, and legal environment.

The five interviewees who stated that the United Kingdom's Islamic finance model is not applicable to Germany gave reasons like population differences among the European countries, varying laws, and varying consumer requirements. As was discussed in the literature review provided in Chapter 6, in Germany most of the migrant population is heterogeneous in nature (Heinen *et al.*, 2015). Dr. Nikolaus Siegfried, former Senior Analyst at Landesbank Berlin AG and pioneer of the QES *Shari'ah*-compliant Islamic finance certificate in 2011 in Germany, highlighted this important point by stating:

> "I think the Muslim community in the UK is very particular in terms of interest in Islamic banking products. I doubt that other countries have similar constituents."

Another interviewee, Nafisa Chaudhry (Former team member of FMF Islamic Banking Germany) who has extensive experience of dealing with Islamic financial products in Germany, stated:

> "The Islamic banking in the UK could be watched by other countries as well, but just for information. Every country has its own laws, rules and regulations and people and demands are different. Therefore every country would have to make their own efforts and do research to find out about their very own market and act accordingly. Just copying the Islamic bank in UK would not make sense."

Mr. Miryusup Abdullaev, Vice President/Head of Unit at Operations, Cash Trading stated that:

> "No, I don't think UK's current model offers a plug and play solution for other European countries due to different structures of economies and societies around Europe."

These findings do not support Hypothesis 7: *The United Kingdom's experience with Shari'ah-compliant financial products provides an Islamic banking model for European countries like Germany.* Alternatively, the findings indicate that Islamic financial institutions should conduct a thorough analysis of not only the potential target market but also the proposed business model.

Table 23 presents a summary of hypothesis based on aforementioned findings from quantitative and qualitative studies.

Table 23: Summary of Hypotheses

No	Hypothesis	Result
H1	Muslims living in Germany are familiar with the concept of Islamic finance.	Supported
H2	Muslims living in Germany are familiar with the *Riba* and consider charging and paying interest is prohibited in Islam.	Supported
H3	Muslims living in Germany consider themselves religious.	Supported
H4	Muslims living in Germany will use *Shari'ah*-compliant Islamic finance products and services if provided with these.	Supported

No	Hypothesis	Result
H5	Muslims living in Germany report a desire for mortgage finance.	Partially Supported
H6	There are market entry barriers for the *Shari'ah*-compliant products in Germany.	Not Supported
H7	The United Kingdom's experience with *Shari'ah*-compliant financial products provides an Islamic banking model for European countries like Germany.	Not Supported

9.8 Concluding Remarks

Chapter 9 presented the analysis of two quantitative surveys, a) the retail Islamic banking, and b) the Muslim umbrella organizations. Both surveys were conducted in Germany. The findings of these surveys are grounded in scientific research methodology. The retail Islamic banking survey was conducted in nine different cities including Berlin, Hamburg, Cologne, Frankfurt am Main, Munich, Duesseldorf, Essen, Duisburg, and Bochum, and used a sample size of 402. The majority of respondents consisted of males and young people. The results of this survey found that the majority of the Muslim population is aware of the fact that Islamic financial institutions avoid *Riba* (50.25%), and 73.43% of the respondents said that they were religious (from religious to very strongly religious). Moreover, 62.31% of the respondents were familiar with the Islamic concept of *Riba*.

More than half of the respondents (55.16%) had a clear awareness about the Islamic banking. Regarding willingness to switch toward Islamic banking, 65.42% said they were willing to switch to Islamic banking. Those respondents who indicated a willingness to use *Shari'ah*-compliant products and services cited three reasons including Islamic banks avoid interest, religious obligation to avoid interest, and personal satisfaction by complying with *Shari'ah* rules. However, 26.62% of the respondents were indecisive. A lack of availability of *Shari'ah*-compliant products and services and a lack of consumer engagement by the Islamic financial institutions are the main reasons for not doing Islamic banking, as stated by the majority of the respondents.

Generally, the respondents mostly desired giro and savings bank accounts and home financing services. Germans, Turkish, and South East Asian nationals showed higher demand for giro and savings accounts, whereas consumers from other nationalities indicated educational loans. Statistically, there is no significant difference in the findings from data collected from individuals of Arabic and Turkish origin. Correlation analysis shows that the respondents who characterize themselves as more strongly religious than others also tended to have heard about Islamic banking more often, considered investing in *Shari'ah*-compliant Islamic products, or avoided non-Islamic products more often.

The results of the survey of Muslim umbrella organizations showed that more than 87.50% of the respondent organizations had awareness about interest-free banking. Giro and savings bank accounts were the most desired products i.e., 80% respectively by the Muslim organizations. The third most highly desired product was educational loans (60%). Furthermore, 75% of the organizations believed that Muslims living in Germany desire Islamic banking products, and 87.50% the respondents agreed that offering Islamic banking products and services will bring benefits for Muslims living in Germany. More than two-third of the Muslim umbrella organizations stated that a current lack of availability in the area of *Shari'ah*-compliant products and services and a lack of consumer engagement by the Islamic financial institutions are the main reasons for not doing Islamic banking. Half of the Muslim organizations (50%) said that their members were religious and over 37% declared their members very religious.

Overall, the results of both surveys revealed that until recently Muslim consumers were unable to use *Shari'ah*-compliant products and services mainly due to a lack of supply. The main results from hypothesis testing are: Muslims living in Germany are familiar with the concept of Islamic finance (charging and paying interest is forbidden in Islam, majority of the Muslim consider themselves religious and showed a willingness to use *Shari'ah*-compliant products including mortgage finance), there are no market entry barriers for the *Shari'ah*-compliant products in Germany, and the United Kingdom's experience of Islamic banking cannot be considered as model for Germany.

The following chapter provides conclusion on the key results of quantitative and qualitative studies and summaries the findings of this study.

Chapter 10: Discussion and Conclusion

10.1 Introduction

The overall objective of this study has been to investigate the knowledge, attitudes, and perceptions of Muslims, including Muslim umbrella organizations, toward Islamic banking and finance products in Germany. In order to achieve desired goals, three different sets of research instruments were designed and tested in Germany. The first instrument was the retail Islamic banking survey that was performed nationwide. The survey returned a sample size of 402 participants in nine different cities. Another survey was used to collect data from eight Muslim umbrella organizations in Germany. Qualitative interviews were the third research instrument that was used in this study. A total of 13 interviews were conducted. After data collection was complete, retail banking and Muslim association surveys were analyzed using Statistical Package for Social Sciences (SPSS) latest version 22 and both descriptive and inferential statistical techniques were applied. However, for the analysis of qualitative data analysis and clustering methods were used.

The aim of the current chapter is to discuss the findings from empirical research and conclude the overall results. Chapter 10 provides an overview of the findings as they pertain to the main research question, the impact of Muslim refugees and asylum seekers in Germany on Islamic banking and finance and recommendations. Research contributions and limitations are also discussed, and recommendations for future research are proposed. Chapter 10 also highlights the outlook for Islamic financial products and services in Germany followed by concluding remarks.

10.2 Summary of Main Findings

Main findings of qualitative research are discussed as follows:

Success Factors of Islamic Banking in Germany and the UK (Research Question 1)

For both countries success factors are different. Following are the main success factors for the United Kingdom:

- Early start of Islamic banking activities during the 1980s
- Close relationship with Muslim countries due to colonization and therefore the ideas of Islamic banking easily spread to the United Kingdom
- Proactive political support from the government
- Positive role of financial and regulatory bodies
- Strategic location of London and its role as an international financial hub
- English language used to conduct business
- Proactive and supportive engagement of Muslim communities in the evolution of Islamic finance

Below are the main success factors for Islamic banking in Germany:

- Presence of largest Muslim population
- Strong economic and political relations between Germany and Turkey
- Leading global economy
- Development of Islamic finance in Turkey may have indirectly but positively influenced the Turkish population living in Germany which supported establishing KT Bank AG in Germany
- Strong economic ties with the Muslim world

Challenges for Islamic Banking in Germany and EU (Research Question 2)

Following are the main challenges for Islamic banking in Germany and the European Union:

- Lack of awareness about Islamic banking and finance
- Cut-throat competition from conventional banks, because these institutions have deep roots in society and they offer relatively cheap products compared to the Islamic banks (such as the case of the United Kingdom)
- Lack of standardized institution on European level is also one of the challenges, because availability of such institutions could enhance the authenticity of products and services as we have established brands like Deutsche Bank AG in conventional finance
- Growing prejudice against Islam due to recent incidents of terrorism in Europe, which has projected a negative image of Islam and may discourage non-Muslims as such incidents may change their perceptions toward Islamic finance
- Lack of legal and regulatory platforms in most of European countries, such as Germany, may leave Islamic finance untapped
- Low demand and less attractive products and services are also important challenges for Islamic finance

Future of Islamic Banking in Germany and EU (Research Question 3)

From discussions in Chapter 4 and qualitative analysis in Chapter 8, it can be concluded that Islamic finance will witness growth opportunities globally. However, growth in Europe, and particularly in Germany, will be slow and gradual. The main reason is that Islamic financial activities are not yet common and Islamic banking has only recently made a formal appearance in Germany. Moreover, Muslims, especially those from Turkish origins, suffered substantial losses due to the Islamic financial products scandal commonly known as Turkish holdings scandal. Therefore, Islamic financial institutions offering *Shari'ah*-compliant products and services need a reasonable amount of time to regain the confidence of this consumer group. On the other hand, the relatively small Muslim population offers only limited growth for

Islamic banking in the United Kingdom. The financial market in the United Kingdom is saturated with Islamic finance. The qualitative portion of this study found that the future of Islamic banking looks good in Europe, but Islamic financial institutions cannot easily make inroads and will face many challenges.

Main findings of quantitative research are discussed as follows:

Perceptions and Willingness Toward Islamic Banking in Germany (Research Question 1&2)

The study found that most Muslims could draw a distinction between conventional and Islamic banks, and concluded that they knew that Islamic banks avoid *interest* and are based on *Shari'ah* principles established in the *Quran*. However, without the presence of Islamic financial institutions (until July 2015), Muslim banking consumers had little information regarding products and services of Islamic banks. Furthermore, the findings of this study indicated that the majority of Muslims were well aware of Islamic banking and finance. More than two-thirds of Muslim respondents considered themselves religious and had a good understanding of *Riba*. They also expressed a belief or understanding that *Riba* is forbidden in Islam. This study also found a positive relationship between their levels of religiosity, awareness, and willingness to switch to Islamic banking. This study also found that two-thirds of the respondents indicated their intention to use *Shari'ah*-compliant products and services.

Relevant Islamic Products or Services in Germany (Research Question 3)

The findings of retail banking and Muslim umbrella organizations survey had shown two common highly desired Islamic products in both surveys. The most desired service was the Giro bank account. As in Germany, a Giro bank account is a necessity because almost all organizations prefer to transfer funds through banking channels. The second most desired was a savings bank account. The reason for this could be that such an account is used to deposit excess money for precautionary savings. However, normally people use investment accounts and services to increase wealth. Mortgage financing was ranked third most desired in the retail banking survey, followed by car financing. Educational loans were ranked third in the Muslim umbrella organizations survey.

Perceptions of Muslim Umbrella Organizations about Islamic Banking in Germany (Research Question 4)

One of the important findings from the survey of Muslim umbrella organizations was that these organizations were well aware of Islamic banking and finance as compared to the retail banking survey. This study also found that more than one-third of Muslim umbrella organizations were not sure of or do not know whether they will use interest-free products and services and recommend those products and services to their members. One of the fundamental reasons that were also common in the banking survey was that most of the respondents were not engaging in Islamic banking because no bank in their region offered such services and no bank has approached them to offer such services.

Another finding of this study was the desire for educational loans by the Muslim umbrella organizations. This means that such organizations were not just looking for loans for consumption purposes but that the education of their children was also a priority. Furthermore, an overwhelming majority of the organizations believed that there was demand for Islamic banking products among Muslims. This study also found that almost all Muslim umbrella organizations indicated that Muslim communities in Germany would benefit from Islamic banking and finance.

10.3 Potential Impact of Muslim Refugees and Asylum Seekers on Islamic Banking

A discussion of the role refugees and asylum seekers will play in the spread of Islamic banking and finance is important to this study. In 2015, the European Union (Germany specifically) witnessed an unprecedented influx of refugees and asylum seekers. According to Pandey (2016), over 1.1 million refugees and asylum seekers were registered in Germany in 2015, five times more than in 2014. The majority of the refugees and asylum seekers were arrived from Muslim countries such Syria, Iraq, and Afghanistan. According to Sola (2016), it is also predicted that by the end of 2020 approximately 5.25 million refugees will arrive in Germany. The current trends suggest that 72.7% of these people will be of working age and the majority of them will be younger men. Therefore, this will lead to important changes in the demography of the country and will have far-reaching implications for the Muslim population, the German economy, and demand for *Sharī'*ah-compliant products and services will shift upward.

Kern (2016) states that the Germany's Muslim population sharply increased to almost 6 million, an increase of 850,000 in 2015 alone. Muslims coming from Syria and Iraq are predominantly of Turkish origin, which might change the findings of the current research in the medium- to long-run as a shift occurs in the pattern of demand for Islamic financial products and services. The quantitative study suggests that the majority of Turkish population in Germany is willing to switch toward Islamic banking, and the presence of the Turkish origin bank in Germany may benefit from this considerable potential.

10.4 Study Recommendations

The findings of this study indicate that most of the Muslims in Germany have a limited understanding of Islamic financial products and services. Therefore, in order to introduce Islamic banking and finance products in Germany, Islamic banks and financial organizations should design appropriate market entry strategies.

To successfully launch Islamic products, financial institutions should gain key insights into the needs and demands of Muslims. The Islamic financial institutions should work to win the confidence of banking consumers because the Turkish holdings scandal is still in the minds of these consumers. It will take effort and time to convince Muslims to buy Islamic financial products, and it will be a challenge to overcome the distrust from past experiences. Before structuring and designing products and services Islamic financial institutions should consult Muslim umbrella organizations. If such organizations are satisfied with *Shari'ah*-compliant aspects of the products or services they can directly or indirect recommend or suggest the products and services to consumers. Because most of the immigrants are well connected to their organizations and it may increase the chances of success.

Most Muslims in Germany are not aware of the existence of Islamic financial institutions in Germany and therefore, it would be necessary to create awareness among target groups about different products and the potential benefits of those products. Informational material in the form of flyers could be distributed among various leading Muslim organizations, and religious scholars (Imams) could be made aware of such products. Imams could play an important role once they themselves know about and approve of the products and services.

The success of any marketing campaign heavily depends on the structure, timing, and content. Therefore, it would be important to design marketing campaigns with different segments of target groups in mind. For instance, the Turkish community is the largest group and focus should be on reaching the maximum number of people through advertisements in Turkish newspapers. Television and radio advertisements, and word of mouth would be helpful in this regard.

Islamic banking in Germany is a very new concept in comparison to that of conventional banking. Therefore, Islamic banks should introduce innovative products and services so that consumers can have a clear differentiation between both models of banking. In addition to this, if products and services of Islamic financial institutions are not cheap or equivalently priced in comparison to conventional banks it might be difficult for *Shari'ah* sensitive consumers to switch to Islamic banking.

This study also found that openness and a proactive role on the part of regulatory bodies was an important factor for the development of Islamic banking and finance in the United Kingdom, because it creates an environment in which Islamic finance flourishes. Thus, it would be important for German regulators to identify the most important challenges faced by Islamic banking and take solid step-by-step measures to resolve them. As was discussed in Chapter 4, the United Kingdom has been successful in attracting the wealth of high net worth Muslim individuals from Muslim countries. London viewed as an international financial hub played an important role in this success. Germany can benefit in a similar nature from leveraging opportunities present in the German banking and finance industry. This study recommends relevant authorities in Germany facilitate Islamic banking and finance in Germany. As was explained in Chapter 1, several rich Muslims from the Middle East have made investments in the real estate sector in Germany. Thus, attractive availability of *Shari'ah*-compliant products and services may create additional investment opportunities in Germany. Moreover, Islamic banking and finance may serve as a tool of financial inclusion for Muslims.

10.5 Research Contributions

This study makes valuable contributions to the existing literature, particularly to the literature pertinent to the financial industry in Germany. The contributions were made in theoretical and practical insights and recommendations. From a theoretical perspective, this study found that Theory of Planned Behavior (TPB) is also valid in the case of Islamic financial products and services in Germany. This study was undertaken with a large sample size from major cities in Germany. As this study used triangulation of quantitative and qualitative data, results were reached in a scientific manner.

This study is also representative of a number of target audiences such as retail banking consumers, Muslim umbrella organizations, and broad-based Islamic banking experts. Therefore, findings of this study are more comprehensive and general in nature. In addition to this, use of mixed research methods (quantitative and qualitative) further enhanced the scope and authenticity of this study. This study is distinctive due to a number of reasons including the fact that it focused on aspects of consumer knowledge and attitudes toward Islamic banking and finance in Germany, and included retail Islamic banking consumers and Muslim umbrella organizations.

Being the first study of its kind, this study has policy implications for a number of stakeholders such as bankers, asset managers, regulators, policy makers, insurance companies and fund managers. Furthermore, this study will also be of interest to academicians including students, professors, and researchers.

On the basis of this study, we can broadly identify two main areas of implications. First, this study has identified key determinants for the success of Islamic banking and financial products in Germany. This study may help existing financial institutions to reconsider their approach toward Islamic banking and finance, which includes innovative products and services, marketing strategies, and business models.

This study highlights the fact that financial institutions offering *Shari'ah*-compliant products and services may study the evolution of Islamic banking in the United Kingdom in order to gain insights about consumer behaviors and the challenges faced by the Islamic financial institutions in Germany. This study could also serve as first-hand information for new market entrants because it sheds light on the knowledge, attitude and willingness of Muslim consumers to engage with Islamic banking and finance. Second, government regulatory bodies may learn lessons from the United Kingdom's experiences with Islamic banking, such as the importance of a level playing field for Islamic financial institutions and the implications of a proactive role on the part of regulators and the government.

10.6 Research Limitations

As there are a large number of Muslim umbrella organizations working in Germany and each has a significant number of members, it was not possible to ascertain whether or not the sample size of eight taken in this study was sufficient.

Due to language barriers (a reasonable size of Turkish population do not speak German, especially females), financial, and time constraints it was not possible to develop a questionnaire that could address in detail every aspect of Islamic banking in Germany. Therefore, the focus of this study was to design a short and easily understood questionnaire to gather data from a large number of Muslims.

As the main objective of this study was to analyze the knowledge, attitudes, and perceptions of retail Islamic banking consumers in Germany, the focus was on retail banking rather than wholesale investment banking or other business entities such as corporates and fund management companies.

The scope of this study was limited to the Muslim population living in Germany. As discussed earlier, the Islamic finance industry in Germany is at an infancy stage and there is a lack of comprehensive empirical research about the buying behaviors of Muslims in Germany. Therefore, it was decided not to include other religious groups such as non-Muslims.

As can be sees in the descriptive profile analysis of the respondents in the quantitative study, only 20% of the respondents had higher secondary school educations and a majority of the respondents represent a higher level of qualification. This was attributed to the fact that many people declined to take part in the survey either due to a lack of information, because of language barriers, or because of some other fear such as negative usage of their personal information.

10.7 Areas for Further Research

The German financial system has witnessed several developments in recent decade, as highlighted in Chapter 5. From an Islamic banking perspective, the most important development was the establishment of KT Bank AG. On the basis of the current study, several areas for further research have been identified.

First, it would be interesting to evaluate the performance of KT Bank AG in coming years to assess the success of Islamic banking in terms of total number of customers, revenue generated, deposit size and base, and range of products offered. These financial indicators might give an initial indication of the actual acceptability of Islamic financial products and services in Germany.

Second, as Islamic banking is in the early stages of development in Germany, it would also be significant to investigate the compatibility of Islamic financial services within an existing conventional financial environment. Moreover, after distribution of Islamic financial services through formal channels, it would be interesting to evaluate the knowledge, awareness, and perceptions of consumers in a later stage to assess whether availability of such products and services has changed the demand pattern.

Third, it could also be important to do an empirical study analyzing non-Muslim consumer perceptions about Islamic banking products in Germany. Finally, the current research only looked into retail banking and did not explore other sectors of banking and finance. It would be good if future researchers explore areas like Islamic fund management and Islamic insurance (*Takaful*).

10.8 Future Outlook

As has already been discussed, Islamic banking products and services were formally launched in Germany in 2015. However, there had been a few previous attempts to introduce Islamic products and services in an informal way, but such efforts were not successful. If we compare the development of Islamic finance with our case study United Kingdom, then we come to know that in the United Kingdom Islamic finance products and services were introduced in an informal way since the 1980s. Until 2004, when regulatory and political support began to increase in the United Kingdom, the market had not witnessed substantial growth. Much of the growth and development in Islamic investment banking after 2004 occurred for five investment banks working there. However, on the retail banking side, the trajectory of growth was not similar to investment banking due to a limited customer base and strong competition from conventional finance institutions. Therefore, in the case of Germany, which launched Islamic banking in a formal manner only recently, this study has concluded (based on data collected in interviews) that growth will be slow.

Germany has a Muslim population of 5.8% (4.76 million), which is the highest Muslim population among European countries. By the end of 2015 the Muslim population in Germany had reached 6 million. According to Flaunet (2014) it is expected that the Muslim population in Germany will reach 5.5 million by the end of 2030, a number which number excludes a high number of immigrants most of whom are Muslims. According to The Guardian (2015), a British newspaper, Germany expects to receive an influx of up to 1.5 million refugees in 2015, and this number could increase in coming years. Keeping in mind an unprecedented large number of asylum seekers in Europe, and particularly in Germany, we can predict that this growth in the Muslim population will affect the demographics of the country and will have economic implications.

Another important factor is that many Muslim countries are strong trading partners with Germany including Turkey, Gulf Cooperation Council (GCC), United Arab Emeritus (UAE), and Pakistan. The development of Islamic finance may indirectly influence these trading relationships. Daimler Financial Services AG, a financial subsidiary of German car manufacturer Daimler AG opened two companies (Mercedes-Benz Leasing Middle East and Mercedes-Benz Finance Middle East) to finance cars under the principles of Islamic law as a strategic approach to increasing sales volume (Spiegel, 2009).

Recently, several countries, including the United Kingdom, have issued Sovereign *Sukuk* bonds to strengthen their capital markets, and Germany might reenter into

Islamic capital markets because the country has already gained the experience of issuing its first *Sukuk* bond in 2004. Therefore, aforementioned factors suggest that Islamic finance will have a positive outlook in Germany, but the growth trajectory will not be same as the United Kingdom; a fact that was also concluded from the data collected in the qualitative study.

10.9 Concluding Remarks

The main objective of this study was to contribute to the existing body of literature in the area of Islamic banking and finance because there is lack of scientific empirical studies on this topic. This study has attempted to fill the gap in the literature. It is expected that the current study will start a healthy discussion about the future prospects of Islamic finance in Germany, and will provide a foundation to undertake in-depth research in areas of Islamic fund management and *Takaful*.

References

Ahmad, A., Zaheer, M., Masood, S. and Usman, S. (2014) Infrastructure project financing. An alternative to debt finance, *IOSR Journal of Business and Management*, 15(5), pp. 48–52.

Ahmed, H. (2009) 'Financial crisis: risks and lessons for Islamic finance', *ISRA International Journal of Islamic Finance*, 1(1), pp. 7–32.

Archick, K., Belkin, P., Blanchard, M.C., Ek,C. and Mix, E.D. (2011) Muslims in Europe: promoting integration and countering extremism, congressional research service,[Online]. Available from: https://www.fas.org/sgp/crs/row/RL33166.pdf [accessed on Jan 20, 2014].

Azad, M.A., Kabir, M. R., Bhuiyan, F. and Masum, A.K.M. (2013) 'Prospects analysis of an Islamic capital market in Bangladesh', *Global Journal of Management and Business Research Finance*, 13(6), pp. 57–61.

Asutay, M. (2007) 'Conceptualization of the second best solution in overcoming the social failure of Islamic banking and finance: Examining the overpowering of Homoislamicus by Homoeconomicus', *IIUM Journal of Economics and Management 15*, 2, pp. 167–195.

Ahmad, K. (2000) 'Islamic finance and banking: the challenge and prospects', *Review of Islamic Economics*, (9), pp. 57–82.

Alim, A. E. (2014) *Global leaders in Islamic Finance – Industry Milestones and Reflections*, Singapore: John Wiley & Sons Singapore Pte. Ltd.

Abu-Alkheil, M.A. (2012) *A theoretical and empirical framework for the cross-country and inter-bank analysis of efficiency, productivity, and financial performance.* PhD. thesis. The University of Hohenheim. [Online]. Available from: http://d-nb.info/1027354092/34 [accessed on Feb 01, 2015].

Abu Bakar, M. (2010) *Broad distinction between Islamic and conventional banking.* [Online]. Available from: http://www.bankislam.com.my/en/Documents/shariah/BroadDistinctionBetweenIslamicConventional.pdf [accessed on Feb 01, 2015].

Al-Saati, R. A. (2003) 'The permissible Gharar (risk) in classical Islamic jurisprudence', *Journal of King Abdul Aziz University: Islamic Economics*, 16(2), pp. 3–15.

Ahmed, H. (2010) 'Islamic finance at a crossroads: the dominance of the asset-based Sukuk', *Journal of International Banking and Financial Law*, 25(6), pp. 366–367.

Ahmed, H. (2006) 'Islamic law, adaptability and financial development', *Islamic Economic Studies*, 13(2), pp. 79–101.

Alrifai, T. (2015) *Islamic finance and the new financial system: An ethical approach to preventing future financial crises*, Singapore: John Wiley & Sons Singapore Pte. Ltd.

Abdel-Khaleq, H.A. (2015) *Venturing into New Territories: Innovative Islamic Funds Structures*, [Online]. Available from: http://www.financialplaces.com/f_article.php?id=8 [accessed on June 10, 2015].

Ajzen, I. (1991) 'Theory of planned behavior', *Organizational Behavior and Human Decision Processes'*, 11, pp. 179–210.

Alam, S.S., Janor, H., Zanariah., Wel, A.C. C. and Ahsan, N.M. (2012) 'Is religiosity an important factor in influencing the intention to undertake Islamic home financing in Klang valley?', *World Applied Sciences Journal*, 19(7), pp. 1030–1041.

Abduh, M. and Omar, A. M. (2012) 'Islamic-bank selection criteria in Malaysia: An AHP approach', *Business Intelligence Journal*, 5(2), pp. 271–281.

Alhojailan, M. I. (2012) 'Thematic analysis: a critical review of its process and evaluation,' *West East Journal of Social Sciences*, 1(1), pp. 39–47.

Amin, H., Rahman, A. R.A., Sondoh, S. L.Jr., and Hwa, M. C. A. (2011) 'Determinants of customers' intention to use Islamic personal financing: The case of Malaysian Islamic banks', *Journal of Islamic Accounting and Business Research*, 2(1), pp. 22–42.

Almanaseer,M., Al Mahamed, S. and Matarneh, B. (2014) 'Islamic finance as an alternative for supplementary loans in commercial banks: a descriptive and analytical study of alternatives', *Research Journal of Finance and Accounting*, 5(15), pp. 142–147.

Ahmed, R. E.,Yahaya, S. and Harashid, Md. (2012) 'Shubuhat on matter of Bai' alinah and Tawarruq', *International Journal of Business and Technoprenership*, 2(1), pp. 95–97.

Andrews, M. (2010) *Islamic Finance*. London: Risk Reward Ltd UK.

Abdul-Rahman, Y. (2010) *The art of Islamic banking and finance: tools and techniques for community-based banking*. New Jersey: USA, John Wiley & Sons, Inc.

Abdullah, V. D. and Chee, K. (2010) *Islamic Finance: why it make sense*. Singapore: Marshall Cavendish International (Aisa) Pte Ltd.

Askari, H., Iqbal, Z., Krichene, N. and Mirakhor, A. (2012) Risk sharing in finance: the Islamic finance alternative. Singapore: John Wiley & Sons Singapore Pte, Ltd.

Almutairi, H. (2010) *A comparison between Islamic and conventional home financing in Kuwait: client perceptions of the facilities offered by the National Bank of Kuwait and Kuwait Finance House*. PhD. thesis. Durham University. Available from Durham E-Theses Online: http://etheses.dur.ac.uk/543/ [accessed on Feb 2, 2016].

Alexander, S., Blume, E. and Braune, I. (2010) 'Potenzial islamischer Bankprodukte in Deutschland. Einstellungen und Erwartungen der Muslime in Deutschland', in Ebert, H. and Thießen, F. (ed.) *Das islamkonforme Finanzgeschäft*. Stuttgart: Deutscher Sparkassen Verlag GmbH, pp. 82–119.

Ahmed, M. (2015) 'Islamic banking: the solution for global financial challenges', *Journal of Islamic Economics, Banking and Finance*, 11(3), pp. 111–121.

Aichbichler, E. (2009) *Islamic banking in Germany and Switzerland.* MA thesis. Universität Wien.

Asutay, M. (2013) 'Islamic moral economy as the foundation of Islamic finance', in Cattelan, V. (ed.) *Islamic finance in Europe: toward a plural financial system.* Cheltenham: Edward Elgar Publishing Limited, pp. 55–68.

Abdullah, S. A. (2007) *The application of the AAOIFI accounting standards by the Islamic banking sector in Saudi Arabia.* PhD. thesis. Durham University. [Online]. Available from: http://etheses.dur.ac.uk/2594/1/2594_605.pdf [accessed on June 23, 2015].

Al-Hares, M. O., AbuGhazaleh, M. N. and El-Galfy, M. A. (2013) 'Financial performance and compliance with Basel III capital standards: conventional vs. Islamic banks', *The Journal of Applied Business Research,* 29(4), pp. 1031–1048.

Azeem, M. M., Marsap, M.A. and Ozari, C. (2015) 'Impact of Basel accord on banking system: evidence from Islamic banks of Pakistan', *Applied Finance and Accounting,* 1(2), pp. 1–9.

Alam, N. (2013) 'Impact of banking regulation on risk and efficiency in Islamic banking industry', *Journal of Financial Report and Accounting,* 11(1), pp. 29–50.

Azmi, S. (2016) *Global Islamic wealth industry faces trust deficit,* [Online].Available from: http://www.zawya.com/story/Global_Islamic_Wealth_Management_Industry_Faces_Trust_Deficit-ZAWYA20160324091858/?v=91 [accessed on March 25, 2016].

Athreya, S. (2014) *Why Basel III in Qatar? Sungard.* [Online].Available from: https://www.sungard.com/~/media/fs/consulting-services/resources/articles/Why-Basel-III-Matters-in-Qatar.pdf?sfdcCampaignId=70150000000ZivD&la=en [accessed on March 21, 2016].

Ahmed, H. (2013) 'Islamic wealth management: goals and instruments', in Ng, W., Peng, P. L. and Yew, K.C. (ed.) *Q Report Issue No1/2013.* Kuala Lumpur: Labuan IBFC Inc., pp. 26–30.

Ariff, M. and Mohamad, S. (2013) 'Islamic wealth management and issues in Waqf management in Malaysia'. in Ng, W., Peng, P. L. and Yew, K.C. (ed.) *Q Report Issue No1/2013.* Kuala Lumpur: Labuan IBFC Inc., pp. 36–44.

Aziz, A. Z. (2016) *Opening remarks at the IFSB meet the members and industry engagement session,* 28 January, Kuala Lumpur.

Ali, S. S. (2013) 'State of liquidity management in Islamic financial institutions', *Islamic Economic Studies,* 21(1), pp. 63–98.

Al-Amine, A.M. M. (2013a) 'Managing liquidity in Islamic finance', in Hunt-Ahmed, K. (ed.) *Contemporary Islamic finance: innovations, and best practices.* New Jersey: John Wiley & Sons, Inc., pp. 121–146.

Al-Amine, A.M. M. (2013b) 'Risk and derivatives in Islamic finance: A Shari'ah Analysis', in Hunt-Ahmed, K. (ed.) *Contemporary Islamic finance: innovations, and best practices*. New Jersey: John Wiley & Sons, Inc., pp. 331–352.

Archer, S. and Karim, A.A. R. (2014) 'The IILM short-term Sukuk for liquidity management: a success story in enhancing financial stability', *Seacen Financial Stability Journal*, 3, pp. 11–23.

Adebayo, I. and Hassan, M. K. (2013) 'Ethical principles of Islamic financial institutions', *Journal of Economic Cooperation and Development*, 34(1), pp. 63–90.

Alvi, A. I. (2009) *Robust standards for Islamic capital and money market*, Paper Presented in "WIBC Pre-Conference Day", Bahrain, 6 December.

Alvi, A. I. (2015) *Global developments in Islamic hedging segment*, Presentation made in "IIFM Workshop on Islamic Hedging & Liquidity Management Hosted by The National Commercial Bank at NCB Regional Office Recreation Building, Al Mather, Riyadh, Kingdom of Saudi Arabia, 26th November.

Alvi, A. Ijlal (2016) ijlal.alvi@iifm.net, Questions about TMA, 27 March 2016.

Alshamrani, A. (2014) 'A critical evaluation of the regulatory framework for the application of Islamic financial derivatives in the Kingdom of Saudi Arabia', *Journal of Islamic Banking and Finance*, 2(1), pp. 269–303.

Al-Taani, K. (2013) 'Challenges facing financial engineering with Islamic rules', *International Journal of Economics, Finance and Management Sciences*, 1(5), pp. 234–240.

Akhtar, S. (2008) *Islamic finance: authenticity and innovation – a regulator's perspective*, Paper Presented in "Harvard Law School", Cambridge, 20 April.

Annuar, N. (2015) 'Derivative and hedging in Islamic finance', *Islamic Finance News*, 12(16), p13.

Ahmed, H. and Khan, T. (2007) 'Risk management in Islamic banking', in Hassan, M. K. and Lewis, K. M. (ed.) *Handbook of Islamic Banking*. Cheltenham: Edward Elgar. pp. 144–158.

Ahmad, A. A., Afifiab, M. and Nordin, N. (2014) 'The viability hedging instruments in current application', *International Business Management*, 8(16), pp. 327–335.

Abdullah, V. D. (2007) *Business operations and risk management in Islamic banking*, Presentation made in "Financial Regulators Forum on Islamic Finance", Kuala Lumpur, 29 March.

Abdul-Rahman, A and Nor, M. S. (2016) 'Challenges of profit-and-loss sharing financing in Malaysian Islamic banking', *Geografia online Malaysian Journal of Society and Space*, 12(2), pp. 39–46.

Abubakar, M. (2016) muhammad.abubakar@bankislami.com.pk, Usage of Islamic financial instruments in Pakistan, 11 July

Al-Rifai, T. (2016) tariq@quorumcentre.com, Cross-country usage of Islamic financial instruments, 06 June

Amin, M. (2016) mohammed.amin@btinternet.com, Cross-country usage of Islamic financial instruments, 07 June

BankIslami Pakistan Limited (2006) *Learn Islamic banking with BankIslami*, Lahore: BankIslami Pakistan Limited.

Belouafi, A. and Belabes, A. (2010) 'Islamic finance in Europe: the regulatory challenge', *Islamic Economic Studies*, 17(2), pp. 34–53.

Belouafi, A. and Chachi, A. (2014) 'Islamic finance in the United Kingdom: factors behind its development and growth', *Islamic Economic Studies*, 22(1), pp. 37–78.

BMBF (2015) *Contemporary integration policy: Islamic theology at German universities.* [Online]. Available from: http://www.bmbf.de/en/15619.php [accessed on May 1, 2015].

BaFin (2015) *Islamic finance conferences in Germany.* [Online]. Available from: https://www.bafin.de/SharedDocs/Veranstaltungen/EN/BaFin_120510_Islamic_Finance_2_en.html [accessed on May 1, 2015].

Burghardt, Ina. and Fuß, C. (2004) *Islamic banking credit products in Germany and in the United Kingdom*, European Business School, Working Paper No.12–2004.

Biswas, Rita., Löchel, Horst (2001) *Recent trends in U.S. and German banking: convergence or divergence?*, Hochschule für Bankwirtschaft, Working Paper No.29.

Bryman, A. and Cramer, D. (2001) *Quantitative data analysis with SPSS for windows: a guide for social scientists.* London: Routledge.

Blaug, M. (1992) *The methodology of economics: or how economist explain.* Cambridge: Cambridge University Press.

Braun, V. and Clarke, V. (2006) 'Using thematic analysis in psychology', *Quantitative Research in Psychology*, 3(2), pp. 4–35.

Bälz, K. (2007) 'Islamic finance for European Muslims: the diversity management of Shari'ah-compliant transactions', *Chicago Journal of International Law*, 7(2), pp. 551–567.

Bank Negara Malaysia (2013b) *Innovation for growth: Basel III creates golden opportunities.* [Online].Available from: http://www.mifc.com/?ch=28&pg=72&ac=49&bb=uploadpdf [accessed on March 21, 2016].

Bank Negara Malaysia (2013a) *Global Islamic liquidity receives IILM boost.* Kuala Kumpur: Bank Negara Malaysia.

BIS (2008) *Principles for sound liquidity risk management and supervision.* Basel: Bank for International Settlements.

Bank Negara Malaysia (2010) *The financial stability and payment systems report.* Kuala Kumpur: Bank Negara Malaysia.

Bacha, I. O. and Mirakhor, A. (2013) *Islamic capital markets: a comparative approach.* Singapore: John Wiley & Sons Singapore Pte. Ltd.

Basu, R., Pras, A. and Rodriguez, S. (2015) *Monetary options and Islamic banking in the GCC: challenges and options.* IMF Working Paper, WP/15/234.

Bacha, I. O. (1999) 'Derivative instruments and Islamic finance: some thoughts for a reconsideration', *International Journal of Financial Services*, 1(1), pp. 1–33.

Banks, E. (2011) *Finance: the basics*, 2nd edn. New York: Routledge.

Bennett, M. and Jain, A. (2015) 'Hedging Sukuk: alternative for issuers', in Macaughtry, L. (ed.), *Islamic Finance News Annual Guide 2015.* Kuala Lumpur: Red Money, p. 30.

Bacha, I. O. (2014) 'Risk management and derivatives in Islamic finance', in Lewis, K. M., Ariff, M. and Mohamad, S. (ed.) *Risk and regulation of Islamic banking.* Cheltenham: Edward Elgar Publishing Limited. pp. 283–300.

BIS (2014) *Basel III: The Net Stable Funding Ratio.* [Online].Available from: http://www.bis.org/publ/bcbs271.pdf [accessed on April 01, 2016].

Colditz, K. (2009) *Islamic banking – a worthwhile challenge for German banks?.* MA thesis, Georg-Simon-Ohm – Hochschule Nürnberg.

Choiruzzad, S. A. and Nugroho, B. E. (2013) 'Indonesia's Islamic economy project and the Islamic scholars', Procedia Environmental Sciences, 17(n.a), pp. 957–966.

Chapra, U. M. (1996) *What is Islamic economics?.* IDB prize winners' lecture series No.9. Jeddah: Islamic Development Bank.

Choudhury, S. (2014) *Islamic retail banking in the UK.* Presentation *In: Turin Islamic Economic Forum*, 18 November 2014, Turin.

Chase, A. (2012) *Divergent political dynamics of Islamic banking in Britain and France*, MA thesis. University of Michigan-Ann Arbor.

Commerzbank AG *Annual report 2014.* [Online]. Available from: https://www.commerzbank.de/media/aktionaere/service/archive/konzern/2015_2/00_CAA_Geschaeftsbericht_2014_Konzern_EN.pdf [accessed on June10, 2015].

Commerzbank AG (2015) *Islamic Finance.* [Online]. Available from: https://www.commerzbank.de/en/hauptnavigation/institutions/products_services/banking_products/islamic_finance/Islamic_finance.html [accessed on June10, 2015].

Commerzbank AG (2012) *Case study: Kuveyt Turk bank.* [Online]. Available from: https://cbcm.commerzbank.com/en/hauptnavigation/credentials/casestudies/kuveyt_turk_bank.html [accessed on June10, 2015].

Chahboune, J. and El-Mogddedi, Z. (2008) 'Islamic banking- das Markpotenzial in Deutschland', *Kreditwesen.* pp. 718–720. [Online]. Available from: http://www.ifibaf.com/uploads/Artikel%20Test/Artikel%20ZfK%20082008gesichert.pdf [accessed on June 10, 2015].

Chowdhury, A.F. M. (2015) 'Why Islamic finance is different? A short review of Islamic jurisprudential interpretation about usury, ambiguity (Gharar), gambling (Maysir) and exploitive commercial arbitrage (Talaqi-Rukban)', *Journal of Emerging Economies and Islamic Research*, 3(3), pp. 1–14.

Casper, Matthias (2014) *Islamic finance – Anspruch und Wirklichkeit.* [Online].Available from: https://www.franz-hitze-haus.de/fileadmin/redakteure/download/Casper_Islamic_Finance.pdf [accessed on Jan 30, 2016].

Claus, I., Jacobsen, V. and Jera, B. (2004) *Financial systems and economic growth: An evaluation framework for policy*, New Zealand Treasury, Working Paper 04/17.

Chia, J.L.,Yahya, M.H. and Muhammad, J. (2015) The impact of Basel III on Malaysian stock performance , *Perkanika Journal of Social Sciences and Humanities*, 23(n.a), pp. 205–218.

Chattha, A. J. and Halim, N.W.A.W. (2014) *Strengthening the financial safety net: the role of Shari'ah-compliant lender-of-last resort (SLOLR) facilities as an emergency financing mechanism*, IFSB Working Paper Series.WP-01/04/2014.

Chisholm, M. A. (2004) *Derivatives demystified: a step-by-step guide to forwards, future, swaps and options.* West Sussex: John Wiley & Sons Ltd.

Dar, H. (2015) *Development of Islamic Finance in the UK* [online]. Available from: http://www.islamicbanker.com/publications/development-of-islamic-finance-in-the-uk. [Accessed 23 November 2015].

Disimino, M. and Hähn, F. fabian.haehn@targobank.de, Bankadas, 17 June 2015.

Deutsche Bank AG (2015) *Islamic finance at Deutsche bank.* [Online]. Available from: https://www.db.com/mea/en/content/islamic_finance.htm [accessed on June10, 2015].

Deutsche Bank AG (2006) *Deutsche bank launches Shari`ah mutual fund capability.* [Online]. Available from: https://www.db.com/medien/en/content/press_releases_2006_3265.htm [accessed on June10, 2015].

Deutsche Asset and Wealth Management (2015*) Facts and figures.* [Online]. Available from: https://deutscheawm.com/Our-Profile/One-Team/Who-We-Are [accessed on June10, 2015].

Djennas, M., Benbouziane, M. and Djennas, M. (2015) 'Currency-banking crises and economic downturns: a comparison between Islamic and conventional banks', in El-Karanshawy *et al.* (ed.) *Financial stability and risk management in Islamic financial institutions.* Doha: Bloomsbury Qatar Foundation, pp. 87–99.

Deutsch-Emiratische Industrie und Handelskammer (2010) *Islamic finance in Germany-factsheet.* [Online].Available from: http://vae.ahk.de/uploads/media/Islamic_Finance_in_Germany_Factsheet.pdf [accessed on Jan 27, 2016].

Deutsche Bank AG (2007) *Deutsche bank academic paper: pioneering innovative sharia compliant solutions.* [Online]. Available from: https://www.db.com/presse/de/downloads/White_Paper.pdf [accessed on June10, 2015].

Dusuki, W. A. (2007) 'Commodity Murabahah Programme (CMP): an innovative approach to liquidity management', *Journal of Islamic Economics, Banking and Finance*, 3(1), pp. 1–22.

Yilmaz̧ D. (2011) Managing liquidity in the Islamic financial services industry, "*Speech at a conference organized by the Islamic Financial Services Board"*, Istanbul, April 6.

Damak, M. and Volland, E. (2008) *Risk management for Islamic financial institutions: a rating perspective.* New York: Standard & Poor's.

Daly, S. and Frikha, M. (2015) 'Islamic finance a support to development and economic growth: the principle of Zakat as an example', *Journal of Behavioral Economics, Finance, Entrepreneurship, Accounting and Transport,* 3(1), pp. 1–11.

Djenic, M., Popovic-Avric, S. and Barjaktarovic, L. (2012) 'Importance of forward contracts in financial crisis, *Journal of Central Banking Theory and Practice,* 2(n.a), pp. 75–96.

Dali, R.S.M. N. and Ahmad, S. (2005) *A review of forward, futures and options from the Shari'ah perspective: from complexity to simplicity.* [Online].Available from: http://www.iefpedia.com/english/?p=4215 [accessed on March 12, 2016].

El Hussein, H. A. N. (2013) 'Islamic finance: is it a viable option to restrain financial crisis?', *Interdisciplinary Journal of Contemporary Research in Business,* 5(4), pp. 579–581.

Ernst, A. (2011) *Promoting Islamic finance and Islamic banking- a legal analysis of the potential for Islamic banking products in Germany.* Trier: Institut für Rechtspolitikan der Universität.

El-Hawary, D., Grais, W. and Iqbal, Z. (2004) *Regulating Islamic financial institutions: the nature of the regulated.* World Bank Policy Research, Working Paper No.3227.

EY (2015) *Luxembourg: the Gateway for Islamic finance and the Middle East,* Luxembourg: EY.

Engels, J. (2010) 'German banking supervision and its relationship to Islamic banks', in Khan, F. F. and Porzio, M. (ed.) *Islamic Banking and Finance in the European Union: a Challenge.* Cheltenham: Edward Elgar, pp. 174–188.

Ernst, D., Akbiyik, D. and Srour, A. (2013) *Islamic banking und and finance.* München: UVK Verlagsgessellschaft mbH.

El-Gamal, A. M. (2006) *Islamic finance: law, economic and practice.* New York: Cambridge University Press.

El-Mogaddedi, Z. (2010) *So sparen Muslime in Deutschland.* [Online].Available from: http://www.dasinvestment.com/fileadmin/images/pictures/1103_islamic.pdf [accessed on Jan 30, 2016].

Evens, R. (2014) *IslamKonforme Versicherungsprodukte: Vermarktung des takaful-Modells in Deutschland.* Wiesbaden: Springer Fachmedian Wiesbaden.

Ebert, H. and Thießen, F. (2010) 'Islamic finance – Facetten eines Phänomens', in Ebert, H. and Thießen, F. (ed.). *Das islamkonforme Finanzgeschäft.* Stuttgart: Deutscher Sparkassen Verlag GmbH, pp. 13–45.

Etzold, V. and Wackerbeck, P. (2012) 'Going West, again – the new offshore opportunities in the Arab world', *The European Financial Review*, pp. 68–74.

Etzold, V. and Wackerbeck, P. (2011) Islamic banking: dawn of a new era, *IESE Business School*, Technical Note No. FN-588-E.

El-Gamal, A. M. (2000) *A basic guide to contemporary to Islamic and finance.* [Online].Available from: https://www.lariba.com/site/pdf/islamic-banking-guide.pdf [accessed on Jan 27, 2016].

E&Y (2015) *Luxembourg: the gateway for Islamic finance and Middle East.* [Online]. Available from: http://www.ey.com/Publication/vwLUAssets/Luxembourg-the_gateway_for_Islamic_finance_and_the_Middle_East/$File/Islamic%20Finance.pdf [accessed on June 19, 2016].

Edbiz Consulting Ltd (2016) *Islamic wealth management report 2016*, London: Edbiz Consulting Ltd.

Ehsan, A. M. (2012) *Islamic perspective on financial derivatives: demand for instruments of risk management in various businesses of Pakistan.* PhD. Dissertation. Durham University.

Elahi, Y. and Aziz, I.A. M. (2011) 'Islamic options (Al-Khiyarat): challenges and opportunities', "*Proceedings of the International Conference on Information and Finance*", Singapore: IACSIT Press, 21 (n.a), pp. 101–104.

Ernawati (2016) 'Risk of Profit Loss Sharing Financing: the Case of Indonesia, *Jurnal Ilmu Ekonomi Syariah (Journal of Islamic Economics)*, 8(1), pp. 101–116.

FSA (2007) *Islamic finance in the UK: regulation and challenges*, London: FSA.

Farhoush, A. and Schmidt, N. (2011) 'Islamic finance in Germany: trends, opportunities, and potential', in Hassan, K. and Mahlknecht, M. (ed.) *Islamic capital markets product and strategies*, West Sussex: John Wiley & Sons Ltd, pp. 235–260.

Folkestad, B. (2008) *Analysing interview data: possibilities and challenges.* Eurosphere Online Working Paper Series. No.13. [Online].Available from: http://eurospheres.org/files/2010/08/Eurosphere_Working_Paper_13_Folkestad.pdf [accessed on March 26, 2016].

Field, A. (2014) *Discovering Statistics Using IBM SPSS Statistics.* 4th ed. London: SAGE Publications Ltd.

Farhoush, A. and Mahlknecht, M. (2013) 'A critical view on Islamic finance in Germany', in Cattelan, V. (ed.) *Islamic finance in Europe: toward a plural financial system.* Cheltenham: Edward Elgar Publishing Limited, pp. 203–212.

Farooq, O. M. (2014) 'Islamic wealth management and the pursuit of positive-sum solutions', *Islamic Economic Studies*, 22(2), pp. 99–124.

Farooq, O. M. (2011) *Qard Hasan, Wadiah/Amanah and bank deposits: applications and misapplications of some concepts in Islamic banking.* [Online]. Available from: http://www.assaif.org/content/download/33323/179191/.../Qardh%20Hasan.pd.[accessed on March 9, 2016].

Flaunet, M. (2014) *Islamic finance in Europe*. Presentation *In:* The 2nd International forum for Islamic banks and financial institutions, 3–4 April 2014, Brussels.

Farooq, M. and Ahmed, M.M.M. (2013) 'Musharakah Financing: Experience of Pakistani Banks', *World Applied Sciences Journal*, 21(2), pp. 181–189.

Guski, N. (2009) *Credit crunch: a chance to develop the Islamic finance market in Germany?* [Online]. Available from http://www.eurekahedge.com/news/09_may_IFNVol6_Iss10_Credit_crunch_IF_in_Germany.asp [accessed on Jan 25, 2014].

Gait, H.A. A. (2009) *Libyan attitudes toward Islamic methods of finance: an empirical analysis of retail consumers, business firms and banks*. PhD. thesis. Griffith University.

Grewal, K. (2013) Overview of the Islamic financial landscape: globally and in Europe. Presentation *In: 4th Islamic Financial Services Forum: The European Challenge*, 9 April 2013, Rome.

Grieser,G. S. (2008) Legal issues in structuring Shariah compliant investments, Presentation given at *Ist IIR Islamic Finance & Real Estate Forum held in Frankfurt/M* on 4–5 November.

Gleisner, F., Hackethal, A. and Rauch, C. (2010) 'Migration and the retail banking industry: an examination of immigrants' bank nationality choice in Germany', *The European Journal of Finance*, 16(5), pp. 459–480.

Gassner,S.M.(2004) *Regulatory framework of Germany-opportunities for structuring Shari'a compliant financial products*, paper presented at 6th Harvard Forum on Islamic Finance held in Cambridge on 8–9 May 2004, pp. 1–10.

Gassner, S.M. (2003b) Islamic finance -Wachstumsmarkt für Deutshe Banken, *Die Bank*, 11(n.a), pp. 732–736.

Gassner,S.M. (2003a) *An obvious gap in the market*. [Online]. Available from: http://www.auslandsmarketing.de/ibf/gap.pdf [accessed on June 10, 2015].

Gould, J. and Kolb, W. (1964) *A dictionary of the social sciences*. London: Tavistock Publications.

Greuning, V. H. and Iqbal, Z. (2008) *Risk analysis for Islamic banks*. Washington DC: The International Bank for Remonstration and Development/The World Bank.

Gassner, S. M. and Wieners, P. J. (2009) *Islamic finance auch am point of sale*. [Online]. Available from: http://www.islamicfinance.de/files/bank-und-markt-02-2009.pdf [accessed on Jan 30, 2016].

Geyer, R. (2002) 'Mit Allahs Segen : Entwicklung und Marktstellung islamischer Investmentfonds', *Zeitschrift für Wirtschafts- und*

Unternehmensethik, 3(2), pp. 257–266.

Global Islamic Finance Report (2014) London: Edbiz Consulting Ltd.

Global Islamic Finance Report (2011) London: Edbiz Consulting Ltd.

Hamed, I. (2013) *Islamic Banking in Germany: Opportunities and Potential Aspects.* MA thesis. [Online]. Available from http://de.slideshare.net/IslamElaziz/islamic-banking-in-germany-opportunities-and-potential-aspects [accessed on June 23, 2015].

Hoque, N., Ather, M. S. and Ahsan, H.M. (2013) 'Islamic business practices in Bangladesh- a survey on some selected firms in Chittagong', *European Journal of Business and Management,* 5(20), pp. 121–129.

Hassan, U.M. (2010) 'Islamic approach of economics: some discourses on Khurshid Ahmad's vision of socio-economic order, self-reliance and economic development', *Kyoto Bulletin of Islamic Area Studies,* 3(2), pp. 216–240.

Hayen, D., Sauer, M., Evers, J., Unterberg, M. and Habschick, M. (2005) *Migranten und Finanzdienstleistungen.* [Online].Available from: http://www.zfti.de/downloads/down_finanzdiensleistungen.pdf [accessed on Feb 01, 2016].

Heinen, N., Alberts, T. and Bitter, L. (2015) *Clients with migrant background: the role of risk preferences in retail banking,* Deutsche Bank Research Management.

Hasan, B. Z. (2011) *Shari'ah governance in Islamic financial institutions in Malaysia, GCC countries and the UK.* PhD. thesis. Durham University. Available from Durham E-Theses Online: http://etheses.dur.ac.uk/810/ [accessed on Feb 2, 2016].

Haug, S., Müssig, S. and Stichs, A. (2009) *Muslimische Leben in Deutschland.* [Online]. Available from: http://www.bmi.bund.de/cae/servlet/contentblob/566008/publicationFile/31710/vollversion_studie_muslim_leben_deutschland_.pdf [accessed on Feb 2, 2016].

Hersh, S. E. (2011) 'Islamic financial and international financial regulation', *Journal of International Service,* pp. 51–63.

Hakim, R. S. (2007) 'Islamic money market instruments' in Hassan, M. K. and Lewis, K. M. (ed.) *Handbook of Islamic Banking.* Cheltenham: Edward Elgar. pp. 161–170.

Haron, A. (2012) 'Integrating Islamic finance to global financial system: the role of the Islamic Financial Services Board (IFSB)', *Money and Economy,* 7(1), pp. 67–85.

Haron, A. (2011) *Basel III: impact on the IIFS and the role of the IFSB,* Paper Presented in "13th AAOIFI-World Bank Annual Conference on Islamic Banking and Finance", Manama, 23 October.

Hassoune, A. (2010) *Derivatives in Islamic finance: examining the role of innovation in the industry.* [Online]. Available from: https://www.moodys.com/research/Moodys-Islamic-finance-industry-faces-need-for-innovation-including-its--PR_196571 [accessed on March 12, 2016].

Hassan, M. Kabir (2010) *An integrated poverty alleviation model combining Zakat, Awqaf and micro-finance,* Paper Presented in "7th International Conference the Tawhidi Epistemology: Zakt and Waqf Economy", Bangi, 6–7 January.

Hassan, M. K. and Kayed, N. R. (2009) 'The global financial crisis, risk management and social justice in Islamic finance', *ISRA International Journal of Islamic Finance*, 1(1), pp. 33–58.

Hunt-Ahmed, K. (2013) 'Introduction: Islamic finance in the world economy', in Hunt-Ahmed, K. (ed.) *Contemporary Islamic Finance: Innovations, and Best Practices*. New Jersey: John Wiley & Sons, Inc. pp. 1–16.

Hassan, B. Z. (2011) *Shari'ah Governance in Islamic Financial Institutions in Malaysia, GCC Countries and the UK*. PhD. thesis. Durham University.

Iqbal, M. and Molyneux, P. (2005) *Thirty years of Islamic banking: history, performance, and prospects*. New York: Palgrave Macmillan.

International Finance Magazine (2015) [online]. Available from: http://www.internationalfinancemagazine.com/search/?searchContent=Difference between Islamic and conventional finance. [accessed on 21 November 2015].

IFSB (2015) *Islamic financial services industry stability report*, Kuala Lumpur: Islamic Finance Services Board.

Islahi, A. A. (2013) *First vs. second generation Islamic economists: deviations and differences in thoughts*, Paper Presented in 9th International Conference "Islamic Economics and Finance, Istanbul, 9–10 September, pp. 1–33.

IslamicFinance.de (2012) *German banking regulator BAFIN organized 2nd conference on Islamic finance*. [Online]. Available from http://www.islamicfinance.de/?q=taxonomy/term/1308 [accessed on March 24, 2016].

IIFM (2016) *Corporate profile*. [Online]. Available from: http://www.iifm.net/about_iifm/corporate-profile [accessed on March 4, 2016].

IFSB (2016) *Background*. [Online]. Available from: http://www.ifsb.org/background.php [accessed on March 4, 2016].

Iqbal, I., Kunhibava, S. and Dusuki, W. A. (2012) 'Application of options in Islamic finance', *ISRA Research Paper No 46/2012*.

Ibrahim, R. (2016) rahizam@bnm.gov.my, Usage of Islamic financial instruments in Malaysia, 03 June

Jamaldeen, F. (2015) *Four ways conventional and Islamic finance differs*. [Online]. Available from: http://www.dummies.com/how-to/content/four-ways-conventional-and-islamic-commercial-bank.html [accessed on November 21, 2015].

Jaffar, A. M. and Musa, R. (2014) 'Determinants of attitude toward Islamic financing among Halal-Certified mirco and SMEs: a preliminary investigation', *Procedia-Social and Behavioral Sciences*, 130 (n.a), pp. 135–144.

Jamaldeen, Faleel (2012) *Islamic finance for dummies*. New Jersey: John Wiley & Sons, Inc.

Jobst, A. A. and Sole, J. (2012) *Operative principles of Islamic derivatives-toward a coherent theory*. IMF Working Paper No.WP12/63.

Jobst, A. A. and Sole, J. (2009) 'The governance of derivatives in Islamic finance'. *J.I.B.L.R.*, 11, pp. 556–565.

Jalil *et al.* (2013) 'Challenges in the Application of Mudarabah and Musharakah Concepts in the Islamic Finance Industry in Malaysia', *ISRA Research Paper No 56/2013.*

Khan F., M. (2014) mfahimkhan@hotmail.com, Islamic finance, 01 February

Karim, A.A. R. (2001) 'International accounting harmonization, banking regulation, and Islamic banks', *The International Journal of Accounting*, 36 (n.a), pp. 169–193.

Kahf, M. and Khan, T. (1992) *Principles of Islamic financing*, Research Paper No.16, Jeddah: Islamic Research Training Institute, Islamic Development Bank.

Khan, M.M. and Bhatti, M.I. (2008) 'Development in Islamic banking: a financial risk-allocation approach', *The Journal of Risk Finance*, 9(1), pp. 40–49.

Kharoufa,A.E. (2000) *Philosophy legislation in Islam, Philosophy of Islamic Shari'ah and its Contribution to the Science of Contemporary Law.* Eminent scholars Lecture Series 19. Jeddah: Islamic Development Bank.

King, J. (2015) Al Rayan bank CEO enjoys UK comforts. *The Banker.* [Online]. Available from:http://www.thebanker.com/Markets/Islamic-Finance/Al-Rayan-Bank-CEO-enjoys-UK-comforts?ct=true. [Accessed 08 November 2015].

KT Bank AG (2015) *KT Bank.* [Online]. Available from: http://www.kt-bank.de/uber-uns/kt-bank.aspx [accessed on June11, 2015].

Kern, S. (2016) *Isalamization of Germany in 2015.* [online]. Available from: http://www.gatestoneinstitute.org/7199/germany-islamization. [Accessed 26 January 2016].

Kettell, B. (2011) *Introduction to Islamic banking and finance.* West Sussex: John Wiley & Sons Ltd.

Kammer, A., Norat, M., Pinon, M., Prasd, A., Towe, C. and Zeidane, Z. (2015) *Islamic finance: opportunities, challenges, and policy options,* IMF Staff Discussion Note SDN/15/05.

Krichene, N. (2013) *Islamic capital markets: theory and practice.* Singapore: John Wiley & Sons Singapore Pte. Ltd.

Kothari, C. R. (1990) *Research methodology: methods and techniques,* 2nd ed. New Delhi: New Age International (P) Limited, Publishers.

Kennedy, M. (2012) *Basel III and Islamic finance: what lies ahead?.* [Online].Available from: http://www.eurekahedge.com/NewsAndEvents/News/96/February_2012_alternative_investment_IFN_Basel_III_and_Islamic_Finance_What_Lies_Ahead [accessed on March 21, 2016].

Khalid, M. (2015) 'Liquidity management in the Islamic financial industry', in Macaughtry, L. (ed.) *Islamic Finance News Annual Guide 2015.* Kuala Lumpur: Red Money, pp. 34–35.

Kamaruzdin, B. T. (2014) *Derivatives and Islamic finance.* [Online].Available from: http://www.inceif.org/research-bulletin/derivatives-islamic-finance/ [accessed on March 14, 2016].

Lewis, K.M. (2009) 'In what ways does Islamic banking differs from the conventional finance', *The Journal of Islamic Economics, Banking and Finance*, pp. 9–24.

Landesbank Berlin AG (2014) *Company Profile.* [Online]. Available from: http://www.lbb.de/landesbank/de/10_Veroeffentlichungen/30_Treasury/02_RZM/03_Rating/04_moodys/20140820_Company-Profile.pdf. [Accessed 24 March 2016].

Liquidity Management Center (2016) *Corporate profile.* [Online]. Available from: http://www.lmcbahrain.com/about-corporate-profile.aspx [accessed on March 4, 2016].

Leedy, D.P. and Ormrod, J.E. (2010) *Practical Research: Planning and Design.* 9th edn. New Jersey: Pearson.

Mauro, F.D., Caristi, P., Couderc, S., Maria, A. D., Ho, L., Grewal, B.K., Masciantonio, S., Ongena, S., and Zaher, S. (2013) *Islamic finance in Europe*, ECB occasional paper series. No 146.

Mohammad, F. (2015) 'The UK continues cementing its position as the Western Islamic finance hub' in Macaughtry, L. (ed.) *Islamic Finance News Annual Guide 2015.* Kuala Lumpur: Red Money, pp. 119–120.

MacEoin, D. (2009) *Sharia law or 'one law for all?* London: Civitas: Institute for the Study of Civil Society.

Marshall, N. M. (1996) 'Sampling for qualitative research', *Family Practice*, 13(6), pp. 522–525.

Mason, M. (2010) 'Sample size and saturation in PhD studies using qualitative interviews', *Forum: Qualitative Social Research*, 11(3), [Online]. Available from: http://www.qualitative-research.net/index.php/fqs/article/view/1428/3027 [accessed on March 26, 2016].

Malhotra, K.N. and Birks, F. D. (2006) *Marketing research: an applied orientation.* 2nd European Edn. Essex: Pearson Education Limited.

Majanga, B. B. (2015) 'Is time ripe to adopt Islamic financial systems in secular developing countries? A review of literature', *Global Journal of Management and Business Research: Economics and Commerce*, 15(8), pp. 11–18.

Msatfa, A. (2012) 'Basel III in the Islamic finance industry', *The Journal of Investing*, pp. 165–170.

Mohammad, S. (2013) 'Liquidity risk management in Islamic banks: a survey', *Afro Eurasian Studies*, 1(2), pp. 215–230.

Maude, D. (2006) *Global private banking and wealth management: the new realties*, West Sussex: John Wiley & Sons, Inc.

Mohamad, S. and Tabatabaei, A. (2008) *Islamic hedging: gambling or risk management?*, Paper Presented in "*21th Australian Finance and Banking Conference*", Sydney, 16–18 December.

Malkawi, H. B. (2014) 'Financial derivatives between Western legal tradition and Islamic finance: a comparative approach', *Journal of Banking Regulation*, 15(1), pp. 41–55.

Mohamad, S., Othman, J., Roslin, R. and Lehner, M. O. (2014) 'The use of Islamic hedging instruments as non-speculative risk management tools', *Venture Capital: An International Journal of Entrepreneurial Finance*, 16(3), pp. 207–226.

Motani, H. (2013) *Islamic finance and derivatives.* A lecture delivered at LSE Islamic finance seminar held on 6 November in London. [Online].Available from: http://www.lse.ac.uk/collections/law/events/2013-Islamic%20Finance.htm [accessed on March 14, 2016].

Motani, H. (2012) *Islamic derivatives and ISDA.* A lecture delivered at Islamic banking and finance conference held on 24 April in Frankfurt. [Online].Available from: http://www.ilf-frankfurt.de/fileadmin/_migrated/content_uploads/Islamic_Derivatives_and_ISDA_-_Motani.pdf [accessed on March 15, 2016].

Muhammad, A.D. (2016) alitahir797@gmail.com, Usage of Islamic financial instruments in Nigeria, 02 June

Mahadik, J. (2016) jmahdik@ALHILALBANK.AE, Usage of Islamic financial instruments in UAE, 09 June

Nawas, T. (2013) 'How serious is the erudite Shariah-compliant business in Europe? Evolution, pivotal challenges and the way forward', *European Journal of Business and Management*, 5(15), pp. 192–202.

Nomani, F. and Rahnema, A. (1994) *Islamic economics systems.* London: Zed Books Ltd.

Newas, T. F. (2014) *Religiosity, generational cohort and buying behavior of Islamic financial products in Bangladesh.* Ph.D thesis. [Online]. Available from: http://researcharchive.vuw.ac.nz/xmlui/bitstream/handle/10063/3392/thesis.pdf?sequence=2 [accessed on June 23, 2015].

Nienhaus, V. (2011a) 'Islamic finance ethics and Shari'ah law in the aftermath of the crisis: concept and practice of Shari'ah compliant finance', *Ethics Perspectives*, 18(4), pp. 591–623.

Nienhaus, V. (2015) 'Self-adjusting profit sharing ratios for Musharakah financing', in El-Karanshawy *et al.*, (Ed.), *Islamic banking and finance–essays on corporate finance, efficiency and product development.* Doha: Bloomsbury Qatar Foundation, pp. 161–172.

Nienhaus, V. (2011b) *Building blocks of Islamic finance: regulation and Shari'ah in perspective*, Speech delivered at the 3rd Securities Commission Malaysia under University of Malaya visiting scholar programme. [Online].Available from: http://

www.iais.org.my/e/index.php/dirasat-sp-1862130118/economic-finance-zakat-awqaf/item/104-building-blocks-of-islamic-finance-regulation-and-shariah-in-perspective.html.[accessed on March 20, 2016].

Nordin, N., Rahman, AB.A. and Omar, H. H. (2014) 'The Islamic management: paving the way for innovation in currency options', *IJMS*, 21(1), pp. 23–37.

Obaidullah, M. (2005) *Islamic financial services*. Jeddah: King Abdul Aziz University.

Omar, A. M., Abduh, M. and Sukmana, R. (2013) *Fundamentals of Islamic money and capital markets*. Singapore: John Wiley & Sons (Asia) Pte.Ltd.

Ozkan, C. (2015) *Regulatory and supervisory challenges of Islamic banking after Basel- III*, Presentation made in "COMCEC financial cooperation working group meeting", Ankara, 19 March.

Önal, I. M. (2013) 'Islamic liquidity management: a way forward', *Afro Eurasian Studies*, 2(1&2), pp. 306–314.

Olaoye, K. I., Dabiri, A. M. and Kareem, R. (2013) 'Islamic banking in Nigeria: challenges and prospects', *International Journal of Management Sciences*, 1(1), pp. 24–29.

Song, I. and Oosthuizen, C. (2014) *Islamic Banking Regulation and Supervision: Survey Results and Challenges*. IMF Working Paper, WP/14/220.

Parker, M. (2008) Islamic finance gaining ground in Germany. *Arab News*. [Online]. Available from: http://www.ifibaf.com/index.php?mact=News,cntnt01,detail,0&cntnt01articleid=17&cntnt01returnid=107 [accessed on Jan 7, 2014].

Perry, V.F. and Rehman, S. S. (2011) 'Globalization of Islamic finance: myth or reality?', *International Journal of Humanities and Social Science*, 1(19), pp. 107–119.

Pew Research Center (2015) *5 Facts about the Muslim Population in Europe*. [Online]. Available from: http://www.pewresearch.org/fact-tank/2015/01/15/5-facts-about-the-muslim-population-in-europe/ [accessed on May 3, 2015].

Pandey, A. (2016) *Europe's refugee crisis: Germany registered over 1 million asylum-seekers in 2015*. [online]. Available from: < http://www.ibtimes.com/europes-refugee-crisis-germany-registered-over-1-million-asylum-seekers-2015-2251590>. [Accessed 26 January 2016].

PwC (2008) *Islamic finance verspricht großes Wachstumspotenzial für deutsche Banken*, [Online].Available from: http://www.strategyand.pwc.com/de/home/Presse/Pressemitteilungen/pressemitteilung-detail/41864791 [accessed on Jan 28, 2016].

Possumah, T. B. and Ismail, G. A. (2012) 'Baitul Mal and legal constraint: public wealth management in Malaysian context', *International Journal of Academic Research in Business and Social Sciences*, 2(11), pp. 27–52.

Parashar, P. S. (2014) 'A case study of liquidity management center in Bahrain', in Lewis, K. M., Ariff, M. and Mohamad, S. (ed.) *Risk and Regulation of Islamic Banking*. Cheltenham: Edward Elgar Publishing Limited. pp. 139–151.

Qaseem, M. (2016) 'Shari'ah perspective on wealth and its management', in Azmi, S. and Malik, R. (ed.), *Islamic Wealth Management Report 2016*, London: Edbiz Consulting Ltd, pp. 26–37.

Rahman, S. Ab. (2005) *The classical Islamic law of guarantee and its application in modern Islamic banking and legal practice.* PhD thesis. University of Wales Aberystwyta.

Raza, F. M. (2010) *Regulation of Islamic finance in the UK and France.* Presentation *in: 3rd Astana Economic Forum*, 2 July 2010, Astana.

Rahman, N.UR. (2012) *Attitude of Muslims toward Islamic banking and finance in the NorthWest of England: a socio-economic perspective.* PhD. thesis. Durham University. Available from Durham E-Theses Online: http://etheses.dur.ac.uk/6394/ [accessed on Feb 2, 2016].

Ribera, A., Etzold, V. and Wackerbeck, P. (2011) 'Soul-search after the crisis: Islamic banking lessons for the financial sector', *IESEinsight*, pp. 52–59.

Rizvi, A.R. S. and Lahsasna, A. (2012) *Derivatives in Islamic finance: the need and mechanisms available for Islamic financial markets*, Paper presented in "2th ISRA colloquium Islamic finance in a challenging economy: moving forward", Sasana Kijang, 27 November.

Razif, F.M.N., Mohamad, S. and Rahman, N.A. N. (2012) 'Permissibility of hedging in Islamic finance', *Middle-East Journal of Scientific Research*, 12(2), pp. 155–159.

Rahman, Y.A. (2016) YARAHMAN@msn.com, Cross-country usage of Islamic financial instruments, 06 June

Schönenbach, R. (2012) Intrinsic barriers of Islamic finance, discussion paper, *Stresemann Foundation.*[Online]. Available from: http://www.stresemann-stiftung.de/wp-content/uploads/2012/11/Stresemann-Foundation-Schoenenbach-Islamic-Finance-in-Germany2012.pdf[accessed on Feb 2, 2016].

Siadat, A. (2013) Islamic banking, nun bald auch bei uns in Deutschland, *Freiburg Law Studen Journal*, 1(n.a), pp. 1–5.

Siadat, A. (2006) alireza.siadat@de.pwc.com, Usage of Islamic financial instruments in Iran, 25 May

Schirrmacher, C. (2007) *Muslims in Germany.* [Online]. Available from: http://en.europenews.dk/_ws/mediabase/_ts_1434707044000/archive/files/BMIStudy.pdf [accessed on March 24, 2016].

Stumpfegger, E. (2015) *Social identity and financial investment decision: empirical insights on German-Turks.* Cham: Springer International Publishing Switzerland.

Sekaran, U. (2003) *Research methods for business: a skill-building approach.* 4th edn. New York: John Wiley & Sons, Inc.

Spiegel (2009) *Selling Mercedes in Sharia: Daimler opens Islamic-friendly financing arm in Dubai.* [Online]. Available from: http://www.spiegel.de/international/

business/selling-mercedes-under-sharia-daimler-opens-islamic-friendly-financing-arm-in-dubai-a-653937.html. [Accessed 12 December 2015].

Sola, K. (2016) *Here's why welcoming refugees is a sound economic investment as well as a moral imperative* [online]. Available from: <http://www.forbes.com/sites/katiesola/2016/01/08/germany-cost-refugees/#6448e5ad66e7>. [Accessed 26 January 2016].

Said, P. (2008) 'Islamic alternative to conventional finance', in Millar, R. and Anwar, H. (ed.), *Islamic finance: a guide for international business and investment.* London: GMB Publishing Ltd, pp. 13–20.

Shanmugam, B. and Zahari R. Z. (2009) *A primer on Islamic finance*, n.a: The research foundation of FCA institute.

Siddiqi, N. M. (2007) 'Economics of Tawarruq: how its Mafasid overwhelm the Masalih', *in Tawarruq: a methodological issue in Sharīʿa-compliant finance*, Position paper presented in Harvard-LSE Workshop dated February 1 in London.

Schuster, F. (2013) *Perspektiven des Islamic Banking im deutschen Bankenwesen unter Betrachtung der Finanzstabilität, des Gewinnstrebens deutscher Banken und Berücksichtigung des deutschen Absatzmarketes.* [Online].Available from: http://www.deutsches-institut-bankwirtschaft.de/wp-content/uploads/2013/12/Schuster-Islamic-Banking-in-Deutschland.pdf [accessed on Jan 29, 2016].

Saunders, M., Lewis, P. and Thornhill, A. (2012) *Research methods for business students.* 6th edn. Essex: Pearson Education Limited.

Schoon, N. (2013) Islamic finance: unique risk management challenges and the impact of Basel III, *Global Risk Update*, pp. 20–24.

Sobol, I. (2013) *Liquidity management practices in Islamic banking*, pp. 567–576. [Online]. Available from: http://zif.wzr.pl/pim/2013_2_1_46.pdf [accessed on March 3, 2016].

Sulaiman, A. A., Mohamad, T. M. and Samsudin, L.M. (2013) 'How Islamic banks of Malaysia managing liquidity? An emphasis on confronting economic cycles', *International Journal of Business and Social Science*, 4(7), pp. 253–263.

Shawamreh, C. (2013) 'The legal framework of Islamic finance', in Hunt-Ahmed, K. (ed.) *Contemporary Islamic Finance: Innovations, and Best Practices.* New Jersey: John Wiley & Sons, Inc. pp. 39–61.

State Bank of Pakistan (2008) *Financial Stability Review*, Karachi, p. 159.

State Bank of Pakistan (2013) *Financial Stability Review*, Karachi, p. 29.

SBP (2015) *Islamic Banking Bulletin.* [Online]. Available from: http://www.sbp.org.pk/ibd/bulletin/2015/IBB-Sep-2015.pdf [accessed on March 37, 2016].

Sadr, M. S (2014) 'Qard Hasan Financing in Islamic Banks', *ISRA International Journal of Islamic Finance*, 6(2), pp. 7–19.

Saleem, M. (2016) Mudassar.saleem@sbp.org.pk, Usage of Islamic financial instruments in Pakistan, 30 May

Trakic, A. (2012) 'The Europe's approach to Islamic banking: a way forward', *Journal of Islamic finance and Business Research*, 1(1), pp. 1–13.

Tarlinton, P. (2004) 'Understanding the adversary', *Australian Army Journal*, II (2), pp. 173–180.

TheCityUK (2015) *The UK: leading Western center for Islamic finance*. London: TheCityUK.

The Z/Yen Group (2015) *The global financial centers index 18*. London: The Z/Yen Group.

Targobank AG (2015) *Facts*. [Online]. Available from: https://www.targobank.de/de/ueber-uns/unternehmen/daten-und-fakten.html [accessed on June 11, 2015].

The Guardian (2015) *Germany expects up to 1.5 million asylum seekers in 2015*. [Online]. Available from: http://www.theguardian.com/world/2015/oct/05/germany-now-expects-up-to-15-mln-migrants-in-2015-report. [Accessed 13 December 2015].

Thomson Reuters (2015) *Global Islamic asset management outlook 2015*. [Online]. Available from: https://www.zawya.com/ifg-publications/Islamic_Asset_Management_2015-260415070526E/ [accessed on March 14, 2016].

UKifs (2013) *Financial market series: UK, the leading Western center for Islamic finance*. London: UKifs.

Uberoi, P. and Evans, N. (2008) *Profit rate swap*. [Online]. Available from: http://www.allenovery.com/sitecollectiondocuments/47753.pdf [accessed on March 14, 2016].

Vizcaino, B. (2014a) What's in a name? Islamic banking rebrands in attempt to go mainstream. *Reuters*. [Online]. Available from: http://www.reuters.com/article/2014/07/02/us-islam-financing-namechange-idUSKBN0F70F520140702 . [Accessed 08 November 2015].

Visser, H. (2009) *Islamic finance: principles and practice*. Cheltenham: Edward Elgar Publishing, Inc.

Vizcaino, B. (2014b) Basel III deposit challenge looms over Islamic ban, *Reuters*, [Online].Available from: http://www.reuters.com/article/us-islam-banking-deposits-idUSKBN0GX0J320140902 [accessed on March 20, 2016].

Vizcaino, B. (2015) Islamic finance body IIFM launches cross currency swap standard. *Reuters*. [Online].Available from: http://uk.reuters.com/article/uk-islam-financing-standards-idUKKBN0TF0XS20151126 [accessed on March 16, 2016].

Veremyev, A., Tsyurmasto, P. and Uryasev, S. (2012) 'Optimal structuring of collateralized debt obligation contracts: an optimization approach', *Journal of Credit Risk*, 8(4), pp. 133–155.

Wilson, R. (2007) *Islamic finance in Europe*. RSCAS Policy Papers, RSCAS PP 2007/02, European University Institute Florence.

Woods, M. (2011) *Interviewing for research and analysing qualitative data: an overview* [online].Available from: http://owll.massey.ac.nz/pdf/interviewing-for-research-and-analysing-qualitative-data.pdf [Accessed 20 July 2015].

Wouters, P. (2013) 'Elements of Islamic wealth management', in Hunt-Ahmed, K. (ed.) *Contemporary Islamic Finance: Innovations, and Best Practices.* New Jersey: John Wiley & Sons, Inc. pp. 147–164.

Wilson, R. (2002) 'The interface between Islamic and conventional banking', in Iqbal, M. and Llewellyn T. D. (ed.) *Islamic banking and finance*, Cheltenham: Edward Elgar, pp. 196–212.

Williams, C. (2007) 'Research methods', *Journal of Business and Economic Research*, 5(3), pp. 65–71.

Wurst, F. (2011) *Immobilienfinanzierung und Islamic Banking: Möglicherkeiten Schariakonformer Immobilienfinanzierungen nach deutschem Recht.* Frankfurt am Main: Peter Lang.

Wilson, R. (2013) *Challenges for Islamic Banks in Complying with Basel III*, Presentation made in "The first annual conference of Islamic economics & Islamic finance at ECO-ENA; Inc., University of Toronto", Toronto, 30–31 August.

Yildiz, A. (2014) *Islamic banking in Deutschland: Herausforderungen und Umsetzung eines unkonventionellen Finanzsystems in Deutschland.* PhD. thesis. Technische Universität Dortmund.

Appendix

Table 8.2: Profiling of the Respondents					
Interviewee	**Organization**	**Job title**	**Industry/ Sector**	**Country**	**Date of Interview**
Mr. Uğurlu Soylu	Kuveyt Türk Katılım Bankası A.Ş. (KT Bank AG)	Managing Director	Banking	Germany	15.12.2014
Dr. Johannes Engels	BaFin	Senior Policy Officer	Banking	Germany	15.12.2014
Mr. Andreas Ernst	Enercon GmbH	Legal Counsel	Corporate	Germany	30.12.2014
Dr.Muhammad Umer Chapra	The Islamic Research and Training Institute- Islamic Development Bank	Advisor	Banking	Saudi Arabia	07.03.2015
Prof. Dr. Abdul Ghafar Ismail	The Islamic Research and Training Institute- Islamic Development Bank	Head Research Division	Banking	Saudi Arabia	07.03.2015
Prof. Dr. Humayon Dar	Edbiz Corporation	Chairman President & CEO	Corporate	UK	18.04.2015
Mr. Waheed Qasir	Maxim Corporate Finance LLP	President	Corporate	UK	18.04.2015
Mrs. Nafisa Chaudhry	Former FMF Islamic Banking	Freelance Consultant	Corporate/ Banking	Germany	12.05.2015
Dr. Nikolaus Siegfried	SlowerCapital	Former Senior Analyst Landesbank Berlin AG	Banking	Germany	28.05.2015
Mr. Miryusup Abdullaev	Deutsche Börse Group	Vice President / Head of Unit at Operations, Cash Trading,	Stock Exchange	Germany	07.06.2015

Table 8.2: Profiling of the Respondents					
Interviewee	**Organization**	**Job title**	**Industry/ Sector**	**Country**	**Date of Interview**
Prof. Dr. Volker Nienhaus	International Center for Islamic Finance (INCEIF)	Adjunct Professor	Academia	Germany	14.06.2015
Dr. Zamir Iqbal	The World Bank Global Islamic Finance Development Center, (GIFDC)	Head	Banking	Turkey	21.06.2015
Dr. Fabian Gleisner	Commerz Business Consulting, Commerzbank AG	Consultant	Banking	Germany	26.06.2015

www.ingramcontent.com/pod-product-compliance
Ingram Content Group UK Ltd.
Pitfield, Milton Keynes, MK11 3LW, UK
UKHW022222051026
15624UKWH00002B/297